In My Opinion . . .

We're working to make the best possible materials available for continuing education and we want to know how we're doing. After you've completed your continuing education course, please take a few moments to answer the following questions and mail the form back to us. Thanks for your help!

1. **What is the title of the continuing education book you are using?**

2. **Did you use this booklet in a:**

    ☐ classroom course   ☐ home study/correspondence course

3. **What license do you hold:**

    ☐ salesperson   ☐ broker   ☐ other_____

4. **Please rate the booklet on the following:**

	Excellent	Good	Fair	Poor
overall content	☐	☐	☐	☐
accuracy	☐	☐	☐	☐
organization	☐	☐	☐	☐
other				

5. **What features or topics did you like the best?**

6. **How can we make this booklet a better continuing education tool?**

7. **What other topics would you like to cover in your continuing education courses?**

NOTE: This page, when folded over and taped, becomes an envelope, which has been approved by the United States Postal Service. It is provided for your convenience.

Return Address:

_____

_____

_____

No Postage
Necessary
if Mailed
in the
United States

BUSINESS REPLY MAIL

FIRST CLASS MAIL   PERMIT NO. 88176   CHICAGO, IL

POSTAGE WILL BE PAID BY ADDRESSEE:

**Real Estate
Education Company**

a division of Dearborn Financial Publishing, Inc.

Attn: Robert Porché, Jr.
155 North Wacker Drive
Chicago, Illinois 60606-1719

NOTE: This page, when folded over and taped, becomes an envelope, which has been approved by the United States Postal Service. It is provided for your convenience.

WE'D LIKE YOUR HELP!

We're working to make the best-possible text materials available to students. We want to know how well this textbook is working for you. Please keep this form until your course is completed. Then answer these quick questions, and mail it back. Thanks for your help!

1. **What is the title and edition number of the textbook you are using?**_____

2. **What is your purpose for taking this course? Are you:**

    _____ preparing for a new career?

    _____ preparing for the broker's exam or to become a broker?

    _____ preparing for career advancement?

    _____ completing part of a general business degree/program?

    _____ seeking information for personal use?

3. **Please rate this textbook on the following:**

Features	Excellent	Good	Fair	Poor
Easy to read	_____	_____	_____	_____
Accurate	_____	_____	_____	_____
Illustrations/Figures	_____	_____	_____	_____
Current	_____	_____	_____	_____
Other_____	_____	_____	_____	_____

4. **What chapters or topics did you find the hardest to understand?**_____

    _____

    _____

5. **How else can we make this book a better learning tool?**_____

    _____

    _____

Name/Address_____

School_____

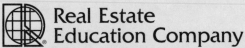

Real Estate Education Company

a division of Dearborn Financial Publishing, Inc.

520 North Dearborn St., Chicago, IL 60610-4354   Phone 312-836-4400 FAX 312-836-1021

NOTE: This page, when folded over and taped, becomes an envelope, which has been approved by the United States Postal Service. It is provided for your convenience.

Return Address:

**No Postage
Necessary
if Mailed
in the
United States**

BUSINESS REPLY MAIL

FIRST CLASS MAIL   PERMIT NO. 88176   CHICAGO, IL

POSTAGE WILL BE PAID BY ADDRESSEE:

**Real Estate
Education Company**

a division of Dearborn Financial Publishing, Inc.

Attn: Marketing Department
520 North Dearborn Street
Chicago, Illinois 60610-9857

NOTE: This page, when folded over and taped, becomes an envelope, which has been approved by the United States Postal Service. It is provided for your convenience.

INVESTMENT ANALYSIS FOR APPRAISERS

JEFFREY D. FISHER & ROBERT S. MARTIN

Dearborn
Financial Publishing, Inc.

While a great deal of care has been taken to provide accurate and current information, the ideas, suggestions, general principles and conclusions presented in this book are subject to local, state and federal laws and regulations, court cases and any revisions of same. The reader is thus urged to consult legal counsel regarding any points of law—this publication should not be used as a substitute for competent legal advice.

Publisher: Carol L. Luitjens
Development Editor: Robert A. Porché, Jr.
Project Editor: Debra M. Hall
Cover Design: Salvatore Concialdi

© 1995 by Dearborn Financial Publishing, Inc.®

Published by Real Estate Education Company,
a division of Dearborn Financial Publishing, Inc.®

Printed in the United States of America.

95 96 97 10 9 8 7 6 5 4 3 2 1

ISBN: 0-7931-1069-6

Library of Congress Cataloging-in-Publication Data

Fisher, Jeffrey D.
    Investment analysis for appraisers / by Jeffrey D. Fisher and
Robert S. Martin.
        p.   cm.
    Includes index.
    ISBN 0-7931-1069-6
    1. Real property—Valuation.   2. Rental housing—Valuation.
3. Commercial buildings—Valuation.   4. Real estate investment—Rate.
of return.   I. Martin, Robert S.   II. Title.
HD1387.F5294   1994
    333.33'2—dc20   94-29512
                                                               CIP

Contents

Preface

Investment Analysis for Appraisers allows readers to develop skills that are essential for analysis of real estate income property investments. Techniques used by real estate investors and appraisers are introduced and illustrated with numerous examples. The concepts discussed in the book are applicable to all types of properties, including small residential rental properties, apartment buildings, office buildings, hotels, motels, shopping centers and other income-producing real estate. Appraisers, real estate brokers, property managers, consultants and others can use the book to improve their understanding of the nature of income property investments. The techniques are applicable for many purposes, including appraisal, lease negotiations, refinancing and analysis for purchase or sale by a broker or investor.

The focus of the book is on learning how to analyze real estate income property from an investor's perspective. Topics covered in the book include an introduction to income property valuation, use of compound interest and discount factors, cash-flow forecasting, investment return calculations, evaluation of mortgage financing, risk analysis and tax considerations in investment analysis.

The book is especially useful in continuing education courses designed to help students further their skills in analyzing real estate income property. Depending on the background of the student, the material can be covered in a 10 or 20 hour module. The first four chapters cover the basics of investment analysis calculations and would be sufficient material for a ten hour module designed for a student with no prior experience with income property investments. Chapters five through seven cover more advanced material that can be covered in a ten hour module designed to challenge the more advanced student who requires only a brief review of the first four chapters.

About the Authors

Jeffrey D. Fisher, PhD, is Director of the Center for Real Estate Studies and Associate Professor of Finance and Real Estate at the Indiana University School of Business. He served as a trustee of The Appraisal Foundation from its formation in 1987 until 1993 and helped develop the content outline for the uniform national appraisal certification exam. Fisher is a past president of the American Real Estate and Urban Economics Association (AREUEA) and past chairman of the Real Estate Center Directors and Chairholders Association. He currently serves on the board of directors of the National Council of Real Estate Investment Fiduciaries (NCREIF) and is on the board of directors of MIG Residential Real Estate Investment Trust. Fisher received the 1992 PREA/Graaskamp Award for Research Excellence from the Pension Real Estate Association. He serves on the board of directors of the Weimer School of Advanced Studies in Real Estate and Land Economics, Homer Hoyt Advanced Studies Institute and is a faculty associate with the Lincoln Institute of Land Policy in Cambridge, Massachusetts. Fisher is the author of seven other books, including *Real Estate Appraisal, Real Estate Valuation, Real Estate Finance and Investments, Questions and Answers to Help You Pass the Real Estate Appraisal Exams,* 2nd Edition and *The Language of Real Estate Appraisal.* He also wrote a chapter on performance measurement for *The Office Building* book, a joint publication of the Counselors of Real Estate, the Appraisal Institute and the Society of Industrial and Office REALTORS®. Fisher developed the "Computer-Assisted Investment Analysis" course and more recently the "Advanced Income Capitalization" course for the Appraisal Institute. He has also developed numerous seminars for the Appraisal Institute, the American Society of Appraisers and other appraisal organizations. Fisher has also been a consultant to appraisers, attorneys, corporations, developers, financial institutions, government agencies and other universities, and has served as an expert witness on several occasions.

Robert S. Martin, MAI, SREA, CRE, is president of Martin and Associates of Winston-Salem, North Carolina. Martin and Associates is a real estate appraisal and consulting firm that specializes in the valuation and evaluation of income producing properties located primarily throughout the Southeastern United States. Typical properties appraised include apartments, office buildings, neighborhood shopping centers, regional malls, hotels, resort properties, golf courses, industrial buildings and subdivisions; and appraisals are prepared for financing decisions, bankruptcies, foreclosures, condemnation and property tax appeals. Martin is the author of three other books, including *Income Property Appraisal, The Language of Real Estate Appraisal* and *Subdivision Analysis*. He is the developer of numerous computer software programs for income property appraisal, including DCFast, DVM2 and Valucom. Martin developed the "Market and Investment Analysis" course for the former Society of Real Estate Appraisers and more recently the "Advanced Applications" for the Appraisal Institute. He has also developed numerous seminars for the Appraisal Institute, including "Appraising Troubled Properties," "Condominium Analysis" and "Preparation of the UCIAR Appraisal Report Form." Martin's clients include financial institutions, attorneys, governmental agencies, corporations, developers and accountants, and he has served as an expert witness on numerous occasions.

(handwritten annotations:)

REAL PROPERTY
PERSONAL PROPERTY
BUSINESS VALUE

4 PRODUCTION MUST EXIST

LAND   (MONEY)
CAPITAL   (BUSINESS)
ONTRAPUNUE   (JOBS) (PEOPLE) (WORK)
LABOR   (DEBT)
              DIFFERENCE BETWEEN OWN — OWE

HOMESICOM   MORTGAGE EQUITY

REAL ESTATE IS NOT ORGANIZED
GOVERNMENT INTERVENTION WILL INCREASE
IN REAL ESTATES FUTURE.
5 YEAR HOLD PERIOD OR MORE
2001 TAXES 15%
DISINTERMEDIATION
INTERUPTION IN SYSTEM
DIRECT

| CHAPTER 1 | # Introduction to Income Property Valuation |

INCOME PROPERTY INVESTMENTS

This chapter provides an introduction to the appraisal techniques that are used to estimate the value of income-producing real estate investments. The income potential of the property generally depends on the willingness of individuals or firms to pay for the use of space. As is the case in the market for other economic goods and services, the price that can be received for renting a particular income property depends on the supply of competing space as well as on the demand for that space by potential users. Property that is capable of producing income has a value to investors who are willing to purchase real estate in anticipation of a return on their investment. Real estate income property is owned by a variety of different types of investors, including individuals, partnerships, corporations, real estate investment trusts, insurance companies, pension funds, and state and local governments.

Income property may be classified as either residential or nonresidential and may have a variety of characteristics. Figure 1.1 summarizes the main classifications of income property. *Residential* income property, in its simplest form, consists of a single-family rental property; in its most complex form it might consist of a highrise apartment project in a downtown metropolitan area. In either case rented space is used as a residential dwelling for one or more individuals.

Nonresidential income-producing real estate includes commercial, industrial, hotels and other special-purpose properties. Commercial space can be further divided into office buildings, shopping centers (superregional, regional, community, neighborhood and specialty), financial institutions, restaurants and other retail stores.

Office space can be classified as highrise, lowrise, single tenant and medical space. Industrial property can be divided into manufacturing, warehouses, lofts, garage space, distribution, and research and development. Hotels can be classified as motels, highrise, convention or resort properties. Special-use properties include hospitals, nursing homes, marinas, shipping facilities, power plants and so forth.

FIGURE 1.1 Classifications of Income Property

Residential   *1–4 family*   *Multifamily*
                                                    Garden apartment
                                                    Lowrise
                                                    Highrise

Nonresidential   *Commercial*   *Industrial*
                         Office   Manufacturing
                           Highrise   Warehouse
                           Lowrise   Office warehouse
                           Single tenant   Lofts
                           Medical   Garage space
                         Shopping centers   Distribution
                           Superregional   Research and development
                           Regional
                           Community
                           Neighborhood
                           Specialty
                         Other retail stores
                         Financial institutions
                         Restaurants

                       Hotel   *Special purpose*
                         Motel   Hospitals
                         Highrise   Nursing homes
                         Convention   Marinas
                         Resort   Shipping facilities
                                                    Power plants
                                                    Other

COMPONENTS OF PROPERTY VALUE

Real estate is a complex economic good that actually consists of various component parts that contribute to the value of a particular property. Figure 1.2 summarizes the major value components. Real estate has two major physical components: the land and the improvements that are added to the land. *Land* is defined as the earth's surface, including land, water and anything attached to it; natural resources in their original state (e.g., mineral deposits, timber, soil). In law, land is considered to be the solid surface of the earth and does not include water. *Improvements* are structures or buildings that are permanently attached to the land.

A distinction is often made between the physical real estate and the legal property rights associated with the physical real estate. The legal rights are referred to as real property. *Real property* is defined as the interests, benefits and rights inherent in the ownership of real estate. *Real estate* is defined as an identified parcel or tract of land, including improvements, if any.[1] When appraising real estate, the appraiser must identify the physical real estate being appraised as well as determine what legal rights are associated with the property being appraised.

All rights to real property are referred to as the *bundle of rights* and are defined as follows: An ownership concept that describes real property by the legal rights associated with owning the property. It specifies rights such as the rights to sell, lease, use, occupy, mortgage and trade the property, among others.

FIGURE 1.2   Value Components

Physical real estate	*Bundle of rights (estates)*
Land	Fee simple
Improvements	Leased fee
	Leasehold
Property rights	
Real property interests	*Financial*
Nonrealty interests	Mortgage
Personal property	Equity
Intangible property	
Business value	
Financing premiums	

These rights are typically purchased by the buyer in a sales transaction unless specifically noted or limited in the sale.

Ownership of the complete bundle of rights is referred to as the *fee simple estate* (or fee simple interest) and is defined as absolute ownership of real estate that is unencumbered by any other interest or estate and is subject to the limitations of eminent domain, escheat, police power and taxation. A fee simple estate can be valuated by the present value of the income generated by market rents.

An owner may convey all or part of the bundle of rights to another entity. For example, when a property is leased to an outside tenant under a written agreement or lease, the landlord has relinquished the right to occupy and use the property until the lease expires. The ownership interest that remains and is held by a landlord subject to the lease is referred to as the *leased fee estate* and is defined as an ownership interest in the real estate held by a landlord who has transferred the right of occupancy to a property through the execution of a lease. The leased fee estate can be valued as the present value of the lease income plus the right to the reversion at the end of the lease. The landlord retains the right to receive rental payment throughout the term of the lease and the right to possess the property at the termination of the lease.

Under a lease arrangement, the tenant holds the right to occupy and use the property as long as the terms of the lease are not violated. The lessee's right of occupancy is forfeited when the lease expires. This interest is known as the *leasehold estate* and is defined as an ownership interest in real estate held by a tenant during the term of a lease. The leasehold estate can be valued as the present value of the difference between the market rent and the rent specified by the lease. The tenant is given the right to use and occupy a property for a time and based on the restrictions contained in the lease.

Under certain circumstances, if the lease allows, the tenant may transfer the right to occupy and use the tenant space. If the lease terms created an advantage for a prospective tenant, the leasehold interest may have value and therefore could be sold for a profit.

A leasehold interest is also created when the land is leased. A developer may enter into a long-term *land lease* (ground lease) and construct the improvements. Under this circumstance, the tenant holds a leasehold interest in the land and owns the improvements until the land lease expires. The owner of the land has a leased fee interest in the land and a reversionary interest in the improvements at the expiration of the land lease. Either party has the right to sell, mortgage or trade the interest, but only the lessee of the land has the right to occupy and use the property. This right is lost when the land lease expires.

Real estate valuation assignments may involve the analysis of any or all of these real estate interests. The task is to identify and estimate the value of the interest.

NONREALTY INTERESTS

Due to the complex nature of many real estate appraisal assignments, nonrealty interests may be involved. *Nonrealty interests* include personal property and intangible property such as business value and contractual arrangements.

Personal Property

The most obvious example of inclusion of a nonrealty interest is when tangible personal property is included. *Personal property* is defined as identifiable, portable and tangible objects that are considered by the general public as being "personal," e.g., furnishings, artwork, antiques, gems and jewelry, collectibles, machinery and equipment—all property that is not classified as real estate.

Examples of real estate projects where personal property may be included are (1) restaurant equipment in a restaurant setting, (2) machinery and equipment in an industrial plant and (3) furniture in a hotel. Personal property is not typically permanently attached to real estate. In some instances, the decision as to whether an item should be considered personal or real property is difficult, especially with regard to industrial property.

Although personal property has value, its value must be separated from that of the real property in an appraisal report. For example, the value of a hotel might include furniture, fixtures and equipment in the hotel that are considered personal property. The appraisal report would indicate the value of this property in addition to the value of the real property (land and improvements).

Business Value

Another nonrealty interest that is frequently part of a real estate transaction is business value. *Business value* is defined as the value resulting from business organization including such things as management skills, assembled work force, working capital, legal rights (trade names, business names, franchises, patents, trademarks, contracts, leases, operating agreements) that have been assembled to make the business a viable and valuable entity in its competitive market. Business value is often associated with properties such as hotels, nursing homes and regional shopping centers.

The term "going-concern value" refers to the total value of the property, including the real property, the tangible personal property and the enhancement to value resulting from an operating business. Going-concern value assumes that the business operation will continue. For example, the appraiser may determine that a hotel has a going-concern value because of its national franchise and above- average management, which have allowed it to capture a higher percentage of the market than other hotels. Thus, in addition to the land, improvements and personal property, the appraiser may assign an additional value to the business enterprise. All of this would be included in the going-concern value of the hotel.

Tax Incentives

For certain property types, governmental agencies have created incentives through the granting of tax credits, depreciation deductions and/or property tax reductions to encourage the development or rehabilitation of certain property types. The value of these incentives would be classified as a nonrealty interest. Analysis of these interests involves a complex process that will not be considered in this book. The analyst should, however, be aware of the possibility that these interests may exist.

MORTGAGE AND EQUITY INTERESTS

Numerous real estate transactions are funded using debt financing. Once the debt is incurred, the lender receives a mortgage interest on the property. The owner's interest becomes an *equity interest*. The mortgage instrument creates a contractual relationship between the owner and borrower. The lender is free to sell his or her mortgage obligation to another lender. The borrower may or may not be able to sell the property and have the subsequent owner assume the loan at its original terms.

If the loan terms are below those typical of the market and the loan is assumable, a potential buyer may pay a premium amount for the right to assume the loan. This premium is referred to as a "financing premium" and would be a nonrealty interest. The additional price does not represent payment for the real property; in effect, a premium is paid for the equity interest in the property. However, because the loan terms are below those typical of the market, the existing mortgage interest in the property is worth less. Should the lender wish to sell the loan to another lender, if the contract terms are less favorable than typical terms, the loan may have a market value less than its current balance. In theory, the additional amount an equity investor would pay for the right to assume the below-market loan is offset by the lower amount the lender would receive if the mortgage interest were sold. Thus, the sum of the mortgage and equity interests is still the same as the value of the real property with market financing.

REAL ESTATE MARKET CHARACTERISTICS

Real estate appraisal differs in many ways from valuation techniques commonly applied to other investments such as stocks and bonds. In part, this is a result of the characteristics of real estate markets versus other capital markets.

A market for an item is created by the interaction of buyers and sellers, all seeking to exchange similar goods. In today's economy, the medium of exchange is typically monetary in nature. The remainder of this book deals with issues and methods used to analyze real estate markets and approaches to estimating the market value for various property types and interests. Following is a review of the various characteristics of the real estate market.

No Organized Market

Unlike the market for stocks and bonds, there is no centralized market for real estate transactions. Thus, it is difficult to know the price of a particular type of real estate at a given point in time.

Availability of Market Information

Information concerning sale prices, lease terms, financing and any other agreements that are part of a transaction may be confidential and unavailable to individuals who are not parties to the sale. There is no recognized source of published information that contains information in the detail needed to analyze a sale accurately. Negotiations for a specific property may involve extended periods of time because of the complexity of a transaction and the need to make judgments concerning construction quality, environmental issues, legal documents, past operating history and so forth.

Because of the time necessary to complete transactions, available information about the transaction price could reflect terms that were agreed on at a point significantly earlier than the actual closing date. Sale prices also may have included consideration paid for interests other than the real estate itself.

Infrequent Trades of Property

Transactions for real estate investments are not continuous, making it difficult to know how prices are changing over time. Appraisers often must use information from property sales that occurred considerably earlier than the date the value is being estimated for the present property appraisal.

Immobility of Real Estate

Unlike many investment opportunities available to the investment community, real estate property is tied to a fixed location. The potential success or failure of a real estate project may be significantly affected by happenings and trends in the general and immediate geographic area that surrounds it. Stocks, bonds and commodities are not tied to a specific location. Even a business can generally be moved to another location if success is not expected at its current location. Real estate, however, is and always will remain a product that is heavily affected by its surroundings. Because the success of an income-producing property is so heavily dependent on the state of its environment, a real estate analyst must place heavy emphasis on an analysis of the area and neighborhood market conditions as well as of the property itself. Another variable factor is that market conditions are not stable and may, therefore, change significantly over time. The change may come abruptly and may have either a positive or a negative impact on the property. If a change is negative, actions to counteract the adverse condition may be physically, politically or financially beyond the capability of a property owner. The immobility of real estate is what makes real estate such a fascinating subject: Identical physical improvements on two lots of the same size may have significantly different market values because of each lot's unique location.

Each Parcel Is Unique

Because of the immobility of real estate, we can say that no two parcels of real estate can ever be *exactly* alike. They will always be at different locations. Whether this difference has a significant impact on value is a different consideration. Because each parcel is unique, the price of one property may or may not be a good indication of the value of another property.

Segmented Markets

The real estate market is divided into numerous segments or submarkets that do not necessarily behave the same way. The division occurs not only by property type and market area but also within each segment itself. For example, the success of one type of building in a particular neighborhood does not automatically ensure that the same building type will be successful in another neighborhood. Construction costs of a Class A office building in Neighborhood X might be absorbed rapidly, and the building might command attractive tenants and rent levels. Because of an oversupply of Class A office space in Neighborhood Y, however, if the same Class A office building were to be constructed in this neighborhood, it might not achieve the same level of success. Technological advances may impact on market segments and change market perceptions. In other words, new segments might be created that would have an impact on existing market segments. For example, the recent rise of small specialty shopping centers has had a significant impact on the tenant mix of neighborhood and community centers. The notion that a neighborhood center cannot be successful without major tenants has disappeared.

Real estate markets may not only be segmented by user type and location but also by investor type. For example, major "investment grade" property may include a multitude of property types but be similar in location, size, effective age, construction quality and, therefore, perceived risk.

GOVERNMENT REGULATIONS

Real estate is heavily regulated and is subject to rules promulgated not only at the local level but also on the state and national levels. New construction must meet the strict requirements set forth in zoning restrictions, development requirements, environmental controls and building inspection requirements. Land use may be further controlled by other public programs. For example, incentives are available for low-income residential housing projects that meet predetermined guidelines. These guidelines are restrictions on the project in addition to the restrictions imposed by zoning, environmental rules and development requirements. It is important to realize that heavy government regulation is a major factor in the real estate market and that changes in rules and laws may significantly affect a real estate investment. In 1981, tax laws were changed to provide incentives to encourage construction of new projects during a period of high inflation and high interest rates. These incentives worked: Significant new construction occurred from 1982 to 1986 in many markets around the country. In 1986, the tax incentives were eliminated. Because the market for certain properties in several market areas had become out of balance, a severe slump in real estate values in oversupplied areas resulted in the late 1980s.

Local controls are emerging as significant factors in the marketplace today, evidenced by severe restrictions that may be placed on new construction. Laws governing such development factors as density, traffic patterns and control, and the impact of new construction on the capacity of public facilities are gradually becoming more restrictive. It appears a developer's options may be reduced even further in the future. Any analysis of the real estate market that does not seriously consider the effect of government controls would certainly be deficient.

MARKET TRENDS

Although there are numerous investment markets that are more volatile (commodities, for example), the real estate market is subject to significantly large shifts over time. Supply and demand for real estate are seldom in balance. Once demand exceeds supply, opportunistic developers typically enter the market and construct new facilities that may exceed the immediate demand. The lead time needed to construct new projects, the size of new projects and the lack of perfect market information and financing alternatives—all contribute to the cyclical nature of the real estate market. Economic factors such as employment, income levels, the level of business activity and the health of financial markets all affect real estate values and are therefore the driving forces behind the fluctuations in real estate markets. Because market information is imperfect, reading and assessing the impact of the cyclical nature of real estate are certainly difficult. A reasonable assessment of market information is obviously needed in an analysis of the real estate market.

Supply Adjusts Slowly

It takes time for the supply of real estate to change through development of new properties or even conversion from one use to another. This adds an additional complication to attempting to measure real estate values. For example, in "equilibrium," value might equal cost if both are accurately and appropriately measured. However, in the short run, value may differ considerably from cost.

Few Buyers and Sellers at One Time

Compared with some other markets, such as stocks and bonds, there are usually relatively few buyers and sellers in the market for a particular property at a particular time. This can result in transaction prices that differ from market value. It also means that in some cases a particular buyer can influence the price. Such a market differs from one characterized by perfect competition, where buyers are "price takers"; that is, a market in which individual buyers do not influence the price. In real estate markets, prices are often influenced by a particular buyer who is willing to bid much more than another bidder. Consequently, some analysts question whether market value is being paid—especially when it is the "optimist" who ends up with the property!

THE ROLE OF CAPITAL MARKETS

We have discussed the characteristics of the market for real estate assets. This is the market in which interests in real property, that is, land and buildings, are traded. Real estate income property is often bought and sold by investors who are primarily interested in the rate of return that they expect to earn on the investment. These investors expect a rate of return commensurate with that available from other capital investments of similar risk. Furthermore, real estate investments are typically financed with mortgages that are obtained from various types of financial institutions, including banks, S&Ls, insurance companies and mortgage real estate investment trusts.

It should be clear that real estate values can be influenced by trends in the broader capital market. Thus, it is important for real estate appraisers to be aware of rates of return that are currently available for alternative investments and have a general understanding of the overall market for real estate capital.

The term *capital market* refers to the market for all the various sources of capital for either lending or investment, including government and corporate bonds and corporate stocks, as debt and equity capital for real estate.

Debt capital is used for construction loans and permanent financing in the form of long-term mortgages. Capital for construction has traditionally come from commercial banks and S&Ls. However, because of the problems experienced by the S&L industry during the late 1980s and early 1990s, it has become more difficult for developers to rely on these sources for construction and development loans. Capital for long-term mortgage loans on single-family residences and smaller residential and nonresidential income property investments typically comes from a bank, S&L or credit union. For larger residential or nonresidential income properties, the debt capital might come from an insurance company, a pension fund or a mortgage real estate investment trust (REIT).

The term *primary market* refers to the initial source of capital received by a user to fund a project. The initial supplier of capital may, in turn, sell the financial instrument that was created when the capital was supplied. For example, a homebuyer might receive a loan from an S&L that results in the creation of a mortgage instrument that indicates the terms of the loan and makes the property collateral for the loan. The S&L might sell this mortgage in what is referred to as the "secondary market." The *secondary market* is the market for existing financial claims. In the case of the secondary mortgage market, purchasers include such entities as the Federal National Mortgage Association (FNMA), referred to as "Fannie Mae," and the Federal Home Loan Mortgage Corporation (FHLMC), referred to as "Freddie Mac." These secondary market participants play an important role in capital markets by providing a source of liquidity for mortgage lenders, a provision that helps ensure the availability of mortgage capital for single-family residential properties.

Equity capital for real estate comes from a wide variety of sources, ranging from small individual investors to large institutional investors such as insurance companies and pension funds. These funds could be invested directly into the real estate project or through a financial intermediary, for example, an equity REIT or some type of syndication such as a public or private limited partnership. The nature of these intermediaries has changed significantly over time. In the early to middle 1980s, syndications were quite active because of their ability to pass the tax benefits associated with real estate through to the investors. With the reduction in tax incentives in 1986, these vehicles became much less attractive. At the same time, the role of pension funds as a source of real estate capital increased in significance. Although some pension funds invest directly in real estate, others prefer to invest through some type of intermediary that can provide expertise in selecting investments and managing the property. Many insurance companies and other money managers responded by establishing funds for pension fund investment. These funds received the capital from the pension fund and invested the money in real estate investments that were then managed by the funds.

TYPES OF REAL ESTATE STUDIES

Real estate studies may be classified in several different categories: market studies, marketability studies, investment analyses, feasibility studies, highest and best use analysis, environmental impact studies, cost-benefit studies, land utilization studies and real estate appraisals. Studies relevant to the preparation of a real estate appraisal include market studies, marketability studies, highest and best use analysis and feasibility studies. Results of each of these studies are vital inputs in an appraisal report. Each category of study is defined below.

Market Study

A thorough real estate analysis of the general market conditions affecting a property includes a *market study* of demographic, economic, political, and cultural trends and conditions that affect the current supply and demand for a particular property type.

Market studies focus specifically on the property *type,* not on the specific property itself. In this sense, market studies are the most general in nature. The other study types focus specifically on a certain property. Key data analyzed in a market study are the demographic and economic factors that affect the subject property as well as governmental policy and social trends.

Marketability Study

A *marketability study* is a real estate analysis that addresses the ability of a property to be absorbed, sold or leased under current and anticipated market conditions.

In contrast to market studies, marketability studies involve analysis of a specific property. Marketability study information is used to test whether current and foreseeable market forces will support development of a specific use and the rate at which absorption could take place. Marketability studies focus closely on competitive facilities to formulate three kinds of conclusions:

1. the price at which a property will be sold or rented;
2. the quantity likely to be sold or rented over the absorption period; and
3. the conditions, marketing techniques and features that will enhance the success of the project.

Marketability study information is used to forecast various key inputs in an appraisal, including rent and expense estimates, the relative contribution of property attributes, absorption periods and absorption patterns. Rent estimates include not only the absolute rent levels but also typical terms: rental increase provisions, options, expense passthroughs, sales overage provisions and so forth.

Investment Analysis

According to the Uniform Standards of Professional Appraisal Practice, an *investment analysis* is a study that reflects the relationship between acquisition price and anticipated future benefits of a real estate investment.

The term "investment analysis" is also used as a general term to describe any of a number of studies that analyze expected future cash flows in relation to money or capital used to purchase an interest in a property. For example, analyses to decide whether to refinance or dispose of a property could be considered investment analyses.

Feasibility Study

According to the Uniform Standards of Professional Appraisal Practice, a *feasibility study* is a study of the cost-benefit relationship of an economic endeavor. It is an analysis of a real estate project that incorporates the results of market and marketability studies to determine whether a project will meet the economic return requirements of a specific market or investor.

The feasibility study focuses directly on the expected performance of the subject property in a real estate appraisal. In undertaking a feasibility study, the appraiser takes information and judgments made based on data from market and marketability studies and applies the analytic techniques associated with investment analysis to calculate benchmarks of expected performance for the subject. If the expected levels of performance meet the standards of an investor for the property, the project passes the test of feasibility. The preparation of feasibility studies will be discussed in a later chapter after the appraiser has been exposed to the analytical techniques used to test the cash-flow inputs forecast using market and marketability study information.

Highest and Best Use Analysis

A *highest and best use (HBU) analysis* is essentially a series of feasibility studies for different use scenarios for the subject property, both for the land as if vacant and for the property as if improved. The use for each that results in the highest value is the use assumed in the appraisal report. In essence, an HBU analysis uses the results of market studies, marketability studies and feasibility studies to arrive at a conclusion regarding the best use of the property.

The HBU is the reasonable and probable use that results in the highest present value of the land after considering all legally permissible, physically possible and economically feasible uses. Capitalization rates or discount rates for each feasible use should reflect typical returns expected in the market. Highest and best use is usually determined under two different premises, as if the site were

1. vacant and could be improved in the optimal manner; or
2. currently improved.

In the latter premise, the choices will be either to keep the existing building or to demolish the building and construct one that would fulfill the highest and best use of the site. In general, it is not feasible to demolish an existing building as long as it contributes value above that of the vacant site.

Environmental Impact Study

An *environmental impact study* is an analysis of the impact of a proposed land use on its environment, including the direct and indirect effects of the project during all phases of use and their long-run implications.

The National Environmental Policy Act of 1969 requires that every recommendation or report on proposals for legislation and other major federal actions significantly affecting the quality of the human environment must be filed with a detailed impact statement. The environmental impact study provides an analysis of any adverse environmental effects that cannot be avoided should the proposal be implemented, alternatives to the proposed action, the relationship between local short-term uses of the environment and the maintenance and enhancement of long-term productivity, and any irreversible and irretrievable commitments of resources that would be involved in the proposed action should it be implemented.

Cost-Benefit Study

A *cost-benefit study* is an analysis of the cost of creating an improvement versus the benefits that will be created by the improvement, including nonmonetary issues.

A cost-benefit study is typically used by public agencies to make decisions concerning capital improvements. A cost-benefit ratio is typically developed through the analysis of a proposed project. The ratio equals the dollar amount of benefits generated by an improvement divided by the cost of that improvement. The ratio must exceed 1.00 for the improvement to be considered desirable.

Land Utilization Study

A *land utilization study* is an analysis of the potential uses of a parcel of land and a determination of the highest and best use for that parcel; a complete inventory of the parcels in a given community or other area classified by type of use, plus (in some cases) an analysis of the spatial patterns of use revealed by this inventory.

Land utilization studies do not embody the viewpoint of any particular investor nor do they focus on any one parcel. Furthermore, the consideration of markets and feasibility is not normally included.

Appraisal

According to the Uniform Standards of Professional Appraisal Practice, an *appraisal* is defined as (1) the act or process of estimating value; an estimate of value and (2) pertaining to appraising and related functions, e.g., appraisal practice, appraisal services.

An appraisal provides an unbiased estimate of the value of an identified interest in real property, related personalty or intangible assets. The appraisal process involves undertaking selective research and analysis of pertinent market data, applying the appropriate analytical approaches, drawing from experience and academic skills, and applying judgment to arrive at an estimate of value. Ultimately, the results of all the key real estate studies are presented in an appraisal report as support for the final value estimate selected.

The three approaches to appraisal include:

1. the cost approach;
2. the sales comparison approach; and
3. the income capitalization approach.

This book illustrates the application of each approach to the appraisal of real estate income property.

NEED FOR AN APPRAISAL PROCESS

Real estate differs from other economic goods or investments in a number of ways. Its value depends on its physical, legal, social and economic characteristics as well as on the dynamics of the market in which it is bought and sold.

The complexity of real estate as well as the lack of market information compared with many other economic goods must be reflected in the appraisal process used to estimate value. The validity of this process is important to market participants such as buyers, sellers, lenders and government agencies that rely on the appraiser's conclusions. The remainder of this book explores the appraisal process in more depth, with emphasis on the valuation of real estate income property.

SUMMARY

Income property can be classified as residential or nonresidential. Nonresidential property includes commercial, industrial, hotel and special-purpose properties. Physical characteristics of real estate include land and improvements. The term *real property* refers to the legal rights associated with the real estate. A fee simple interest in the property owns the complete bundle of rights. When a property is leased, the lessor transfers some of the rights to the lessee. The lessor's interest is referred to as a leased fee interest, and the lessee's rights are referred to as the leasehold interest.

A property may include nonrealty interests in addition to real property. Examples include personal property and business value. When there is a business value, the going-concern value of the property exceeds that of the real property and the personal property.

When a mortgage is used to finance a property, a mortgage interest and an equity interest are created. Mortgages that have favorable terms can result in a financing premium, which is an amount paid for the right to assume the mortgage. This premium does not add value to the real property.

Real estate markets are characterized by lack of an organized national market, difficulty in obtaining market information, infrequent sales and a small number of active buyers and sellers at a particular point in time. Real estate is also immobile and each parcel is unique. Markets tend to be segmented and real estate is subject to many government regulations.

A market study is an analysis of general market conditions, whereas a marketability study is an analysis of the ability of a specific property to be absorbed, sold or leased under current or anticipated market conditions. A feasibility study combines the results of the market and marketability studies to determine whether a project will meet the economic return requirements of a specific market or investor. A highest and best use analysis combines the results of market studies, marketability studies and feasibility studies to determine the use that results in the highest value. An appraisal is an unbiased estimate of the value of an identified interest in real property, related personal property and any intangible assets such as business interests and financing premiums. The need for an appraisal can arise from a variety of sources, including owners, sellers, buyers, lenders, insurance companies and government agencies.

The value of real estate is affected by local market trends, slow adjustments in supply and changes in the capital market. Because of the unique characteristics of real estate assets and the complexities of real estate markets, appraisers follow a well-defined process when estimating value.

KEY TERMS

appraisal	land utilization study
bundle of rights	leased fee estate
business value	leasehold estate
capital market	marketability study
cost-benefit study	market study
environmental impact study	mortgage interest
equity interest	nonrealty interests
feasibility study	nonresidential property
fee simple estate	personal property
improvements	primary mortgage market
income	real estate
income property	real property
investment analysis	residential property
land	secondary mortgage market
land lease	segmented market

QUESTIONS

1. What are the ways of classifying income property?
2. What is the difference between real estate and real property?
3. What is meant by the term "bundle of rights"? How can these rights be separated?
4. What are the sources of nonrealty interests? Do nonrealty interests have value?
5. What interests are created when a property is financed with a mortgage?
6. What is meant by the term "appraisal"?
7. Why is it necessary to appraise real estate income property?
8. What distinguishes real estate markets from the market for other investments?
9. How could changes in the capital market affect the value of real estate-income property?
10. What is the difference between a marketability study and a market study?
11. What is a highest and best use analysis?

END NOTE

1. In some jurisdictions, the terms "real estate" and "real property" have the same legal meaning. The separate definitions recognize the traditional distinction between the two concepts in appraisal theory.

CHAPTER 2

Compound Interest and Discount Factors

IMPORTANCE OF THE TIME VALUE OF MONEY

The income approach assumes that the value of a property equals the present value of anticipated future benefits. This chapter reviews the concepts of compound interest and discounting that form the foundation for converting estimated future income into a *present value.*

Someone unfamiliar with the concept of compound interest might believe that we could merely add up the anticipated future benefits, as demonstrated below.

Year	Annual Cash Flow
1	$ 10,000
2	10,000
3	12,000
4	12,000
5	130,000
Total	$174,000

If the present value of future benefits were calculated in this manner, and the investor paid $174,000 for the property, he or she would not earn a rate of return on the capital invested. The annual cash flow would be just sufficient to return the investor's initial investment in the property. This is not likely to occur for two reasons. First, investors must expect to receive a return of more than their original investment to be induced to invest money rather than spend it. Second, alternative investment opportunities of comparable risk are likely to be available that could be expected to give the investor an additional rate of return on capital invested. Thus, there is an opportunity cost associated with making an investment that does not provide the same return for the same level of risk. This can be summarized by the financial principle of the *time value of money,* which is defined as a financial principle based on the assumption that a positive interest can be earned on an investment and, therefore, money received today is more valuable than money received in the future.

To properly capture the time value of money, *compound interest* theory was developed. Compound interest theory assumes periodic interest is earned on funds that have been deposited. It further assumes that interest for a specific period is also earned on the interest that has accumulated from prior periods.

A second theory was developed under which expected future cash flows could be reduced to a present value estimate by calculating what would be needed today to grow at compounded interest to the future expected value. This mathematical process is referred to as *discounting,* which is defined as the process of converting future income to a present value by mathematically reducing future cash flow by the implied interest that would have been earned assuming an initial investment, an interest rate and a specified time period.

The discounting process is used extensively by appraisers to estimate the present value of expected future cash flows.

VARIABLES IN THE DISCOUNTING PROCESS

Any problem involving calculations using the discounting process involves four variables:

1. time period;
2. interest rate;
3. expected future cash flow (or cash flows); and
4. present value.

Once any three of these variables are known, the fourth can usually be calculated by using published tables, a hand-held calculator or a computer.[1] The two variables most likely to be calculated by appraisers are the interest rate and the present value.

Interest Rate

If the present value is known or assumed to be known, along with the expected future cash flows over a specified time period (holding period), the *interest rate* can be calculated. For example, the present value might represent the price recently paid for a comparable property. If the appraiser knows what cash flows the buyer projected over time, the interest rate can be calculated. This interest rate represents the rate of return or *yield rate* (also referred to as an *internal rate of return*) that the investor would expect to earn.

Present Value

Appraising income property requires the appraiser to estimate the present value of anticipated future cash flows. Depending on the particular capitalization technique chosen, the appraiser may be required to forecast the expected cash flows over a specific time period and calculate the present value of those cash flows, using a specified interest rate as a *discount rate.* The interest rate selected as a discount rate should be the rate of return investors would require to invest in properties of comparable risk.

COMPOUND INTEREST AND DISCOUNT FACTORS

Before the invention of hand-held calculators, appraisers relied mainly on published tables of factors for specific interest rates and holding periods. These factors were precalculated either for a present value of one dollar or for periodic payments of one dollar. Most tables included six different columns of factors calculated on an annual basis (see Appendix A). To use these factors, the appraiser needed only to multiply the dollar amount being considered by the appropriate factor to arrive at present or future value calculations. The tables assumed equal periodic compounding periods, for example, annual or monthly compounding.

With the introduction of calculators and widespread use of computers, the tables have virtually disappeared from use. Financial calculators have the compounding and discounting formulas built in. The table information is, therefore, at the fingertips of the appraiser and accessible by entering a few simple keystrokes. A discussion follows, covering each of the common six factors typically used. These factors are generally referred to as the "Six Functions of One Dollar." All six factors are mathematically related to each other. This relationship will be demonstrated after a discussion of each of the six factors.

Future Value of One Dollar S^n

The *future value of one dollar* signifies the amount to which an investment of $1 grows with compound interest after a specified number of years at a specified interest rate (column 1 of the compound interest tables in Appendix A). The factor for the future value of one dollar is arrived at by adding one to the interest per period (i) and taking this to the exponent that represents the number of years (n): $(1 + i)^n = S^n$.

Formula: $(1 + i)^n = S^n$ (column 1 in the table in Appendix A)

where i equals the effective interest rate and n equals the number of time periods (column 1 in the table in Appendix A).

Table Relationship.   This factor is the reciprocal of the *present value of one dollar* (column 4 in the table in Appendix A).

Example 2-1

What will a $10,000 investment made today grow to at the end of 5 years, assuming a 12 percent rate of return?

Year	Beginning Value	Annual Return (12%)		Ending Balance
1	$10,000	+ ($10,000 × 0.12)	$1,200 =	$11,200
2	11,200	+ (11,200 × 0.12)	1,344 =	12,544
3	12,544	+ (12,544 × 0.12)	1,505 =	14,049
4	14,049	+ (14,049 × 0.12)	1,686 =	15,735
5	15,735	+ (15,735 × 0.12)	1,888 =	17,623

Present Value	Future Value	Future Value Factor
$10,000	$17,623	$17,623 ÷ $10,000 = 1.7623

Factor Solution.   The 12 percent annual future value of one factor for five years may be found in the tables in Appendix A. The factor is 1.762342. The factor also can be found using the financial functions of a financial calculator by entering 1.00 as the present value, five years as the number of periods (holding period) and 12 percent as the interest, then pressing the future value key. Alternatively, it can be found by solving the following mathematical relationship, using the powers option:

$$(1 + 0.12)^5 = (1.12)^5 = 1.762342$$

Discussion.   The factor represents the basic compound interest concept and is used to convert a single lump-sum payment into a future value estimate. In investment analyses, this factor is used in the first step of calculating an adjusted rate of return to estimate the future value numbers for each interim cash flow using a reinvestment rate.

Future Value of One Dollar per Period

The *future value of one dollar per period* is defined as a compound interest factor to which a constant periodic investment of $1 per period will grow, assuming compound growth at a specific rate of return for a specific number of compounding periods (column 2 of the compound interest tables in Appendix A). In an appraisal (and a real estate investment analysis), these payments are generally assumed to be made at the *end* of each period.

NOTE: The annuity factors in the table assume each payment will be received at the end of the year. This type of annuity is referred to as an *ordinary annuity.* Annuities can also be assumed to start at the beginning of the year. This would be referred to as an *annuity in advance.* An example of an annuity in advance is provided later in this chapter.

Formula: $\dfrac{(1 + i)^n - 1}{i} = S_{\overline{n}}$ (column 2 in the tables in Appendix A)

where *i* equals the effective interest rate and *n* equals the number of time periods.

Table Relationship.   This factor is the reciprocal of the sinking fund factor (column 3 in the tables in appendix A).

Example 2-2

What will a $1,000 investment made at the end of each of the next five years grow to at the end of the five-year period, assuming a 12 percent rate of return?

Annual Investment	Future Value	Future Value Factor
$1,000 (EOY)	$6,352	$6,352 ÷ $1,000 = 6.352

* Proof *

Year	Beginning Balance	Annual Return (12%)	Additional Investment	Ending Balance
1	$ 0	+ $0	+ $1,000	= $1,000
2	1,000	+ (1,000 × 0.12) $120	+ 1,000	= 2,120
3	2,120	+ (2,120 × 0.12) 254	+ 1,000	= 3,374
4	3,374	+ (3,374 × 0.12) 405	+ 1,000	= 4,779
5	4,779	+ (4,779 × 0.12) 573	+ 1,000	= 6,352

(handwritten in left margin:) 1,000 PMT   12 I   5 N   FV

Factor Solution. The 12 percent annual future value of one dollar per period factor for five years may be found in the tables in Appendix A. The factor is 6.352847. The factor may also be found using the financial functions of a calculator by entering 1.00 for the payment, five years as the number of periods (holding period) and 12 percent as the interest rate. When the future value key is pressed, the factor for 12 percent will appear.

The future value of one dollar per period can also be calculated by adding the future value of 1.00 factors for $(n-1)$ periods and adding 1.00. For example, if we add the future value of 1.00 factors for years one through four at a 12 percent interest rate and then add 1.00, we obtain the same answer as the future value of an annuity of 1.00 factor for five years.[2]

Discussion. This factor may be used to calculate the future value for a series of equal payments in the first step of calculating an adjusted rate of return. This factor is probably used the least by an appraiser in typical assignments.

Sinking Fund Factor

The *sinking fund factor* is a compound interest factor that represents the level payment percentage required to be periodically invested and compounded at a specific interest rate to grow to an amount equal to $1.00 over a specific time period (column 3 of the compound interest tables).

Formula: $\dfrac{i}{(1+i)^n - 1} = 1/S_{\overline{n}}$ (column 3 in the tables in Appendix A)

where i equals the effective interest rate and n equals the number of time periods.

Table Relationship. This factor is the reciprocal of the future value of one dollar per period (column 2 in the tables in Appendix A).

Example 2-3

What level annual payment must be paid at the end of each of five years, assuming a 12 percent rate of return to grow to $10,000 in five years?

Future Value		Sinking Fund Factor		Sinking Fund Payment
$10,000	×	0.1574	=	$1,574

* Proof *

Year	Beginning Balance	Annual Return (12%)		Additional Payment		Ending Balance
1	$ 0	+ $0		+ $1,574	=	$ 1,574
2	1,574	+ (1,574 × 0.12) $189	+	1,574	=	3,337
3	3,337	+ (3,337 × 0.12) 400	+	1,574	=	5,311
4	5,311	+ (5,311 × 0.12) 638	+	1,574	=	7,523
5	7,523	+ (7,523 × 0.12) 903	+	1,574	=	10,000

Factor Solution.   The 12 percent annual sinking fund factor for five years may be found in the tables in Appendix A. The factor is 0.157410. The factor may also be found using the financial functions of a calculator by entering 1.00 for the future value, five years for the holding period and 12 percent as the interest rate. When the payment key is pressed, the factor for 12 percent will appear.

Discussion.   This factor can be used to estimate the amount necessary to set aside in a reserve for replacements. The factor is also used in some of the formula approaches to yield capitalization. It also can be used by appraisers to estimate the periodic annual payment needed to cover a projected loss in value. A complete understanding of the operation and assumptions made when using a sinking fund factor is required if the appraiser is to understand fully some of the appraisal techniques presented later.

Present Value of One Dollar

The *present value of one dollar* is a compound interest factor typically calculated for an annual interest rate used to discount an expected future cash flow to arrive at its current present value (column 4 of the tables in Appendix A).

Formula: $\dfrac{1}{(1 + i)^n}$ $= 1/S^n$ (column 4 in the tables in Appendix A)

where *i* equals the effective interest rate and *n* equals the number of time periods.

Table Relationship.   This factor is the reciprocal of the future value of one dollar (column 1 in the tables in Appendix A).

Example 2-4

What is the present value of $10,000 to be received at the end of five years, assuming a 12 percent interest rate?

Future Value		Present Value Factor		Present Value
$10,000	×	0.5674	=	$5,674

* Proof *

Year	Beginning Balance		Additional Return (12%)			Ending Balance
1	$5,674	+	($5,674 × 0.12)	$ 681	=	$ 6,355
2	6,355	+	(6,355 × 0.12)	763	=	7,118
3	7,118	+	(7,118 × 0.12)	854	=	7,972
4	7,972	+	(7,972 × 0.12)	957	=	8,929
5	8,929	+	(8,929 × 0.12)	1,071	=	10,000

Factor Solution.   The 12 percent annual present value factor for five years may be found in the tables in Appendix A. The factor is 0.567427. It may also be found using the financial functions of a financial calculator by entering 1.00 as the future value, five years as the holding period and 12 percent as the interest rate and pressing the present value key. Alternatively, it can be calculated by solving the following mathematical relationship, using the powers and reciprocal options:

$$\frac{1}{(1 + 0.12)^5} = \frac{1}{1.765435} = 0.567654$$

Discussion. This factor is probably the most important one used by an appraiser. It is the principal factor used to transform either a single-year or a multiple-year cash-flow forecast into a present value estimate. Many of the appraisal techniques used in the income approach mirror this concept. It is, therefore, important that an appraiser completely understand the present value concept and the method used to calculate this present value factor.

Present Value of One Dollar per Period

The *present value of one dollar per period* is a compound interest factor typically calculated for an annual interest rate that is used to discount a series of equal future cash flows in order to arrive at a current present value of the total stream of income (column 5 of the tables in Appendix A).

Formula: $\dfrac{1 - \dfrac{1}{(1 + i)^n}}{i} = a_{\overline{n}}$ (column 5 in the tables in Appendix A)

where *i* equals the effective interest rate and *n* equals the number of time periods.

Table Relationship. This factor is the reciprocal of the payment to amortize one dollar (column 6 in the tables in Appendix A).

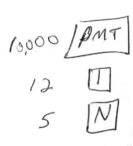

Example 2-5

What is the present worth of receiving five annual payments (end of year) of $10,000 over each of five years assuming a 12 percent rate of return?

Year	Cash Flow		Present Value Factor (12%)		Present Value
1	$10,000	×	0.8929	=	$ 8,929
2	10,000	×	0.7972	=	7,972
3	10,000	×	0.7118	=	7,118
4	10,000	×	0.6355	=	6,355
5	10,000	×	0.5674	=	5,674
Total					$36,048

Present Value	Annual Payment	Present Value Factor
$36,048	$10,000	$36,048 ÷ $10,000 = 3.6048

Factor Solution. The 12 percent annual present value of one dollar per period for five years may be found in the tables in Appendix A. The factor is 3.604776. It may also be found using the financial functions of a calculator by entering 1.00 as the payment, five years as the holding period and 12 percent as the interest rate. When the present value key is pressed, the factor for 12 percent will appear.

Discussion. This factor is the sum of the present value factors (column 4 factors, Appendix A) for the holding period, as shown below.

Year	Present Value Factors
1	0.892857
2	0.797194
3	0.711780
4	0.635518
5	0.567427
Total	3.604776

This factor is extremely useful to an appraiser who wishes to calculate the present value of a forecast cash-flow schedule containing equal cash flows.[3]

NOTE ON THE PRESENT VALUE OF ANNUITIES IN ADVANCE: The present value of the one dollar per period factor discussed above assumes that the cash flows are received at the *end* of each year. This is why the first-year cash flow is also discounted.

This is referred to as an "ordinary annuity" and is the assumption normally used in financial tables. It is also the assumption used in financial calculators, unless the user changes the mode of the calculator to assume the first cash flow occurs at the *beginning* of the year. When the payments for an annuity are assumed to start at the beginning of the first year, the annuity is referred to as an "annuity in advance." The present value of this annuity will be higher than that of an ordinary annuity that uses the same interest rate and number of payments because all cash flows are received one year sooner. In fact, because each cash flow is received one year sooner, the present value of this annuity will be higher by a factor of $(1+i)$. Using the previous example, if the payments of $10,000 began at the beginning of the first year, the present value of five years of payments discounted at a 12 percent interest rate would be

Present Worth of Ordinary Annuity	$\times$	$(1 + i)$	$=$	Present Worth of Annuity in Advance
$36,048	$\times$	1.12	$=$	$40,374

Payment To Amortize One Dollar

The *payment to amortize one dollar* is the periodic payment necessary to repay a $1 loan with interest paid at a specified rate over a specified time on the outstanding loan balance (column 6 of the tables in Appendix A).

Formula: $\dfrac{i}{1 - 1/(1 + i)^n} = 1/a_{\overline{n}|}$ (column 6 in the tables in Appendix A)

where i equals the effective interest rate and n equals the number of time periods.

Table Relationship.   This factor is the reciprocal of the present value of one dollar per period (column 5 in the tables in Appendix A). This factor is also equal to the effective interest rate plus the sinking fund factor for the year selected or, in terms of columns:

$$\text{Column } 6 = \text{Column } 3 + i$$

Example 2-6

What level of annual end-of-year payment would be needed to amortize a $10,000 loan payment over 5 years, assuming a 12 percent interest rate?

		Installment to		
Loan Amount		*Amortize Factor*		*Annual Payment*
$10,000	×	0.2774	=	$2,774

Payment	$2,774
Interest	−1,200
Sinking Fund Payment	$1,574

NOTE: For proof that five annual payments of $1,574 each, assuming compounding at 12 percent, will grow to $10,000, see the sinking fund factor discussion.

In the above example, the annual payment is $2,774. This is the amount necessary to repay the loan in five years (with annual payments) and pay the bank 12 percent interest on the outstanding balance each year. A loan schedule for this example is shown following:

Typical Amortization Schedule

Year	Beginning Balance	Interest	Payment	Principal	Ending Balance
1	$10,000	$1,200	$ 2,774	$ 1,574	$8,426
2	8,426	1,011	2,774	1,763	6,663
3	6,663	800	2,774	1,974	4,689
4	4,689	562	2,774	2,212	2,477
5	2,477	297	2,774	2,477	0
Total		$3,870	$13,870	$10,000	

Factor Solution. The 12 percent annual payment factor for five years may be found in the tables included in Appendix A. The factor is 0.277410. The factor may also be found using the financial functions of a calculator by entering 1.00 as the present value, five years as the holding period and 12 percent as the interest rate. When the payment key is pressed, the factor for 12 percent will appear.

Another method of obtaining the payment factor is to add the sinking fund factor to the effective interest rate. The sinking fund factor in this instance is 0.157410 (based on a 5-year holding period and a 12 percent interest rate), and the interest rate is 0.120000. The sum is 0.277410. Viewed in this manner, we might say that the installment to amortize 1.00 factor consists of two components:

1. an allowance for interest on the loan (*return on capital*) and
2. repayment of the loan (referred to as *return of capital*).

This can be interpreted as meaning that a borrower could pay interest of 12 percent per year and set aside 15.74 percent of the loan ($1,574.10) in a sinking fund (for example, a bank account) earning 12 percent and accumulate enough money in the sinking fund ($10,000) to repay the loan after 5 years.[4]

Loan Constant. The payment to amortize one dollar factor can be used to calculate loan payments for level-payment amortizing loans and can be referred to as a *loan constant.* Level-payment amortizing loans are fixed-payment loans over a specific time period (*amortization* period), whose payment includes a combination of interest and principal that would result in total repayment over the amortization period.

In the previous example, the loan constant would be for a 5-year loan with *annual* payments. Note that the loan constant (27.741 percent) in the above example is greater than the interest rate of 12 percent. It must be higher for the loan to be amortized. In fact, in this example it is quite a bit higher, because the loan is being amortized over only 5 years.

MORTGAGE CAPITALIZATION RATE

In general, a *capitalization rate* is the ratio of some measure of cash flow from an investment to the value of that investment. The measure of cash flow is usually the cash flow during the first year of the investment. In the case of a mortgage loan, the cash flow is the annual payment on the loan and the investment is the initial amount of the loan. In the example considered above, the payment during the first year (which is the same each year) is $2,774. The amount of the loan (which is the lender's investment) is $10,000. Thus the capitalization rate for the mortgage (referred to as a *mortgage capitalization rate*) is $2,774 ÷ $10,000 = 27.74 percent. This is obviously the same as the mortgage constant. The point is that the mortgage constant can be referred to as the "mortgage capitalization rate."

The concept of a capitalization rate is used so frequently in appraisal theory and practice that it is essential for the appraiser to have as much insight into this concept as possible. Therefore, it is important to begin to think about the interpretation of this ratio. Our example and the discussion were related to the relationship between loan payments and the value of that loan (which is the present value of the payments). More generally, a capitalization rate is a relationship between the cash flow on any investment and the present value of those cash flows. If, in the example considered above, the annual payments were for an investment in a property (rather than a loan) that would produce income of $2,774 for the next five years (and nothing thereafter), then we could say that the capitalization rate for the property would be 27.74 percent.[5] The relationship between capitalization rates and compound interest theory is discussed extensively in later chapters.

Monthly Payments

As mentioned above, the installment-to-amortize factor is used primarily to calculate loan payments for level-payment, self-amortizing loans. Frequently, loan payments are made monthly. For a 25-year loan at 12 percent interest with monthly payments, the installment-to-amortize factor would be calculated as follows.

$$\text{Formula: } \frac{i}{1 - 1/(1 + i)^n} = \frac{1}{a_{\overline{n}|}}$$

$$i = 0.12/12 = 0.01$$

$$n = 25 \times 12 = 300$$

$$\frac{1}{a_{\overline{n}|}} = \frac{0.01}{1 - 1/(1 + 0.01)^{300}} = \frac{0.01}{0.949466} = 0.010532$$

For a $10,000 loan, the monthly payment would therefore be:

$$\$10,000 \times 0.010532 = \$105.32$$

We can also determine the loan constant for a loan with monthly payments. In this case it is customary to express the loan constant on an *annual* basis, even though the payments are actually made on a monthly basis. For the above example, the annual constant would be

$$\text{Annual mortgage constant} = [\$105.32 / \$10,000] \times 12 = 12.64\%$$

Effective Annual Rate

The *effective annual rate* is the rate based on annual compounding that is equivalent to a rate that assumes more frequent compounding. For example, if a loan is made at a 12 percent rate with monthly payments, the effective rate is higher than it would be if payments were made only on an annual basis, because interest compounds each month. The effective annual rate could be calculated as follows:

$$(1 + i)^{12} - 1 \text{ or } (1 + 0.01)^{12} - 1 = 1.1268 - 1 \text{ or } 0.1268 \text{ or } 12.68\%$$

A loan with a nominal annual rate of 12 percent that has monthly payments is equivalent to a loan that has annual payments and an interest rate of 12.68 percent. Thus, we could say that the effective annual rate is 12.68 percent.

INTERRELATIONSHIP AMONG THE FACTORS

It is informative to understand that all of the six factors are mathematically related. Some of the relationships were presented earlier. They are summarized as follows:

- Column 1 is the reciprocal of Column 4
- Column 2 is the reciprocal of Column 3
- Column 5 is the reciprocal of Column 6
- Column 6 = Column 3 + i
- Column 1 × Column 3 = Column 6
- Column 2 × Column 4 = Column 5
- Column 1 × Column 3 × Column 5 = 1
- Column 2 × Column 4 × Column 6 = 1

NOTE: The last two relationships enable the appraiser to calculate what one factor is in terms of the other factors. For example:

$$\text{Column 3} = \frac{1}{\text{Column 1} \times \text{Column 5}} = \frac{\text{Column 4}}{\text{Column 5}}$$

PRESENT VALUE APPLICATIONS

Historically, the tables in Appendix A were used by real estate appraisers to estimate the present value of various types of incomes. Today, calculators and computers do the same task, but it is important to understand how the tables can be used to calculate present value.

Present Value of a Level Income Stream

Example 2-7

Find the present value of the following end-of-year (EOY) cash flows, assuming a 15 percent annual discount rate.

Year	Cash Flow
1	$2,000
2	2,000
3	2,000
4	2,000
5	2,000

Cash Flow		Present Value of an Annuity Factor @ 15%		Present Value
$2,000	×	3.352155	=	$6,704

(handwritten marginal notes: 2000, 15, 5, PMT, I, N, PV)

The present value of a given level income stream can be found once a discount (interest) rate is selected, because at that point three of the four essential elements in a compound interest problem would be known (future cash flows, time period and interest rate).

Because the five cash flows are equal and equal time periods are assumed in the analysis, the answer can be readily calculated by multiplying the periodic cash flow by the 5-year present value of one dollar per period for 15 percent as shown above. The same answer could have been found by discounting each payment by the appropriate present value of one dollar factor for each year. (This approach is necessary when the cash flows are uneven and tables are used.)

Year	Cash Flow		Present Value @ 15%		Present Value
1	$2,000	×	0.869565	=	$1,739
2	2,000	×	0.756144	=	1,512
3	2,000	×	0.657516	=	1,315
4	2,000	×	0.571753	=	1,144
5	2,000	×	0.497177	=	994
Total					$6,704

Note that the capitalization rate for the above example is $2,000/$6,704, which is 29.83 percent. Based on our earlier discussion about the relationship between factors, it should not be a surprise that the same rate can be found in column 6 (Payment to Amortize $1) of the 15 percent compound interest tables in Appendix A.

Present Value of a Level Income Stream Plus a Reversion

Investments are often analyzed for a holding period that is shorter than the time period over which the investment will generate income. In this case the resale price of the property at the end of the holding period must be considered. The term *reversion* is used in real estate appraisal and investment analysis to refer to the proceeds from resale. In the following example it is assumed that income will be $5,000 per year and the property can be sold for $50,000 at the end of a 5-year holding period.

Example 2-8

What is the present value of the following 5-year cash flows, assuming a 15 percent annual rate of return?

Year	Cash Flow (EOY)
1	$ 5,000
2	5,000
3	5,000
4	5,000
5	5,000
5	50,000

Cash Flow		Annuity Factor @ 15%		Present Value
$5,000	×	3.352155	=	$16,761

Cash Flow		Present Value Factor @ 15%		
$50,000	×	0.497177	=	24,859
Total				$41,620

An alternative way of solving the above problem is to determine the present value of each cash flow individually, then add the results of each present value. This is shown as follows:

Year	Cash Flow		Present Value Factor @ 15%		Present Value
1	$ 5,000	×	0.869565	=	$ 4,348
2	5,000	×	0.756144	=	3,781
3	5,000	×	0.657516	=	3,287
4	5,000	×	0.571753	=	2,859
5	55,000	×	0.497177	=	27,345
Total					$41,620

The answer is obviously the same for each approach. The answer also could have been found by using the present value function of a calculator or using a computer.

Present Value of Variable Income

Frequently, an appraiser is faced with the task of estimating the present value of a variable cash-flow forecast. Because this type of income stream is not level, the shortcut method using the present value of one dollar per period cannot be used. In this case, the appropriate math is to find the sum of the present values of the income for each year, including any reversion. This is illustrated in the following example, in which income during each year differs and there is a reversion at the end of the holding period.

Example 2-9

What is the present value of the following 5-year variable cash flows, assuming a 15 percent annual rate of return?

Year	Cash Flow		Present Value Factor @ 15%		Present Value
1	$ 5,000	×	0.869565	=	$ 4,348
2	5,250	×	0.756144	=	3,970
3	5,600	×	0.657516	=	3,682
4	5,850	×	0.571753	=	3,345
5	65,000	×	0.497177	=	32,317
Total					$47,662

In this case, the capitalization rate (ratio of the *first* year cash flow to the present value) is $5,000 ÷ $47,662 = 10.49 percent. Because the income is not a level annuity and because there is a reversion, the exact mathematical relationship between the capitalization rate and the discount rate (interest rate) is not obvious. That is, the capitalization rate is *not* the factor in column 6 of the tables in Appendix A and it cannot be found by the simple table relationships described earlier. However, there is still a conceptual relationship between the capitalization rate and the discount rate. This relationship will be explored extensively throughout this text.

Typically, most real estate cash-flow forecasts today have a variable cash-flow pattern, unless the payments have been fixed by a long-term absolute net lease. Thus, the approach illustrated in the above example is the most common and most general approach. It can be used to handle any income pattern, as long as the expected future cash flows can be estimated in dollars.

Example 2-10

What is the present value of the following 5-year cash flows, assuming the payments are received in advance and assuming a 15 percent rate of return?

Year	Cash Flow		Present Value Factor @ 15%		Present Value
1	$2,000	×	1.000000	=	$ 2,000
2	3,000	×	0.869563	=	2,609
3	3,500	×	0.756144	=	2,646
4	4,000	×	0.657516	=	2,630
5	5,000	×	0.571753	=	2,858
Total					$12,743

Present Value of Cash Flows Received in Advance

Typically, real estate cash flows are assumed to have been received at the end of a period. Sometimes, however, an appraiser may be faced with estimating the value of income received at the beginning of the period (in advance).

Receiving a cash flow at the beginning of year 2 (for example) is the same as receiving it at the end of year 1. The appropriate approach to calculate present value, therefore, is to add the entire beginning payment (because the present value of receiving $2,000 today is $2,000) to the present value of the future cash flows. In this case, the present value of the cash flows received at the beginning of year 2 is the same as the present value of the same cash flow assumed to be received at the end of year 1.

Interest Rate Calculation

Whenever a complete set of cash flows is known or assumed, the present value tables may be used to calculate the interest rate. In this case, three of the four elements of compound interest must be known or assumed: the present value, the holding period and the future cash flows. Because of the mathematical complexity of calculating an interest rate, trial and error is the only method of finding an answer. Calculators and computers can be programmed, however, to undertake the trial-and-error process rapidly and find the answer in only a few seconds. The first method illustrated to calculate an interest rate will be trial and error using the table factors. (See Example 2-11.)

The interest rate can also be found using a hand-held calculator. The answer is found by entering $10,000 as the beginning cash flow, entering *each* future cash flow in the proper register, then pressing the IRR (internal rate of return) key. The calculator will rapidly search for the correct answer and finally print the answer on the display. In this case, the interest rate found was 14.318796, rounded to 14.32 percent.

Year	Cash Flow
0	($10,000)
1	1,200
2	1,200
3	12,000

The answer also could have been found using a computer. For example, spreadsheet programs have an internal rate of return calculation option as a built-in function.

To prove that the correct interest rate is 14.32 percent, the analyst need only calculate the present value of the future cash flows using 14.32 percent interest factors to determine whether the present value of the future cash flows is equal to the present value of the investment. Following is the proof:

Year	Cash Flow		Present Value Factor @14.32%		Present Value
1	$ 1,200	×	0.874738	=	$ 1,050
2	1,200	×	0.765166	=	918
3	12,000	×	0.669319	=	8,032
Total					$10,000

In this instance, the interest rate calculation of 14.32 percent is correct, because the present value of the future cash flows discounted at this rate is equal to the present value of the investment.

Example 2-11

Find the interest rate, given an initial investment of $10,000 and expected cash flows as follows:

Year	Cash Flow	
0	($10,000)	(Initial Investment)
1	1,200	
2	1,200	
3	12,000	

Solution—Trial and Error

Try 15%:

Year	Cash Flow		Present Value Factor @ 15%		Present Value
0	($10,000)				
1	1,200	×	0.8696	=	$1,044
2	1,200	×	0.7561	=	907
3	12,000	×	0.6575	=	7,890
Total					$9,841

$9,841 < $10,000, therefore, 15% is too high

Try 14%:

Year	Cash Flow		Present Value Factor @ 14%		Present Value
0	($10,000)				
1	1,200	×	0.8772	=	$ 1,053
2	1,200	×	0.7695	=	923
3	12,000	×	0.6750	=	8,100
Total					$10,076

$10,076 > $10,000, therefore, 14% is too low

IRR	Present Value
14%	$10,076
15%	9,841
Difference	$ 235

IRR	Present Value
14%	$10,076
?%	10,000
Difference	$ 76

Interpolation

$14\% + (76/235)1\% = 14.32\%$

The Internal Rate of Return

The *internal rate of return,* or IRR for short, is defined as a rate of return that discounts all expected future cash flows to a present value equal to the original investment. It represents the rate of return on an investment.

The internal rate of return is recognized as a more general term than "interest rate," but the two represent the same concept. In real estate, the term "interest rate" is more commonly used when discussing mortgage financing. In this case, the mortgage interest rate would be the interest rate that discounts all future loan payments to a present value equal to the initial mortgage balance. In other words, the mortgage interest rate calculated would be the internal rate of return to the lender. (If points are charged on the loan, the internal rate of return to the lender would be higher.)

The internal rate of return can also be referred to as a "discount rate" or "yield rate." Typically, when an interest rate is used to discount future cash flow to a present value estimate, it is referred to as a "discount rate." When calculating the interest rate for a set of cash flows, the rate found is usually referred to as a "yield rate" or "internal rate of return." Although the terminology may appear confusing, it is important for an appraiser to understand the terminology and the meaning of each rate. Conceptually, internal rates of return, interest rates, discount rates and yield rates are similar, because each represents the return on an investment and is the rate that discounts all expected future cash flows to a present value. When used in practice, each should have a descriptor attached to it that describes the ownership interest to which the rate applies. For example, a rate used to discount future property cash flows to present value equal to the total property value is referred to as the "property discount rate." Following is a table of the typical internal rates of return used in real estate analyses:

Typical Real Estate Internal Rates of Return

Interest	Discount / Yield Rate	Symbol
Total property	Property discount rate	Y_O
Building value	Building discount rate	Y_B
Land value	Land discount rate	Y_L
Equity	Before-tax equity yield rate	Y_E
Mortgage	Mortgage interest rate	Y_M or i

In using or calculating any of the rates listed above, the only cash flows used are those that are applicable to the property interest appraised, and the present value estimates represent the value of the interest to which the cash flows accrue. For example, when estimating the value of the land, the land discount (Y_L) is used to discount the cash flow attributable to the land.

MORTGAGE LOAN CALCULATIONS

The compound interest concept is the basis for calculating loan payments for level-payment, self-amortizing loans. Each payment includes interest and principal portions that vary over time, as explained earlier in this chapter in discussion of the installment to amortize factor.

The following discussion covers only the mathematics of calculating mortgage payments, interest rates, remaining loan terms and loan balances, using compound interest tables and calculators.

Calculating Loan Payments—Level Amortizing Mortgages

Calculating a mortgage payment for a self-amortizing loan is a typical compound interest problem. In this case, the analyst is given three of the four variables needed to calculate an answer—the holding period (the amortization term), the interest rate (the mortgage interest rate) and the present value (the beginning loan balance)—and is asked to find the future payments. An example follows:

Example 2-12

What is the monthly payment required to amortize a $100,000 loan over 25 years, assuming a 10.5 percent interest rate?

Solution 1 (Compound Interest Table)

Loan Amount		Payment Factor		Monthly Payment
$100,000	×	0.009442*	=	$944.20

*The 0.009442 factor is from the monthly compound interest tables in Appendix B.

As in any basic compound interest problem, the time interval between payments must be equal. In many cases, loan payments are required monthly, so the interest rate and number of periods over which the compounding is to take place must be adjusted accordingly.

The answer also could have been found using the financial functions of a calculator by inputting 300 as the number of periods (12 × 25), 0.875 as the monthly interest rate (10.5 ÷ 12) and $100,000 as the present value.

Once the payment key is pressed, the monthly payment is displayed.

Example 2-13

Solution 2 (Calculator)

n	=	300
i	=	0.875%
PV	=	$100,000
PMT	=	?
Payment	=	$944.18

In this instance, 300 monthly payments of $944.18 (difference due to rounding) would totally pay off the $100,000 loan and provide the lender with an 0.875 percent monthly rate of return, or 10.5 percent on an annual basis. The effective interest rate would not be 10.5 percent but would be $(1.00875)^{12}$, that is, 1.1102 or 11.02 percent. The IRR to the lender would be 0.875 percent per month.

Calculating a Loan Balance—Level Amortizing Mortgages

The compound interest tables or a calculator may be used to calculate the loan balance for a level amortizing loan at any point in time. Conceptually, the easiest way to calculate a loan balance is to realize that the balance at any time is the present value of the remaining series of payments discounted at the effective mortgage interest rate. The example that follows illustrates this point:

Example 2-14

What would be the balance of the loan in the previous example after six years of payments?

Solution 1 (Compound Interest Tables)

Payment		Monthly Present Value Annuity Factor @ 10.5%, 19 Years		
$944.18	×	98.605822	=	$93,102

In the above example, the present value of one dollar per period for 228 payments (19 × 12) at an 0.875 percent interest rate (10.5 ÷ 12) is 98.605822. Multiplying this factor by the expected monthly payment of $944.18 results in a present value estimate for the income stream of $93,102, which is the loan balance after 72 (6 × 12) months of payments.

The answer also may be found using the financial functions of a calculator by entering the number of remaining time periods (228), the effective interest rate (0.875 percent) and the monthly payment of $944.18, and pressing the present value key. Several additional automatic functions are also built into most calculators that calculate a loan balance.

Example 2-15

Solution 2 (Calculator)

n	=	228
i	=	0.875
PMT	=	$944.18
PV	=	?
Loan Balance	=	$93,102

SUMMARY

Because the value of real estate income property depends on anticipated future benefits, a thorough understanding of time value of money concepts is very important. Although most appraisers use financial calculators or computers to solve the types of problems illustrated in this chapter, a review of the *six functions of one dollar* that form the basis for the traditional financial tables provides insights into the interrelationships between the different compound interest and discounting concepts important in appraisal theory. Whether tables, a financial calculator or a computer is used, appraisers should be able to find the present value of any given series of cash flows, whether the cash flows represent a level annuity, an annuity plus a reversion or an uneven series of cash flows with or without a reversion. All of these situations can be encountered in practice.

Many terms have virtually the same meaning: interest rate, discount rate, yield rate, return on capital and internal rate of return. It is important to understand how to calculate and interpret the meaning of each of these terms because they form the basis for yield capitalization. Because the discount rate used in yield capitalization should reflect the internal rate of return that a typical investor requires if he or she is to invest in the property, it is also important to know how that investor might view the reinvestment assumptions implicit in the interpretation of the internal rate of return, as well as the possibility of there being multiple IRRs for the same investment.

KEY TERMS

adjusted internal rate of return
amortization
annuity in advance
capitalization rate
compound interest
compound interest factor
discounting
discount rate
effective annual rate
future value of one dollar
future value of one dollar per period
interest
interest rate
internal rate of return
Inwood annuity factor
loan constant

mortgage capitalization rate
net present value
ordinary annuity
payment to amortize one dollar
present value
present value annuity of one dollar
present value of one dollar per
   period
principal
return of capital
return on capital
reversion
sinking fund factor
six functions of one dollar
time value of money
yield rate

QUESTIONS

1. What is meant by the term "discounting"? How is discounting related to the financial principle of the time value of money?
2. Which financial functions do you think an appraiser would be most likely to use?
3. Which financial function do you think an appraiser could use to determine how much money would have to be set aside in an interest-earning account to replace a roof in five years?
4. Why does an appraiser need to distinguish between an ordinary annuity and an annuity in advance?
5. What is the relationship between a loan constant and the interest rate for a fully amortized mortgage?
6. Suppose an investment is estimated to have a cash flow of $100,000 per year for the next five years. At the end of the fifth year, the property is expected to be sold for $1 million. What is the present value of the investment at a 10 percent discount rate?
7. Refer to question 6. Suppose the income is $100,000 for the first year but then increases 5 percent per year over the next four years. What is the present value at the same 10 percent discount rate?
8. Suppose a loan is made for $5 million. Interest is to be charged at an 8 percent interest rate with payments amortized over 30 years. What is the monthly loan payment? What is the balance of the loan after five years?

END NOTES

1. If the future cash flow is the unknown variable and the future cash flow involves more than one period, then it must be assumed to follow a well-defined mathematical pattern (for example, a level annuity) in order to solve for the future cash flow using tables or a financial calculator in a straightforward manner.

2. The reason the future worth of 1.00 factors are for $(n-1)$ years rather than n years is the assumption that the cash flows are deposited at the end of the year. Thus, the deposit during the last year does not earn interest and is worth only 1.00. Only the previous years' cash flows earn interest.

3. Some appraisal textbooks refer to this factor as an "Inwood factor," especially when the resulting present value is contrasted with that found under an alternative way of valuing annuities referred to as the "Hoskold" premise. This is discussed later.

4. Of course, we might question the ability of the borrower to earn 12 percent on the money. However, by making the principal payment to the bank, the net result is the same as if the borrower earned 12 percent on the funds given to the bank.

5. An example of an investment in a property interest that would have this type of income pattern might be a leasehold estate in a property that has a below-market lease that expires in five years.

| CHAPTER 3 | # Cash-Flow Forecasting |

REAL ESTATE CASH-FLOW FORECASTS

The income approach theoretically is based on the premise that the value of real estate property is the present value of the anticipated future benefits. These future benefits manifest themselves in the income approach as expected future cash flows, both from the operation of the income-producing property and the expected net proceeds from a forecast resale of the property at the end of a holding period. Preparing a reliable and supportable cash flow can be a difficult task, especially in a highly volatile market, but methods have been developed to test and refine these forecasts. It is important for the appraiser not only to be able to identify and quantify expected cash flows but also to understand the important effect that changes in assumptions have on any final value estimates. Because forecasts reflect expectations for the future and will probably prove to be incorrect, their accuracy should not be judged from a historical perspective but from the perspective of how logical the forecasts appeared at the moment they were made, given the data available to the appraiser.

FORECASTING

Forecasting is accomplished by assimilating information from the past, identifying relationships between influencing factors and drawing conclusions about what will probably happen in the future. The final conclusion will be reached after application of typical forecasting techniques such as modeling, applied judgment, time series analyses and various additional approaches. The sources of forecasting information include historical data and behavior patterns, as well as current trends and performances. Key considerations in the forecasting process include:

- Forecasts must be timely, that is, based on the most recent trends.
- Forecasts must be in the units appropriate for the decision (dollars, units, units per period and so forth).
- Forecasts must be as detailed as needed to capture key factors that affect the item being forecast.
- Forecasting assumptions and limitations should be clearly spelled out.

Items usually in a forecast for a real estate appraisal include income, rent, expenses, vacancy, sales prices, interest rates and value. In addition, market demand, supply, absorption, capture rate, market capacity and market potential are key elements in a highest and best use analysis, as well as in economic feasibility studies. Note that all forecasts involve estimation of actual cash flows versus cash flows based on accounting or accrual concepts. The purpose of forecasting in real estate appraisal is to identify the dollar amounts actually to be received or paid by typical investors in the property under analysis.

TYPES OF INCOME

Application of the income approach to real estate income property requires one or more measures of the income potential of the property. Commonly used measures include potential gross income, effective gross income, net operating income, before- and after-tax cash flow, and reversion (resale) proceeds.

- Potential gross income (PGI) is the total potential income that could be expected from property at full occupancy before operating expenses are deducted. PGI can be calculated for the first year of ownership of the property and estimated for each year of operation over a typical holding period.
- Effective gross income (EGI) is the anticipated income from operation of the property after vacancy and collection losses. EGI is often based on a percentage of potential gross income that is typical for the area. For a leased fee estate, vacancy losses should include losses due to tenant turnover. Net operating income is the income remaining after all operating expenses are deducted from effective gross income but before mortgage debt service, tax depreciation or any state or federal income taxes are deducted. NOI is usually expressed as an annual amount.
- Before-tax cash flow (BTCF) is the portion of net operating income that remains after debt service is deducted but before tax depreciation or income taxes are deducted. BTCF is also referred to as "equity dividend" or "pretax cash flow."
- After-tax cash flow (ATCF) is the portion of cash flow that remains after state and federal income taxes have been deducted. The amount of ordinary income tax depends on the taxable income that results from owning the property. Taxable income is determined by the amount of interest and tax depreciation that can be deducted from NOI when calculating taxable income. The tax liability depends on the investor's other taxable income.
- Reversion is the cash that an investor receives when the investment is sold. The amount depends on the value of the property at the time of sale, which depends on the income anticipated by the next owner. Thus, the reversion can be viewed as selling the rights to future income to the next investor. The income from reversion may be calculated before or after deduction of the mortgage balance and income taxes and should be consistent with the way cash flow is calculated during the operating years. For example, if the appraiser is analyzing the property before considering financing and taxes, NOI would be estimated during the operating years, and the reversion would be equal to the net resale proceeds (sales price less any selling costs). If, on the other hand, the appraiser wanted to project BTCF, then debt service would be deducted from NOI during each operating year and the mortgage balance would be deducted from the net resale proceeds.

CASH-FLOW FORECASTS FROM OPERATIONS

The cash flow generated annually from the operation of an income-producing property is, basically, the income received less operating expenses. Usually, these estimates are made on an annual basis, assuming that the net cash flows are received at the end of each year. Cash-flow forecasts may be prepared that assume receipt at the beginning of the year, but it is rare to receive all income and pay all expenses at the beginning of the year. There is one instance in which it would be logical to assume that receipt of income would occur at the beginning of the year, namely, when a building is leased on an absolute net basis (tenant pays all operating expenses). Such a lease requires a full annual payment at the beginning of each year. Leases requiring this specific payment structure are rare.

Sources of Annual Income

Income from a real estate property is produced primarily by charging a tenant to occupy the space; in other words, to rent the space through the execution of a lease. It is often said that appraisals are "lease based," because one of the basic assumptions made, whether the space is leased or owner occupied, is that the space could be leased at a certain rental rate. This rental or implied rental typically becomes the primary source of income from the property. The relative level of rent for a specific building is based on the perceived utility and the effective demand for the property as determined by current market conditions for the property type being appraised based on rental ranges for comparable properties. An appraiser may imply a certain level of rent or may actually consider any existing leases for tenant space. If the income forecast includes rent from existing leases, the ownership interest becomes the leased fee interest. If the income forecast is based on market rent levels, the ownership interest appraised is the fee simple interest.

There are a few specialized property types where the income usually analyzed is not actual or implied lease income, for example, hotels, nursing homes and recreational facilities. In each of these cases, the source of the income is the actual charges to tenants to occupy or use the facilities. Conceptually, use charges are similar to rent, but the operating expenses are structured in a different format.

Some properties are able to generate income from sources other than rent. Apartment buildings may contain laundry facilities and/or vending machines that generate additional income from their use. Office buildings may generate income from parking, concessions, antenna rent (on the top of highrise buildings) and so forth. Shopping centers can generate additional income from such things as selling advertising services and equipment rental. In some instances, it becomes difficult to decide whether the additional funds are income to the real estate or income attributable to nonrealty interests such as business value and personal property rental. When making judgments about whether additional income is attributable to the real estate, the appraiser should weigh all the facts carefully—especially whether additional management expertise is necessary to generate additional income.

Land rent and easement fees are other sources of income prevalent in the market. These incomes would be the result of transferring ownership rights in vacant land.

Operating Expenses

All expenses to operate an income-producing property are deducted from the income in the year the expenses are incurred. Typically, the expenses fall into two categories: fixed expenses or variable expenses.[1] *Fixed expenses* are annual costs that generally do not vary based on the occupancy level of a building. These expenses include property taxes, insurance and some maintenance contracts (an elevator maintenance contract, for example). *Variable expenses* generally do vary with the level of occupancy of the building. Examples include the basic costs of operating the building, including utility costs, janitorial fees, management expenses, maintenance costs (interior, exterior and site) and professional fees.

Each expense must be identified directly as a cost to operate the building. Expenses to manage or operate the ownership entity, such as partnership fees, profit distribution and individual income taxes, are not building operating expenses and should not be included in the calculation of net operating income (NOI). In addition, deductions for depreciation and interest costs for mortgage financing are not included in calculating the NOI for the building. Determination of whether the landlord or tenant pays all or portions of each expense item is typically controlled by a lease contract.

Net Operating Income

The difference between income and operating expenses is referred to as *net operating income* or *NOI*. It is the income an owner would expect to receive prior to making any debt service payments. Forecasts of future NOI are based on expected relative changes in income and expenses over a selected holding period. Practically, a change in income may directly affect the level of an expense. For example, in many cases, management fees are based on income collected. If income were to rise, a corresponding increase in management fees would be expected.

RESALE PROCEEDS FORECAST

In addition to annual income from operations, an owner of an income-producing property could expect to receive *resale proceeds,* that is, the net proceeds generated by resale of the property at the end of a holding period. In most income-producing real estate properties, the property has some value at the end of a typical holding period. In development properties such as subdivision and condominium projects, where lots or units, respectively, are gradually sold, there may be nothing remaining to sell at the end of a typical sellout period. The level of the reversion can have a significant impact on value, so care must be taken when forecasting the reversion.

Holding Period

One of the first inputs to be selected by an appraiser when preparing a cash-flow forecast is the holding period. The period selected should represent the "typical" holding period for the particular class of property. Sometimes it is difficult to determine what a typical holding period is. In the middle 1980s, properties tended to be held from 5 to 10 years. After that, the tax incentives associated with turning over the property to a new owner tended to result in a sale before the 15th year of ownership. After the 1986 tax law change, many of the incentives for shorter holding periods disappeared, which currently makes selecting a "typical" holding period difficult. For the purpose of discounted cash-flow analysis, the appraiser should attempt to select a holding period for the property being valued that is representative of the typical investor, because the market value of a property should reflect the investment motivations for the typical investor.

Frequently, the terms *holding period, marketing period, absorption period* and *sellout period* are confused. *Holding period* is the time period over which an investor holds the property before deciding to sell. *Marketing period* is the time period required to actually sell the property once the decision to sell is made. *Absorption period* is the time required to either rent-up a property or sell out lots in a development. The *sellout period* and *absorption period* are basically the same. In appraisal theory, cash flows for an investment property are forecast over a typical holding period and discounted to a present value. There is, however, no adjustment for marketing period, if the value estimate is to represent market value, because the market value definition assumes a typical buyer and seller and a reasonable marketing period. If, on the other hand, an appraisal is made that requires or limits the marketing period to a time period less than what would be considered typical or reasonable by the appraiser, the value estimate would be considered a forced, or liquidation, value.

Because the purpose of most appraisal assignments is to estimate market value, the appraiser generally selects the holding period and simply reports a typical marketing period under current market conditions. As mentioned earlier, selecting and supporting a so-called typical holding period is difficult; in the final analysis, the "correct" period would not necessarily be based on historical evidence. On the contrary, the correct estimate is the "typical" period used in a forecast by "typical" investors when analyzing a real estate investment, rather than how long the investor actually expects to hold the property. In most cases, investors use 5- to 15-year projections, so projections in this range would be reasonable. In theory, an appraiser using a 5-year cash-flow forecast should arrive at exactly the same value as an appraiser using a 15-year forecast. In practice, there may be slight value differences when different holding periods are used, but according to appraisal theory, the appraisers should arrive at identical market values if the values are based on the same premise.

Resale Value

The resale value is the forecast of the price to be received by the property owner at the end of the holding period. It is frequently referred to as the *reversion*. In essence, it represents the probable price that will be paid by the next owner. That price, in theory, depends on the expectations of the next owner at that future time. Again, as in forecasting other values, the quality and reliability of the resale forecast can be judged only against what is logical given today's information, rather than what actually happens to the sales price over time.

There are various methods of estimating resale value. Each is discussed in detail later in this chapter. All methods are designed to mirror typical buying strategies.

Disposition Costs

The actual proceeds from resale used in a discounted cash-flow analysis or yield capitalization (concepts to be explained in detail later) should reflect the actual dollars that will be received by the current owner. Selling costs such as sales commissions and legal fees are usually incurred in a real estate transaction. The magnitude of these *disposition costs* to the seller at reversion depends on the property type, local customs, property size and selling strategy. An appraiser, therefore, must make a judgment of how the estimated disposition costs for the property being appraised would affect its net proceeds from sale (reversion). Sometimes selling costs are not explicitly deducted from the sales price used in a discounted cash-flow forecast. This does not mean that the appraiser does not believe there will be any selling costs. Rather, it is done to simplify the presentation of the cash flows. In this case, the sales price shown in the analysis would be assumed to be already net of selling costs. This approach is used in the examples in this book. In appraisal practice the appraiser should be consistent in either showing or not showing an explicit estimate of selling costs in a discounted cash-flow analysis so that cash-flow estimates will be comparable.

CASH-FLOW FORECASTS

This chapter introduces the key types of income that are relevant in cash-flow forecasts. We will now look in more detail at the estimation of net operating income (NOI), that is, cash flow that is available before deduction of any mortgage financing.

Rental Income Calculations

The rental income forecast is made after comparing the subject with similar properties in its market segment. The rental rate may be calculated on the following basis:

- *Gross lease*—Landlord pays all operating expenses.
- *Net lease*—Tenant pays a portion of the operating expenses (usually everything except taxes, insurance, management and exterior maintenance).
- *Absolute net lease*—Tenant pays all operating expenses (usually with the exception of management fees).[2]

The rental rate is applied to the net usable area, the net leasable area or the gross building area. *Net usable area* is space that can be occupied by tenants. *Net leasable area* may include a pro rata share of the common area. *Gross building area* is the total floor area of the building.[3] Contractual rental payments may or may not be at market rent levels. All rental projections made in the remainder of this chapter will be assumed to reflect market rental rates.

Rental rates may vary within a building, based on location, quality of tenant space, condition of the improvements and use of the space. Any rental rate selected should represent the best estimate of what the space would rent for under current market conditions. The typical *rental units of comparison* for income-producing properties are:

- rent per square foot of gross building area;
- rent per square foot of net leasable area; and
- rent per unit.

In addition, some income-producing properties are rented on a specialized unit basis, such as rent per seat, rent per door and rent per room.

An integral part of any income forecast is the expected pattern of change over the holding period. Historical trends are important considerations in forecasting future rental rate changes, but historical patterns should not be the sole source of support for the rental rates selected for future years. The appraiser must analyze current and expected market conditions in selecting future rental rates. Again, any forecast change must be logical, given current market conditions, and must represent the thought process of a typical investor.

The basic valuation example that will be used frequently in the remainder of the book assumes that NOI is based on a net leasable area of 20,000 square feet and a market rent of $15 per square foot. The *potential gross income (PGI)* for this example is $300,000:

$$20,000 \text{ sq. ft. @ } \$15 \text{ per sq. ft.} = \$300,000$$

Vacancy and Credit Loss Estimate

It would be highly unusual for the subject property and all properties in the market segment in an area to be fully occupied. Low vacancy levels encourage developers to construct new, competing projects. Most cash-flow forecasts, therefore, contain an adjustment for *vacancy and credit loss.* The vacancy and credit loss percentage used when estimating the fee simple interest in a property should be the typical rate for the market. This typical rate may change from year to year, and it could vary from property type to property type and from market to market. In rapidly growing markets, you could expect the typical vacancy rate to be higher than in stable or slowly growing markets. The higher vacancy rate in growing markets is caused by the need to create new space to satisfy the growing need. The higher rate exists because of the lead time needed to receive the proper approvals and construct a new project. Vacancy allowance can also be affected by existing leases on a property.

Vacancy and collection are often expressed as a percentage of potential gross income. Our example will assume a 6 percent stabilized vacancy and credit loss allowance. The vacancy allowance in the first year, therefore, would be

Potential Gross Income		*Vacancy and Credit Loss*		*Vacancy Amount*
$300,000	×	0.06	=	$18,000

Effective Gross Income

The rental income that remains after adjusting for vacancy and credit loss is the *effective gross income (EGI).* The effective gross income often includes any other income directly attributable to the real estate. Income generated by any nonrealty interest such as personal property or business income would not be included as a part of either potential gross income or effective gross income. For the previous example, the effective gross income for the first year is

Potential Gross Income	$300,000
Less Vacancy and Credit Loss	−18,000
Effective Gross Income	$282,000

OPERATING EXPENSES

As mentioned earlier, *operating expenses* fall into two categories: fixed expenses and variable expenses. The expenses are only those needed to operate the property. Five methods usually used to estimate operating expenses include:

1. direct dollar estimate;
2. expenses per square foot of gross building area;
3. expenses per square foot of net building area;

4. percentage of effective gross income; and
5. expenses per unit.

As a rule, the option used to estimate an expense item either is the method used in the market to quote or calculate an expense or reflects a common unit of comparison used in the market. For example, maintenance contracts for elevators are set by contract. The usual method of forecasting the expense for this item is, therefore, a direct dollar estimate. Management fees are usually quoted as a percentage of actual income collected, so the typical estimate is a percentage of effective gross income. Utility expenses are usually compared on the basis of a price per square foot of gross building area, so utility expenses are typically forecast on the same basis.

As with income, forecasting future changes in any expense over a holding period requires thorough market analysis. Historical trends are important, but they should not be the sole basis for estimating future trends. Any forecast change must be logical, given market conditions, and represent the expectation of a typical investor. Following is an expense forecast for the property example used in several valuation problems later in this book:

Example 3-1

Gross Building Area = 24,000 Square Feet (sq. ft.)

Net Building Area = 20,000 Square Feet (sq. ft.)

Fixed Expenses:	
Property Tax (Actual)	$11,900
Insurance	4,000
Maintenance Contract	4,000
Variable Expenses:	
Management Fee (5% of Effective Gross Income)	14,100
Utilities ($1.25/sq. ft. of Gross Building Area)	30,000
Janitorial ($.90/sq. ft. of Net Building Area)	18,000
Total Operating Expenses	$82,000

After estimating expenses, the appraiser should test the reasonableness of the estimate by calculating the applicable key ratios:

- expenses per square foot of gross building area;
- expenses per square foot of net building area;
- operating *expense ratio* (total expenses divided by effective gross income); and
- expenses per unit (Expenses per unit are calculated most often for multifamily income-producing properties.)

In the example above, the key ratios are

- expenses per square foot of gross building area:

$82,000 ÷ 24,000 sq. ft. = $3.42 per sq. ft.

- expenses per square foot of net building area:

$82,000 ÷ 20,000 sq. ft. = $4.10 per sq. ft.

- operating expense ratio:

$$\$82,000/\$282,000 = 0.2908, \text{ or } 29.08\%$$

The ratios should appear reasonable when compared with similar ratios for competitive properties. If not, the expense forecasting process should be reviewed to confirm the reasonableness of each forecast. The operating expense ratio is sometimes calculated using potential gross income rather than effective gross income. The appraiser should be consistent.

REPLACEMENT RESERVES

Frequently, appraisers include a *reserve for replacements* adjustment in an expense forecast. The reserve is a deduction that reflects the fact that components of the building with short economic lives may need to be replaced (requiring a lump-sum payment) before the end of the economic life of the building. For example, assume an air-conditioning compressor with a current replacement cost of $50,000 will need to be replaced in ten years. An appraiser could adjust for this possibility in six ways.

1. Build a replacement reserve to be deducted in each year that is equal to today's cost of $50,000 divided by the remaining life of the component (10 years): ($50,000 ÷ 10) = $5,000.
2. Estimate the replacement cost in 10 years. Assume this will increase to $70,000 because of inflation. Then calculate the sinking fund payment needed to grow to $70,000 in ten years and deduct this amount each year from the cash flow. The interest rate chosen for the sinking fund factor is typically a "safe rate" earned on an account in which funds would be deposited each year. Note that it would be incorrect to base a sinking fund payment on $50,000, because $50,000 would not be enough to replace the unit in ten years.
3. Deduct a lump-sum payment of $70,000 in year 10. In this case, at least a 10-year holding period would need to be used.[4]
4. Reduce the estimated resale price at the end of the holding period by an amount that represents the effect that the physical deterioration of the compressor would have on the price. In our example, this alternative could be used if the holding period were less than ten years. For example, if the building were to be sold at the end of the ninth year, the purchase price might be reduced by slightly less than $70,000, because the compressor would have to be replaced one year later.
5. Include the potential periodic cost as part of the annual maintenance expense for the building. Maintenance expenses usually vary widely from year to year for both the subject property and its competitors, so the maintenance assumption basically reflects a contingency fee.
6. Make no adjustment in the cash flows, which basically means that the risk of possibly having to replace the unit would be reflected in the discount rate used in the analysis.

Any of the above alternatives could be considered a proper way to treat the replacement in appraisal theory. The method of treatment should have no bearing on the final value estimate if that estimate is done logically and consistently. Occasional arguments against using reserves are that reserve items are often not reported in profit-and-loss statements for comparable properties[5] and investors usually do not build reserve replacements into the cash-flow projections used when analyzing investments. The method an appraiser chooses to use is not the important issue. The important issue is that once a method is chosen, to ensure consistency the appraiser should use the same method when analyzing both comparable data and the subject property. In the valuation examples in the remainder of this book, a reasonable level of maintenance expenses will be assumed and the risk of possible replacement items will be compensated for in the discount rate.

CASH-FLOW EXAMPLE

Following is an example of a typical annual cash flow:

Example 3-2

Assumptions:

Income:	Increasing 4 percent per year.
Vacancy:	Level at 6 percent per year.
Management:	5 percent of effective gross income.
Property tax:	$11,900 level for 3 years, increasing to $15,000 in years 4, 5 and 6.
Insurance:	$4,000, increasing by 3 percent per year.
Utilities:	$30,000, increasing by 5 percent per year.
Janitorial:	$18,000, increasing by 4 percent per year.
Maintenance:	$4,000, increasing by 3 percent per year.

	Year 1	Year 2	Year 3	Year 4	Year 5	Year 6
PGI	$300,000	$312,000	$324,480	$337,459	$350,958	$364,996
Vacancy	−18,000	−18,720	−19,469	−20,248	−21,057	−21,900
EGI	$282,000	$293,280	$305,011	$317,211	$329,901	$343,096
Management 5%	$ 14,100	$ 14,664	$ 15,251	$ 15,861	$ 16,495	$ 17,155
Property tax	11,900	11,900	11,900	15,000	15,000	15,000
Insurance	4,000	4,120	4,244	4,371	4,502	4,637
Utilities	30,000	31,500	33,075	34,729	36,465	38,288
Janitorial	18,000	18,720	19,469	20,248	21,057	21,899
Maintenance	4,000	4,120	4,244	4,371	4,502	4,637
Total Expenses	$ 82,000	$ 85,024	$ 88,183	$ 94,580	$ 98,021	$101,616
NOI	$200,000	$208,256	$216,828	$222,631	$231,880	$241,480

The end result of the income and expense forecast is a series of estimated NOIs.[6] The appraiser should test the reasonableness of the estimates by calculating the implied change in NOI over the holding period. In the above instance, the implied change is ($241,480 ÷ $200,000) − 1 = 20.74 percent, or approximately 4 percent per year. Typically, the relationship between income and expense is such that each tends to move in relation to the other. An implied NOI trend that is not logical, given the trends assumed for the incomes and expenses, may be a result of faulty forecasts.

ESTIMATING RESALE PROCEEDS

There are three common methods used to estimate a reversionary value:

1. Estimating the resale price as a dollar amount
2. Estimating a percentage change over the holding period
3. Applying a terminal (going-out) capitalization rate to estimated income one year after the end of the holding period

Direct Dollar Forecast

Making a direct dollar forecast of *resale proceeds* without basing it on a calculation method used by typical investors is rare. Using this method, however, may be logical if there is a contractual purchase arrangement that specifies a resale amount, for example, an option to purchase the property at the end of the lease. It is also possible that a dollar estimate was made using some other method, such as another independent discounted cash-flow valuation calculation or a discounted cash-flow approach to the subject after analysis of a holding period following the first assumed investment holding period. For example, a reversion assumed at the end of a 10-year analysis might be logically estimated by first undertaking an analysis of the cash flows to be received in years 10 through 20, then calculating the value of those cash flows in 10 years. This method of analysis may be used in valuing leased fee interests.

Estimated Percent Change

A second method is to assume a percent change in value over the holding period. The percent change could be expressed as either an annual or a total change and could reflect either a total increase, a decrease or no change in value over the time period. The relationship of the two should be logical, given the parameters of the appraisal problem. For example, suppose the value of the property with the cash flows illustrated previously is $2 million. What will its value be after five years, assuming (1) a 3 percent per year increase in value and (2) a total increase in value of 15 percent? The calculations are as follows:

$$\text{Value} = \$2,000,000 \qquad \text{Holding Period} = 5 \text{ Years}$$

- Reversion assuming a 3 percent annual change in value:

$$\$2,000,000 \times (1.03)^5 = \$2,318,548$$

Note that this is slightly more than a 15 percent total increase, due to compounding.

- Reversion assuming a 15 percent total increase in value:

$$\$2,000,000 \times 1.15 = \$2,300,000$$

The Terminal Capitalization Rate

A third method used to forecast the resale proceeds is to use the concept of a capitalization rate to estimate the resale price. Recall that a capitalization rate is the ratio of a single year's cash flow to the value of the total cash flows. Usually, the capitalization rate is based on the first-year cash flow, as illustrated in the previous chapter. As discussed in that chapter, although the capitalization rate uses only the first-year cash flow when it is calculated, the resulting capitalization rate is related to the assumptions used to calculate the present value of the cash flows, because the present value is based on anticipation of all future cash flows. Thus, if we knew the appropriate capitalization rate, we could estimate the present value of the future cash flows by dividing the first-year cash flow by the capitalization rate.

What is important at this time is that there is a relationship between the cash flow at a given time and the present value of all future cash flows that can be captured by selection of an appropriate capitalization rate. We can use this relationship to estimate the resale price of the property at the end of the holding period, because the resale price is theoretically based on the present value of the future cash flows that the new owner will receive.

Thus, we can think in terms of a capitalization rate that expresses the relationship between the first-year cash flow to the new owner and the price that the new owner should be willing to pay for the property at that time. Stated slightly differently, we can estimate the resale price of the property by dividing the estimated first-year income to the next buyer by an appropriate capitalization rate. This can be thought of as a shortcut approach to estimating the resale price rather than as attempting to project cash flows over a holding period for the new buyer and discount those cash flows.[7]

When a capitalization rate is used to estimate the resale price, it is referred to as a *terminal capitalization rate*.[8] In theory, the terminal capitalization rate should represent the typical rate that would be expected at the time the property is sold. A slightly higher rate is sometimes used because of the additional uncertainty associated with estimating what the cash flow will be when the property is sold to the new owner, and because the building is older and may not have the same income potential as it had at the beginning of the holding period.

As an example of using the terminal capitalization rate, consider the NOI forecast shown earlier. The NOI in year 6 was estimated to be $241,480.

Now assume that an appropriate terminal capitalization rate (R_T) would be 10 percent. Our estimated resale price would then be as follows:

$$\text{Reversionary value} = \frac{\text{NOI (6th year)}}{R_T} = \frac{\$241,480}{0.10} = \$2,414,800$$

Note that the terminal capitalization rate was applied to the year 6 NOI, rather than to the year 5 NOI. The logic here is that the value at the *end* of year 5 is the present value of income that starts in year 6. This is consistent with the way the capitalization rate was calculated in Chapter 2. In that case the cash flow was for the end of year 1 and the value was for the beginning of year 1 (which is the *end* of year 0).

Once the value is found, the overall capitalization rate should be compared to the terminal capitalization rate to ensure that the implied relationship is logical. In addition, an appraiser should also calculate both the implied change in NOI and the implied change in value to ensure that the implied assumptions are reasonable and supported by current market data.

For example, suppose we discount the cash flows for the above example at a 13 percent discount rate. A summary of the calculation is as follows:

Year	Cash Flow
1	$200,000
2	208,256
3	216,828
4	222,631
5	231,880 + $2,414,800 = $2,646,680

The present value of the above cash flows at a 13 percent discount rate is $2,063,414, or approximately $2,065,000.

Using this present value, note that the capitalization rate based on the first-year NOI would be $200,000 ÷ $2,065,000, or approximately 9.70 percent. This is slightly less (30 basis points lower) than the terminal capitalization rate of 10 percent. This difference is logical if we believe that the outlook for future cash flows for the next buyer (starting in year 6) would be about the same as for the first five years. The slightly higher terminal capitalization rate could reflect being a little conservative when estimating the resale price, that is, building a slight risk premium into the terminal capitalization rate.

NOTE: Some appraisers prefer to apply the terminal capitalization rate to the income during the last year of the holding period rather than the income one year later. For example, in the five-year cash-flow forecast illustrated above, the terminal cap rate would be applied to the income during the fifth ($231,880) rather than the sixth year (holding period plus one year). This would give the same answer if the correct terminal capitalization rate is used. In this case, the terminal capitalization rate would have to be 9.60 percent to arrive at the same estimated resale price. Dividing $231,880 by 9.60 percent results in approximately the same resale price of $2,414,480. In this case, we are using a capitalization rate that is for the same year as the calculated value. To be consistent, this would have to be compared with an initial capitalization rate (going-in capitalization rate) calculated in the same manner. In our example, the year 1 NOI was estimated to be $200,000. This is the NOI at the end of the first year. What would the NOI be at the beginning of year 1 (end of year 0)? Assuming the increase in NOI from year 0 to year 1 would be the same rate of approximately 3 percent per year, NOI would have been about $194,000 at the beginning of year 1. Using this NOI to calculate a capitalization rate (assuming the same present value), we obtain an answer of $194,000 ÷ $2,065,000, about 9.39 percent. Note that the difference between the going-in capitalization rate and the terminal capitalization rate is still about 30 basis points, the same as it was before. Thus, the same conclusions will be reached as long as the appraiser is consistent in his or her thinking.

Conceptually, the choice as to which method to use is based on the position an appraiser takes on the definition and method of calculation of the overall capitalization rate. No matter which approach is used, the reversionary value should be the same, because the appraiser is estimating the value on the same date. If the NOI data used to estimate the overall rates for comparable sales reflect last year's or a year 0 forecast, then to be consistent, the appraiser would capitalize year 5's NOI to estimate the resale in the example above. If, on the other hand, the appraiser believes the NOI data used to calculate overall rates for comparable sales represent an end-of-year estimate, year 6's net operating income would be used. An appraiser can make this decision only after a close analysis of comparable data and the methodology used to estimate NOI.

Care should be taken when determining the appropriate relationship between the going-in capitalization rate and the terminal capitalization rate (the "going-out" rate). When estimating ownership interests other than fee simple or when occupancy is not stabilized, there may be little relationship between the two. There are logical circumstances where either one could be higher than the other. In estimating the fee simple interest, however, most appraisers select a terminal rate that is slightly higher than the current rate. As discussed above, one reason given for using a higher rate is that the future forecast is less certain and, therefore, has greater risk. The riskiness of the property, however, is generally reflected in the discount rate. The appropriate reversionary value to use is the one used by typical investors. The issue, therefore, concerning the relationship between the two is what relationship reflects the current investor thought process. Unless it can be demonstrated either that older buildings sell for higher capitalization rates than newer buildings or that investors always use higher going-out than going-in rates, simply using a higher capitalization because of the risk would not mirror investor expectations.

No matter what relationship is expected, the appraiser should compare the implied current rate with the terminal rate used to see whether the relationship is logical.

SOURCES OF INCOME AND EXPENSE DATA

Income and expense information can be gathered from either primary or secondary sources. Primary sources include building owners and managers, utility companies, accountants, real estate brokers, leasing agents and other appraisers. Secondary sources include professional journal articles, publications by building management associations and lender publications. In all cases, the data must be reported in a format suitable for application to the subject property.

Where possible, any income and expense forecast should be compared with the historical performance of the property itself. The subject building may have attributes that would place cost levels for certain expenses outside normally expected levels. For example, a poorly designed or insulated building may have utility costs that exceed normal levels. The expense forecast should reflect what aspects of the property may not fall within a typical range.

SUMMARY

The income approach is based on the premise that the value of real estate property is the present value of anticipated future benefits. For real estate income property, these benefits come from anticipated cash flow that must be forecast by assimilating information from the past, identifying relationships between influencing factors and drawing conclusions about what will probably happen in the future. Forecasts of cash flows usually begin with an estimate of net operating income. When calculating net operating income, only expenses associated with operating the property are deducted. These expenses are categorized as either fixed expenses or variable expenses, depending on whether they vary with the level of occupancy. A reserve for replacement of short-lived items is sometimes included with operating expenses.

Depending on the interest being appraised, a resale or reversion value of the property may have to be estimated. Two common ways of estimating the resale price are to (1) assume an annual or total change in value from the time the property is purchased until it is sold and (2) use a terminal capitalization rate. Terminal capitalization rates are often estimated by taking the going-in capitalization rate and adding a premium for the uncertainty of estimating income at the time the property is sold. Differences in income potential for the property at the time of resale versus at the time of purchase could also affect the choice of an appropriate capitalization rate.

KEY TERMS

absolute net lease
absorption period
disposition costs
effective gross income (EGI)
fixed expenses
forecasting
going-in capitalization rate
gross building area
gross lease
holding period
marketing period
net leasable area
net lease

net operating income (NOI)
net usable area
operating expense ratio
operating expenses
potential gross income (PGI)
resale proceeds
reserve for placement
reversion
terminal capitalization rate
units of comparison
vacancy and collection loss
variable expense

QUESTIONS

1. What is meant by forecasting? Why is it necessary for appraisers to forecast income?
2. What is the difference between potential gross income and effective gross income?
3. What are the main categories of operating expenses?
4. How is the holding period determined?
5. What is the difference between a holding period, a marketing period and an absorption period?
6. What is the difference between usable area and leasable area?
7. What is meant by "disposition costs"? How does the appraiser usually consider disposition costs in a discounted cash-flow analysis?
8. What is the difference between a gross lease and a net lease?
9. What are the typical "units of comparison" for rental rates?
10. What are the typical ways that operating expenses are estimated?

END NOTES

1. A third category of expenses that is often included in the calculation of net operating income is called a "reserve for replacements." This category of expenses will be discussed later in this chapter.

2. This is sometimes referred to as a net-net-net lease, where the three items that are net are taxes, insurance and exterior maintenance. This terminology is not common today.

3. It is usually measured from the exterior of the walls and includes all enclosed areas, including the basement area.

4. The effect of this alternative on the value of the property would be equivalent to alternative two *if* the rate for the sinking fund were assumed to be the discount rate used to calculate the present value rather than a safe rate.

5. Replacements of items that contribute value to the property over a significant number of years would be considered a "capital expenditure" for accounting purposes, not an expense item.

Capital expenditures are depreciated for tax purposes and, thus, would not be deducted as an expense in the year of the replacement.

6. Depending on the appraisal technique being used, there may be a further reduction from NOI to calculate cash flow to a particular interest in the property, for example, deduction of a mortgage payment to estimate cash flow to the equity investor. This will be discussed in the next chapter.

7. In fact, this would not eliminate the need to estimate a resale price for the second investor at the end of the second holding period. To eliminate the need to estimate a resale price, we would have to estimate cash flows for the entire economic life of the property, which is not very practical.

8. Sometimes the terminal capitalization rate is referred to as a "residual capitalization rate."

The capitalization rate we discussed earlier, which expresses the relationship between the first-year income to the present value of the property (year 0), is sometimes referred to as a "going-in capitalization rate" to contrast it with the terminal capitalization rate.

CHAPTER 4	# Investment Return Calculations

The purpose of an appraisal is to estimate the market value of a property, assuming its purchase by a knowledgeable, typical investor. Implicit in this approach to estimating market value is that the analytical techniques used by an appraiser to arrive at the market value are duplicates of the methodology used by the typical investor to arrive at a purchase price. For example, when using yield capitalization as an income approach, the appraiser estimates the future benefits (usually in the form of net operating income [NOI] and net proceeds from a forecast resale) and discounts the expected cash flows by a rate of return that reflects the return required by a typical investor, given the ownership interest being appraised. In applying this methodology, it is assumed that:

- the appraiser understands the various investment techniques usually used by investors to analyze an income property and
- the appraiser can select an appropriate discount rate based on rates of return implied by actual sales from the market.

To promote a deeper understanding of appraisal techniques, the various investment analysis measures of return are presented in this chapter.

INVESTOR MOTIVATIONS

An investor usually has two goals when investing funds: preservation of the capital invested and a desire to earn a competitive profit on the capital invested. Numerous investment opportunities are available to an investor in the marketplace. Each has its own specific set of characteristics and its own level of risk. Some investments, such as publicly traded stocks, are highly marketable. Some, including real estate, may require extended periods to sell. There are short-term investments and long-term investments. There are investments with low risk (T-bills backed by the federal government) and investments with high risk (commodities futures). Some provide for gradual payback of the original investment and profit; others have a lump-sum payment at maturity. Investors select the investments that they perceive match their investment goals.

As discussed in Chapter 1, real estate has its own set of investment characteristics, including lack of liquidity, differential tax treatment, need for competent management and dependence on location. Because investors do have many alternatives for investing their money, real estate operates in the market-place and must compete with alternative investments for funds. Expected returns from real estate must be comparable to returns from other investments with similar risk. When an analyst compares the returns from one investment with those from another, the returns must be compared after considering the relative risk of each alternative.

Preservation of Capital

Naturally, the first goal of any investor is the *preservation of capital,* that is, not to lose money. Certainly, in some risky investments losing the original capital is a distinct possibility. An investor generally expects to have the original investment returned through periodic payment, through the receipt of a lump-sum payment at some time in the future or through a combination of the two. This is sometimes referred to as "return of capital" or "recapture." When a lender advances funds for a loan requiring level amortizing payments over a specific amortization period, the repayment of the loan will occur gradually through periodic payments.[1] Other investments may be expected to hold their value over time, in which case the original capital will be returned at resale. In the early and middle 1900s, when inflation was virtually nonexistent, real estate was expected to lose some value over time because of depreciation of the improvements from age, wear and tear. The investor, therefore, did not expect to recover all the investment at resale, and typical investment approaches required periodic repayment of a portion of the invested capital.

In the 1960s inflation became a fact in the marketplace, driving land prices and construction costs up year by year. The rising land prices and costs resulted in a rise in nominal property value even after adjustment for depreciation. Investors, therefore, could expect return of the invested capital at resale. Investment techniques that assumed the return of capital would occur at resale became popular. In fact, inflation moved at such a rapid pace that an investor could expect to resell the property for more than the original investment, resulting in additional profit. The issue of preservation of capital will be discussed for each of the investment techniques presented in this chapter.

Earning Investment Profit

The second motive of an investor is to earn a profit on invested capital. The amount of expected profit is directly related to the risk inherent in the invest-ment. Low-risk investment would be expected to earn low profits; high-risk investment would be expected to generate high profits. Through the competitive bidding process, the market forces interact and set the return range for each class of investment. Real estate is a major segment of this market, and prices paid for properties, in theory and in practice, reflect the market's perception of the risk in real estate. Unfortunately, because of the lack of a formally organized market and the characteristics of the real estate itself, actual returns are not readily available. In the market for corporate bonds, for example, the returns are published daily for actively traded bonds. In real estate, the returns can be implied only after a detailed analysis of the potential of the property.

When doing an appraisal, several of the techniques used require the input of return measures that are typical for the market. The interesting aspect of real estate is that there are a multitude of interests that could be valued, as well as financing and tax implications to be considered. As a result, there are a number of different returns that can be calculated that use information from the same property but have a different meaning. An appraiser must understand the interrelationship of all possible measures of return for real estate and understand how each can be affected by the structure of a transaction.

REAL ESTATE RETURN MEASURES

Several income investment measures can be extracted from a real estate sale, including payback period, first-year cash-flow ratios, internal rates of return, net present values, profitability indexes and adjusted rates of return.

Payback period is the time that elapses until an initial investment is returned. *Cash-flow ratios* (sometimes called *income rates*) are calculated by dividing the cash flow available to an ownership interest for a single year by the value of the ownership interest itself. Usually, the cash flow is the first year of the investment holding period. In real estate, these first-year cash-flow rates are typically referred to as *capitalization rates* and are preceded by a description identifying the applicable ownership interest. For example, the cash-flow rate that is calculated by dividing the first-year NOI by the total overall property value is referred to as the *overall capitalization rate* (R_O) (or going-in capitalization rate).[2]

Internal rates of return are calculated either by hand or by electronic means using an iterative process to calculate the rate of return that would discount a specific set of forecast periodic cash flows to be received by an ownership interest to a present value equal to the ownership interest itself. In real estate, these internal rates of return are usually called "yield rates" and are preceded by a description identifying the applicable ownership interest. For example, the internal rate of return calculated by comparing the cash flows to be received by the equity investor on a before-tax basis to the equity investment is the *before-tax equity yield rate,* or *equity yield rate* for short.

The cash-flow ratios discussed earlier do not specifically address profitability but are only "snapshot" ratios, which can be used for comparison with comparable real estate sales. Yield rates, however, directly address profitability and can be compared with measures of return for alternative investments (real estate as well as other investments) after consideration for relative differences in risk.

Net present value and profitability index calculations are similar to the internal rate of return approach in that profitability is addressed and a complete schedule of future cash flows (income from operations and a forecast resale) are analyzed. However, there are some differences in the calculations. First, a level-of-investment yield rate is selected that represents a target yield rate for the investment. Second, the total present value of future cash flows is calculated, using the target yield rate as a discount rate. Third, the original investment is compared to the total present value to arrive at investment decisions. In the case of the net present value, the original investment is subtracted from the present value. That is,

Net present value = Present value of future cash flows — Original investment

The profitability index is equal to the present value of the cash flows divided by the original investment. That is,

$$\text{Profitability index} = \frac{\text{Present value of future cash flows}}{\text{Original investment}}$$

The calculation of each of these measures is illustrated later.

An *adjusted internal rate of return (AIRR)*[3] calculation is similar to the internal rate of return calculation, except that expected future cash flows are compounded forward at a reinvestment rate to arrive at a total expected future value of the future cash flow. Then the future cash flows are compared with the original investment to calculate an implied annual rate of return.

Recall that the adjusted internal rate of return was discussed and illustrated in Chapter 2.

CALCULATION OF INVESTMENT RETURN MEASURES

In this chapter, the various measures of return are calculated on a before-tax basis only, without consideration for financing. The impact of financing on real estate measures of return is discussed in Chapter 9. The following set of cash flows will be used to calculate each return measure:

Example 4-1

Sample Data

Given:

Value	= $1,000,000	Resale price (10 years) = $1,200,000
Land Value	= $150,000	

Year	1	2	3	4	5
GPI	$140,000	$145,000	$150,000	$155,000	$160,000
Vacancy and Credit Loss	−10,000	−10,500	−11,000	−11,500	−12,000
EGI	$130,000	$134,500	$139,000	$143,500	$148,000
Operating Expenses	−30,000	−32,500	−35,000	−37,500	−40,000
NOI	$100,000	$102,000	$104,000	$106,000	$108,000

Year	6	7	8	9	10
GPI	$165,000	$170,000	$175,000	$180,000	$185,000
Vacancy and Credit Loss	−12,500	−13,000	−13,500	−14,000	−14,500
EGI	$152,500	$175,000	$161,500	$166,000	$170,500
Operating Expenses	−42,500	−45,000	−47,500	−50,000	−52,500
NOI	$110,000	$112,000	$114,000	$116,000	$118,000

Payback Period

Payback period is the length of time needed to return the initial investment to an investor. Following is a payback calculation for the sample data.

Investment = $1,000,000

Year	NOI	Cumulative Total Cash Flow
1	$100,000	$ 100,000
2	102,000	202,000
3	104,000	306,000
4	106,000	412,000
5	108,000	520,000
6	110,000	630,000
7	112,000	742,000
8	114,000	856,000
9	116,000	972,000
10	118,000	1,090,000

In this instance, payback did not occur until year 10. That is, after ten years the cumulative NOI totaled more than $1 million, which is the amount of the initial investment. The weakness of using payback as an investment measure is that it ignores the time value of money.

Income Multipliers

Ratios calculated by dividing the value of the property by the potential gross income (PGI), effective gross income (EGI) or net operating income (NOI) are called *income multipliers*. If the divisor is the potential gross income, the ratio is referred to as a *potential gross income multiplier (PGIM)*. If the divisor is the effective gross income, the ratio is referred to as an *effective gross income multiplier (EGIM)*. If the divisor is the net operating income, the ratio is referred to as a *net income multiplier (NIM)*. The gross income multipliers (potential and effective) are expressed as factors rather than as ratios simply because of tradition. In the case of the NIM, it is more common to use the reciprocal of this ratio, which is the overall capitalization rate, discussed previously as a cash-flow ratio or income rate. Following are calculations for each income multiplier using the sample data:

$$PGIM = \$1,000,000 \div \$140,000 = 7.654$$

$$EGIM = \$1,000,000 \div \$130,000 = 7.692$$

$$NIM = \$1,000,000 \div \$100,000 = 10.00$$

NOTE: The overall capitalization rate (R_O) is the reciprocal of the NIM, that is, 1/10, or 10 percent.

The income multipliers do not explicitly address profitability and are simple bench-mark relationships used to compare real estate sales.

Overall Capitalization Rate

The *overall capitalization rate* is calculated by dividing first-year NOI by the value of the property. It is the reciprocal of the NIM and is more typically calculated in this format. The symbol R_O is used to represent the overall capitalization rate (overall rate). Following is the overall rate calculation using the sample data:

$$R_O = \$100,000 \div \$1,000,000 = 0.10 \text{ or } 10\%$$

Like the income multipliers, the overall capitalization rate does not explicitly address profitability and is simply a bench-mark relationship used to compare real estate sales. If two real estate properties are highly comparable, then an appraiser would expect their income multipliers and overall rates to be similar for each property. There are, however, factors that may logically cause the income multipliers and overall capitalization rates for relatively comparable properties to be substantially different. Following is a list of the key factors:

- differences in financing;
- differences in the ownership interest purchased;
- existence of excess land;
- differences in vacancy and credit loss percentages;
- differences in expense ratios;
- differences in expected future income; and
- differences in expected resale (reversion) proceeds

Differences in Financing. Investors will pay a premium for a property that has financing terms more favorable than usual, such as a below-market interest rate. Thus, given two properties, if the price of one of them included an additional premium paid for favorable financing, the amount of the premium must be deducted from that property's price before the income multipliers or overall capitalization rate can be expected to be consistent.

Differences in the Ownership Interest Purchased. If the price of either property represented a different interest, the income multipliers may not be consistent. For example, suppose the land for one of the properties is leased rather than owned. Then one sale may represent a fee simple interest in the land and building, whereas the other may represent a fee simple interest in the building and a leasehold interest in the land. Thus, the purchase price would not be for comparable property interests. This could make comparison of income multipliers or overall capitalization rates misleading.

Excess Land. If one sale contained excess land (land in excess of that required by the improvements), the value of the excess land must be deducted before the income multipliers or overall capitalization rates can be expected to be similar, because the excess land may not be generating any income. It may be owned to allow for future expansion or as a speculative land investment.

Differences in Vacancy and Credit Loss Percentages. Depending on the reason for differences in vacancy and credit loss allowance, the gross income multipliers may not be comparable. For example, suppose two properties are purchased by investors at prices that result in EGIMs of 6. If the properties have different amounts of vacancy and credit loss, clearly their PGIMs are not the same. Alternatively, suppose two properties are purchased by investors for about the same PGIMs. If one of the properties has a temporarily higher vacancy rate because some of the space is being renovated, the EGIMs, NIMs and overall capitalization rates would not be comparable.

Differences in Expense Ratios. If the operating expense ratios for the properties are different (and expected to remain different),[4] the PGIMs and the EGIMs are likely to differ, because, all else being equal, investors will pay less for the property with greater operating expenses. Because PGI and EGI are calculated before operating expenses, measures that rely on these ratios could be misleading. For example, suppose two properties are purchased by investors at a price that results in a 10 percent overall capitalization rate. However, one of the properties has a 40 percent operating expense ratio and the other has a 50 percent operating expense ratio. Clearly, the gross income multipliers could not be the same.

Differences in Expected Future Income.   Because income multipliers and capitalization rates are usually calculated using income for the first year of the holding period, differences in expectations for future years can cause the ratios to differ. All else being equal, investors will pay more for a property with greater future income potential. For example, suppose two properties are expected to have the same internal rates of return (property yield rates) over a typical investment holding period. Both properties have the same first-year NOI. Because of differences in lease terms, however, the NOI for one of the properties will be level, whereas the NOI for the other will increase 5 percent each year. Clearly, a higher price will be paid for the second property. Thus, any ratios based on the first-year income are going to differ for the two properties. For example, the overall capitalization rate will be lower for the property with the greater income potential.

Differences in Expected Resale (Reversion) Proceeds.   The reason differences in expected resale prices will cause any measures based on first-year income to differ is similar to that for future income, discussed above. All else being equal, investors will pay more for a property with a higher expected resale price.

Land and Building Capitalization Rates

Another method of analyzing real estate is by considering its physical components, land and building, separately. In the early and middle 1900s, the values of these components were viewed as moving in different patterns. With the absence of significant inflationary trends, land value was viewed as remaining relatively stable, whereas the improvements were viewed as losing value over their economic life as a result of gradual depreciation. The total value was separated into building value and land value and the NOI was divided into income attributable to the land and income attributable to the building. Once both were split, the analyst could then calculate a first-year ratio for the land and a first-year ratio for the building. The first-year ratio for the land, calculated by dividing the income attributable to the land by the land value, became the *land capitalization rate* (R_L); the first-year ratio for the building, calculated by dividing the income attributable to the building by the building value, became the *building capitalization rate* (R_B). Following is the calculation of each, using the sample data and assuming the income attributable to the land is $13,500, based on the amount someone would have to pay to lease the land.

Example 4-2

Value	$1,000,000	NOI	$100,000
Less land value	−150,000	Less land income	−13,500
Building value	$ 850,000	Building income	$ 86,500

$$R_B = \$86,500 \div \$850,000 = 0.1018 \text{ or } 10.18\%$$

$$R_L = \$13,500 \div \$150,000 = 0.09 \text{ or } 9\%$$

The preceding example assumes the land value is known. Historically, the land capitalization rate and the internal rate of return or land discount rate were assumed to be equal because the land value was assumed to remain constant over time. Today we realize that this is not necessarily true. Depending on the expected change in land value, the land capitalization rate could be higher or lower than the internal rate of return on the land.

Property Yield Rate

The *property yield rate* (Y_o) is the internal rate of return to the total property value and is calculated by finding the interest rate that discounts the expected NOI and net proceeds from resale to a value equal to the total property value. Following is the property yield rate calculation, using the sample data:

Year	Cash Flow
0	($1,000,000)
1	100,000
2	102,000
3	104,000
4	106,000
5	108,000
6	110,000
7	112,000
8	114,000
9	116,000
10*	$1,318,000

$$IRR = Y_O = 0.1187 \text{ or } 11.87\%$$

*Year 10 includes NOI of $118,000 and resale proceeds of $1,200,000.

The property yield rate in this instance is a measure of profitability for the property. If two real estate properties are highly comparable, the appraiser could expect their property yield rates to be similar. In fact, expected yield rates for different investments should normally be the same unless there are differences in risk. (Differences in tax benefits could also result in differences in before-tax yield rates.) The riskiness of the investment depends on factors such as:

- whether it is an existing project or a development project;
- the lease terms (e.g., whether there are CPI adjustments and expense pass-throughs);
- the credit rating of the tenants; and
- the type of ownership interest purchased.

Net Present Value

Net present value (NPV) is a standard measure of return for many investment analysts. It is calculated by selecting a target rate of return, calculating the present value of the future cash flows and comparing this present value estimate to the initial investment. Following is an NPV calculation, assuming an 11 percent target rate and using the sample data:

Year	Cash Flow		Present Value Factor @ 11%		Present Value
1	$ 100,000	×	0.900901	=	$ 90,090
2	102,000	×	0.811622	=	82,785
3	104,000	×	0.731191	=	76,044
4	106,000	×	0.658731	=	69,825
5	108,000	×	0.593451	=	64,093
6	110,000	×	0.534641	=	58,810
7	112,000	×	0.481658	=	53,946
8	114,000	×	0.433926	=	49,468
9	116,000	×	0.390925	=	45,347
10	1,318,000	×	0.352184	=	464,179
Total present value					$1,054,587

Total present value	$1,054,587
Less investment	−1,000,000
Net present value	$ 54,587

Once the present value is calculated, the NPV is found by subtracting the original investment. If the NPV is greater than 0, the investment promises to provide a return in excess of 11 percent. If the NPV is negative, the expected return would be less than 11 percent and the investment would be rejected. In the above example, an additional $54,587 could be invested and the investor could still expect to earn 11 percent.

The NPVs may not be comparable for two similar properties if the investments required for each are different. A $2 million investment would be expected to have a higher NPV than a $1 million investment, all other things being equal.

Profitability Index

Conceptually, the *profitability index (PI)* and the NPV approaches are basically the same. In each the future cash flows are discounted by a target rate of return and the total present value is compared to the initial investment. In calculating the PI, however, the initial value is divided into the total present value, rather than subtracted from it, as shown below:

$$\frac{\text{Total present value}}{\text{Investment}} = \frac{\$1,054,587}{\$1,000,000} = 1.0546$$

The resulting ratio becomes the PI. An index greater than 1.00 indicates expectations that the investment will earn greater than an 11 percent return. If the index is less than 1.00, the investment is not forecast to earn an 11 percent annual return. Comparing two investments in this manner eliminates the problem found when using the NPV when the investments are of unequal value.

Adjusted Internal Rate of Return (Optional)

The adjusted internal rate of return approach is similar to the internal rate of return approach, except that it assumes future cash flows are compounded forward at a specified reinvestment rate. The reinvestment rate is not necessarily the same as the internal rate of return, which is why the adjusted internal rate of return can differ from the internal rate of return.[5] The reinvestment rate is usually either a *safe rate,* which represents the amount that funds could earn if reinvested in an account in which they would accumulate interest at little risk until the property was sold, or a *speculative rate,* which represents the rate that typically could be earned on comparable real estate investments. In the latter case, the assumption is that funds would be used to purchase other real estate investments, but the other investments might earn an internal rate of return that would be less than the specific project being evaluated.

Following is an adjusted internal rate of return calculation assuming a 10 percent reinvestment rate, using the sample data:

Year	Cash Flow		Future Value Factor @ 10%		Future Value
1	$ 100,000	×	2.357948	=	$ 235,795
2	102,000	×	2.143589	=	218,646
3	104,000	×	1.948717	=	202,667
4	106,000	×	1.771561	=	187,785
5	108,000	×	1.610510	=	173,935
6	110,000	×	1.464100	=	161,051
7	112,000	×	1.331000	=	149,072
8	114,000	×	1.210000	=	137,940
9	116,000	×	1.100000	=	127,600
10	1,318,000	×	1.000000	=	1,318,000
Total future value					$2,912,491

The total future value of $2,912,491 represents the amount of funds that the investor will have accumulated, including interest earned on the reinvested cash flows, after ten years. We now want to calculate the rate of return associated with making an investment of $1,000,000 in year zero and receiving a total of $2,912,491 after ten years. Note that the investor does not receive any cash flows during years 1 to 9 because they were assumed to be reinvested. The adjusted rate of return can be calculated mathematically as follows:

$$\text{AIRR} = (\$2,912,491 \div \$1,000,000)^{1/10} - 1 = 0.1128, \text{ or } 11.28\%$$

Alternatively, we could have used a financial calculator as follows:

PV	=	$1,000,000
FV	=	$2,912,491
PMT	=	0
n	=	5
i	=	?
i	=	11.28%

In this instance, the adjusted rate of return assuming reinvestment at 10 percent is 11.28 percent, which is less than the property yield or pure IRR of 11.87 percent. The adjusted rate of return is an excellent measure of the potential profitability of an investment if the IRR is higher than one might expect to earn on the interim cash flows.

SUMMARY

It is important to understand investment return calculations, because the motivations of the actions of the typical investor ultimately affect the market value of the property. An investor is motivated to purchase income property in anticipation of future benefits in the form of cash flows that recapture the investor's initial investment capital, as well as provide a yield rate on the capital.

Cash-flow ratios and income multipliers are often examined by investors to see whether they are in line with those of comparable properties. There are, however, many reasons that these ratios could differ for properties that have the same expected yield rate. Thus, appraisers must be careful when these ratios are used as indications of the relationship between income and value.

A number of measures can be used by investors to determine whether the investment meets a target yield rate. These include the internal rate of return, net present value and profitability index. The internal rate of return would be compared with a target yield rate. If the internal rate of return is greater than the target yield rate, then it is a good investment. The target yield rate can also be used as a discount rate to calculate the present value of the expected future cash flows. If the internal rate of return is greater than the target yield rate, the net present value will be positive (greater than zero) and the profitability index will be greater than one.

An adjusted internal rate of return is similar to the internal rate of return but allows the cash flows to be reinvested at a specified reinvestment rate, which might be either the same as the target yield rate or a lower safe rate. When the reinvestment rate is less than the internal rate of return, the adjusted internal rate of return will be less than the internal rate of return.

KEY TERMS

adjusted internal rate of return (AIRR)
before-tax equity yield rate
building capitalization rate (R_B)
capitalization rate
cash-flow ratio
effective gross income multiplier (EGIM)
equity yield rate (Y_E)
income multiplier
income rate
land capitalization rate (R_L)

modified internal rate of return (MIRR)
net income multiplier (NIM)
net present value (NPV)
overall capitalization rate (R_O)
payback period
potential gross income multiplier (PGIM)
preservation of capital
profitability index (PI)
property yield rate (Y_O)
safe rate
speculative rate

QUESTIONS

1. What are the primary motivations for investing in real estate income property?
2. What is meant by the term "payback period"?
3. What is the difference between a cash-flow ratio and an internal rate of return?
4. What is meant by a net present value?
5. Why do you think an adjusted internal rate of return is typically less than an internal rate of return?
6. Suppose a property was just purchased for $1 million that is expected to have net operating income during the first year of $90,000. After the first year, the cash flow is expected to increase by $5,000 per year for ten years because of the terms of the lease. At the end of the tenth year, the property is expected to be sold for $1.4 million to the lessor because of an option in the lease. There will be no loan on the property. Calculate the following:
   a. Overall capitalization rate
   b. Net income multiplier
   c. Internal rate of return (property yield rate)

    d.   Net present value by using a 12.5 percent discount rate

    e.   Profitability index by using a 12.5 percent discount rate

    f.   Adjusted internal rate of return, using a 6 percent reinvestment rate

---

END NOTES

    1.   Recall that in Chapter 2 we showed how the interest rate on a loan (return *on* capital) plus the sinking fund factor for the same interest rate (return *of* capital) was equal to the loan constant (mortgage capitalization rate).

    2.   Sometimes the overall capitalization rate is simply referred to as the "cap rate." Another synonymous term is "overall rate."

    3.   The adjusted rate of return is also referred to as the "adjusted internal rate of return," or "adjusted IRR" for short. Another synonymous term is *modified internal rate of return (MIRR).*

    4.   For example, one of the properties may have a much less efficient HVAC system, causing utility expenses to differ.

    5.   If the reinvestment rate is less than the internal rate of return, the adjusted internal rate of return will also be less than the internal rate of return.

CHAPTER 5

Investment Measures with Mortgage Financing

IMPACT OF FINANCING ON REAL ESTATE CASH-FLOW FORECASTS

In the 1960s, mortgage financing became an important factor in many real estate transactions. Currently, a multitude of financing options are available to an investor. When an investor secures a mortgage loan for an income producing property, the investor becomes the owner of the *equity interest* and the lender has a *mortgage interest*. In essence, the two have become partners in the real estate. Under the terms of a mortgage loan agreement, for advancing a portion of the funds to finance the purchase, the lender receives periodic payments over a specified time period known as the *amortization period*. The periodic loan payments include provisions for a complete return of the principal balance (return *of* capital), as well as a competitive profit (return *on* capital) to the lender. Generally, the lender has first right to receive the payments required by the loan contract and is in what is typically referred to as first position. Should the equity investor fail to meet the required payment schedule, the investor will ultimately lose the property and, therefore, the equity investment. Since the lender is in first position, the mortgage position usually involves less risk. This suggests that the expected profit level rate (mortgage interest rate) for the lender would be less than the equity investor's profit rate (*equity yield rate*).

An owner has, basically, two motives when financing a real estate purchase with a mortgage. The first is to secure the level of funds needed to purchase the property, and the second is to increase the equity profits through the use of financial leverage. The concept of financial leverage will be discussed later in this chapter.

Real estate cash flows are affected because the periodic debt payments are deducted from each year's forecast net operating income (NOI) and any remaining loan balance is deducted from the resale proceeds. Once the mortgage payments have been deducted, the resulting annual cash flows are referred to as the *before-tax cash flows (BTCF)* from operations. In appraisal literature, these cash flows have also been referred to as the *equity dividend* or *cash throw off (CTO)*. The net reversion after deducting any remaining loan balance is referred to as the "before-tax cash flow from reversion."

CALCULATION OF INVESTMENT RETURNS, ASSUMING FINANCING

The typical investment measures calculated in Chapter 4, including payback, capitalization rates, internal rates of return, net present value, profitability index and adjusted rates of return, can also be calculated for the equity investor. The same set of cash flows used in Chapter 4 to calculate investment measures on an unleveraged basis will be used to calculate the leveraged return, except that a $750,000 loan at a 10 percent interest rate for 25 years will be assumed.

Example 5-1

Given:

Mortgage interest rate	$1,200,000 (10 Years)
Value	$1,000,000
Loan amount	$750,000
Mortgage interest rate	10
Amortization period	25 Years (Monthly)
Equity value	$250,000
Resale price	$1,200,000 (10 Years)

Year	1	2	3	4	5
NOI	$100,000	$102,000	$104,000	$106,000	$108,000
Annual debt service	− 81,783	− 81,783	− 81,783	− 81,783	− 81,783
BTCF	$ 8,217	$ 20,217	$ 22,217	$ 24,217	$ 26,217

Year	6	7	8	9	10
NOI	$110,000	$112,000	$114,000	$116,000	$118,000
Annual debt service	− 81,783	− 81,783	− 81,783	− 81,783	− 81,783
BTCF	$ 28,217	$ 30,217	$ 32,217	$ 34,217	$ 36,217

Resale price (reversion)	$1,200,000
Loan balance	− 634,210
BTCF from reversion	$ 565,790

NOTE: In this instance, the mortgage capitalization rate (R_M), sometimes referred to as the mortgage constant, is 0.1090 ($81,783/$750,000).

Payback Period

Payback period is the length of time it takes an equity investor to regain the initial equity investment. The following demonstrates how payback is calculated for the sample data.

Equity Investment = $250,000

Year	Before-Tax Cash Flow	Cumulative Total Cash Flow
1	$18,217	$ 18,217
2	20,217	38,434
3	22,217	60,651
4	24,217	84,868
5	26,217	111,085

6	28,217	139,302
7	30,217	169,519
8	32,217	201,736
9	34,217	235,953
10	36,217	272,170

In this instance, payback did not occur until year 10. That is, it took ten years of BTCF from operations to receive sufficient cash flow to return the original equity investment.[1] The weakness of using payback as an investment measure is that it ignores the time value of money.

Equity Capitalization Rate

The *equity capitalization rate* (R_E), frequently referred to as the *equity dividend rate*, is calculated by dividing the first-year BTCF by the equity value. Following is the R_E calculation using the sample data.

$$R_E = \text{BTCF}/V_E = \$18{,}217/\$250{,}000 = 0.0729, \text{ or } 7.29\%$$

where V_E represents equity value.

The equity capitalization rate does not explicitly address profitability and is simply a benchmark relationship used to compare real estate sales. If two real estate properties are highly comparable, the appraiser could expect their equity dividend rates to be similar. One must be very careful, however, if financing of the properties differs. For example, equity dividend rates can and should in theory differ for different loan-to-value ratios. As we will see later, the higher the loan-to-value ratio, the greater the risk.

Before-Tax Equity Yield Rate

The *before-tax equity yield rate* or "equity discount rate" is the internal rate of return to the equity value calculated by finding the interest rate that discounts the expected BTCF and the equity proceeds from resale to a value equal to the original equity investment. The symbol used to represent the before-tax equity yield rate is Y_E. Following is the before-tax Y_E calculation using the sample data.

Year	BTCF
0	($250,000)
1	$18,217
2	20,217
3	22,217
4	24,217
5	26,217
6	28,217
7	30,217
8	32,217
9	34,217
10*	602,007

$$\text{IRR} = Y_E = 0.1590, \text{ or } 15.9\%$$

*Year 10 BTCF and resale proceeds.

The yield rate in this instance is a measure of profitability for the equity investor. The before-tax Y_E of 15.90 percent is significantly higher than the property yield rate of 11.87 percent (from Chapter 4). The increase in the yield rate is a result of positive leverage, which will be discussed in a later section of this chapter.

If two real estate properties are highly comparable, the appraiser could expect the before-tax equity yields to be similar. As with the equity capitalization rate, however, the before-tax yields may not be comparable if the financing structures are not similar. If, for example, the property was financed with a loan for $650,000 instead of $750,000 but at the same interest rate (10 percent) for the same time period (25 years) with monthly payments, the before-tax Y_E would be

---

Example 5-2

Given:

Value	$1,000,000
Loan amount	$650,000
Mortgage interest rate	10
Amortization period	25 Years (Monthly)
Equity value	$350,000
Resale price	$1,200,000

Year	1	2	3	4	5
NOI	$100,000	$102,000	$104,000	$106,000	$108,000
Annual debt service	– 70,879	– 70,879	– 70,879	– 70,879	– 70,879
BTCF	$ 29,121	$ 31,121	$ 33,121	$ 35,121	$ 37,121

Year	6	7	8	9	10
NOI	$110,000	$112,000	$114,000	$116,000	$118,000
Annual debt service	– 70,879	– 70,879	– 70,879	– 70,879	– 70,879
BTCF	$ 39,121	$ 41,121	$ 43,121	$ 45,121	$ 47,121

Resale price	$1,200,000
Loan balance	– 549,649
Before-tax proceeds	$ 650,351

The before-tax Y_E, assuming a $650,000 loan, is calculated as follows:

Year	BTCF
0	($350,000)
1	29,121
2	31,121
3	33,121
4	35,121
5	37,121
6	39,121
7	41,121
8	43,121
9	45,121
10	697,472

$$\text{IRR} = Y_E = 0.1458, \text{ or } 14.6\%$$

By dropping the loan-to-value ratio from 75 percent to 65 percent, the before-tax Y_E for the same set of cash flows, interest rate and amortization structure dropped from 15.9 percent to 14.6 percent. It should be noted, however, that there is also less risk for the equity investor when less debt is used. This is discussed in Chapter 6.

Net Present Value

The net present value (NPV) may be calculated using the equity cash flows. The NPV under these circumstances becomes the NPV for the equity investment. It is calculated by selecting a target rate of return, calculating the present values of the forecast before-tax cash flows and comparing the present value estimate with the initial equity investment. Following is an NPV calculation assuming a 15 percent target rate and using the sample data.

Year	BTCF		Present Value Factor @ 15%		Present Value
1	$ 18,217	×	0.869565	=	$ 15,841
2	20,217	×	0.756144	=	15,287
3	22,217	×	0.657516	=	14,608
4	24,217	×	0.571753	=	13,846
5	26,217	×	0.497177	=	13,034
6	28,217	×	0.432328	=	12,199
7	30,217	×	0.375937	=	11,360
8	32,217	×	0.326902	=	10,532
9	34,217	×	0.284262	=	9,727
10	602,007	×	0.247185	=	148,807

Total present value $265,241
Less equity investment −250,000
NPV $ 15,241

Once the present value is calculated, the NPV is found by subtracting the original value. If the NPV is greater than zero, the investment promises to provide a return in excess of 15 percent. If the net present value were negative, the expected return would be less than 15 percent and would be rejected. In the above example, the investor could invest an additional $15,241 of equity capital and still earn 15 percent. This assumes the amount of the loan would remain the same.

Differences in NPV could occur for the same reasons that differences in the yield rate could occur. In addition, the NPVs are not comparable for two similar properties if the equity investment required for each one is different.

Profitability Index

Conceptually, the *profitability index* approach and the NPV approach are basically the same. In each, future cash flows are discounted by a target rate of return and the total present value is compared to the initial investment. In calculating the profitability index, however, the initial equity value is divided into the total present value rather than subtracted from it, as shown below.

Total present value/Equity investment = $265,241/$250,000 = 1.061

The resulting ratio becomes the profitability index. An index greater than 1.00 indicates that the investment is expected to earn greater than a 15 percent return. If the index is less than 1.00, the investment is not forecast to earn a 15 percent annual return.

Adjusted Internal Rate of Return

As we have discussed, the *adjusted internal rate of return (AIRR)* approach is similar to the internal rate of return approach, except that it is assumed that future cash flows will be compounded forward at a typical investment rate. Following is an AIRR calculation, using a 12 percent reinvestment rate and the sample data we have been analyzing in this chapter.

Year	BTCF		Present Value Factor @ 15%		Present Value
1	$ 18,217	×	2.773079	=	$ 50,517
2	20,217	×	2.475963	=	50,057
3	22,217	×	2.210681	=	49,115
4	24,217	×	1.973823	=	47,800
5	26,217	×	1.762342	=	46,203
6	28,217	×	1.573519	=	44,400
7	30,217	×	1.404928	=	42,453
8	32,217	×	1.254400	=	40,413
9	34,217	×	1.120000	=	38,323
10	602,007	×	1.000000	=	602,007
Total future value					$1,011,288

$$\text{AIRR} = (\$1,011,288/\$250,000)^{1/10} - 1 = 0.1500, \text{ or } 15\%$$

In this instance, the AIRR, assuming reinvestment at 12 percent, is 15 percent, which is less than the before-tax equity yield or unadjusted internal rate of return (IRR) of 15.90 percent. The AIRR is an excellent measure of the potential profitability of an investment if the IRR is higher than an investor might expect to earn on the interim cash flows.

FINANCIAL LEVERAGE

Financial leverage is defined as the use of borrowed funds in the purchase of an investment. If the addition of the mortgage increases the return to the equity, the addition of the mortgage has resulted in *positive leverage*. If the addition of the mortgage decreases the return to the equity, the addition of the mortgage has resulted in *negative leverage*.

As shown earlier in this chapter, borrowing funds at an interest rate or mortgage yield rate (Y_M) that is below the property yield rate (Y_O) results in a positive impact on the before-tax equity yield rate (Y_E). In addition, generally the higher the loan-to-value ratio the higher the before-tax Y_E. This circumstance is referred to as "positive (or favorable) leverage" because the equity investor is able to increase the rate of return through borrowing funds. Should the mortgage interest rate, however, be higher than the property yield rate (Y_O), the before-tax Y_E will be lower than the Y_O, which would result in "negative (or unfavorable) leverage." The phenomenon of negative leverage is presented in the next example by using the sample data, except, in this case, the $750,000 mortgage is assumed to have a 12.5 percent interest rate for 25 years (monthly payments). The before-tax Y_E is calculated as follows:

Example 5-3

Given:

Value	=	$1,000,000
Loan amount	=	$750,000
Mortgage interest rate	=	12.5%
Amortization period	=	25 years (Monthly)
Equity value	=	$250,000
Resale price (10 Years)	=	$1,200,000

Year	1	2	3	4	5
NOI	$100,000	$102,000	$104,000	$106,000	$108,000
Annual debt service	− 98,132	− 98,132	− 98,132	− 98,132	− 98,132
BTCF	$ 1,868	$ 3,868	$ 5,868	$ 7,868	$ 9,868

Year	6	7	8	9	10
NOI	$110,000	$112,000	$114,000	$116,000	$118,000
Annual debt service	− 98,132	− 98,132	− 98,132	− 98,132	− 98,132
BTCF	$ 11,868	$ 13,868	$ 15,868	$ 17,868	$ 19,868

Resale price	$1,200,000
Loan balance	−663,490
Before-tax proceeds	$ 536,510

Year	BTCF
0	($250,000)
1	$ 1,868
2	3,868
3	5,868
4	7,868
5	9,868
6	11,868
7	13,868
8	15,868
9	17,868
10	$556,378

$$\text{IRR} = Y_E = 0.1066, \text{ or } 10.66\%$$

With the interest rate at 12.5 percent instead of 10 percent, the before-tax Y_E is only 10.7 percent, which is less than the 11.87 percent Y_O. By borrowing the money at an interest rate higher than the Y_O, the before-tax Y_E was negatively affected, an example of negative leverage. Normally we would expect positive leverage based on anticipated cash flows at the time the property is purchased. We expect the Y_E to be greater than the mortgage yield rate (Y_M) because of the additional risk incurred by the equity investor compared with the mortgage lender. Of course, it may turn out after the property is purchased that the equity investor does not earn the originally expected return.

Cash-Flow Leverage

The concept of positive and negative leverage can also be viewed on a first year cash-flow basis alone. In essence, if the mortgage capitalization rate (R_M) is less than the overall rate (R_O), then positive leverage will result, and the equity dividend rate (R_E) will be greater than R_O. In periods of no inflation or deflation this would be the case. Caution should be exercised, however, when analyzing leverage on a first-year cash-flow basis only. Unfavorable leverage can occur on a cash-flow basis even though it is favorable over the holding period.

This was true for the first example using the sample data in this chapter. The overall yield rate (Y_O) of 11.87 percent exceeded the interest rate on the mortgage (Y_M) of 10 percent, which magnified the equity yield rate (Y_E) to 15.9 percent with a 75 percent loan-to-value ratio. Thus, there was favorable financial leverage based on yield rates. For this same example, the overall capitalization rate (R_O) is 10 percent, which is less than the mortgage constant (R_M) of 10.90 percent.* Recall that the equity dividend rate (R_E) calculated earlier for this sample data is 7.29 percent. Thus, there is negative leverage when viewed in terms of the effect of leverage on the equity dividend rate whereas there is positive leverage when viewed in terms of the effect of leverage on the equity yield rate.

Effect of Leverage on Equity Dividend Rate

The effect of leverage on the equity dividend rate can be shown as follows:

$$R_E = R_O + (R_O - R_M) M / (1 - M)$$

where M is the loan-to-value ratio. Using the above example, we have

$$
\begin{aligned}
R_E &= 10 + (10 - 10.90) \times .75 / .25 \\
&= 10 - (.90 \times 3) \\
&= 10 - 2.70 \\
&= 7.30
\end{aligned}
$$

This is the same equity dividend rate as calculated earlier. (The difference from 7.29 percent is due to rounding.) The formula shown above makes it clear that R_O must exceed R_M for leverage to be positive and increase R_E. Furthermore, the effect of leverage increases as the loan-to-value ratio (M) increases.

Effect of Leverage on Equity Yield Rate

The effect of leverage on the equity yield rate Y_E can be *estimated* using a similar formula as follows:

$$Y_E = Y_O + (Y_O - Y_M) M / (1 - M).$$

Note that in this case we use the mortgage interest rate Y_M, which is a yield rate rather than the loan constant that is a cash flow rate. Using the same example, we have

$$
\begin{aligned}
Y_E &= 11.87 + (11.87 - 10) \times .75 / .25 \\
&= 11.87 + (1.87 \times 3) \\
&= 17.48
\end{aligned}
$$

This is higher than the equity yield rate calculated earlier which was 15.9 percent. This is because the above formula uses the initial loan-to-value ratio (M) and assumes that the loan-to-value ratio (M) is constant over the investment holding period. This is not true when the loan is amortized and/or the property value changes. In the example above the loan balance decreases over a period

---

* Note that the mortgage constant is higher than the interest rate of 10 percent because the loan is amortized.

FIGURE 5.1   Positive Leverage

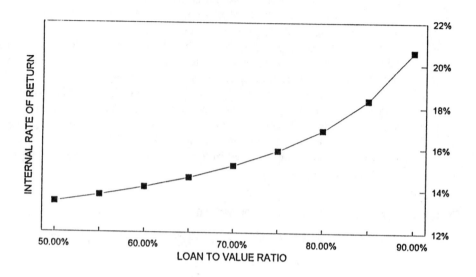

of time and the property value increases over a period of time. Both of these factors result in a buildup of equity over the holding period that reduces the loan-to-value ratio each year. This is why the equity yield rate is overestimated when the above formula is used. The formula gives an exact answer if the loan is not amortized, i.e., interest only, and the property value does not change over the holding period. Even when this is not true, however, the formula is still useful in understanding the relationships between Y_O, Y_M and Y_E.

Figure 5.1 uses the sample data from the beginning of this chapter (loan at a 10 percent interest rate) where there is positive leverage to illustrate how the investor's return on equity (Y_E) increases with increasing amounts of leverage, i.e., higher loan to value ratios. In that example, the property value was assumed to increase from $1 million to $2 million over the ten year holding period. But what if the property value does not actually increase? Suppose instead that the property value decreases to $800,000. Figure 5.2 shows what would happen to the investor's return on equity (Y_E) at different amounts of leverage if the property value decreases to $800,000. In this case there is negative financial leverage. The more the investor had borrowed, the lower his or her expected rate of return on equity. This illustrates the risk associated with the use of financial leverage. We don't know what will actually happen to the property value over a period of time. The investor may have expected the property value to increase to $1.2 million and borrowed money based on the expectation of positive financial leverage. That is, if no money had been borrowed, the investor's expected return on equity would have been 11.87 percent whereas with a 75 percent loan, the expected return on equity would be 15.9 percent. If the property value actually declines to $800,000, however, the investor's actual rate of return would have been 9.47 percent if no debt had been used but it would be 8.06 percent with a 75 percent loan. Leverage works against the investor in the latter case. This is why the investor must expect a higher rate of return if he

FIGURE 5.2   Negative Leverage

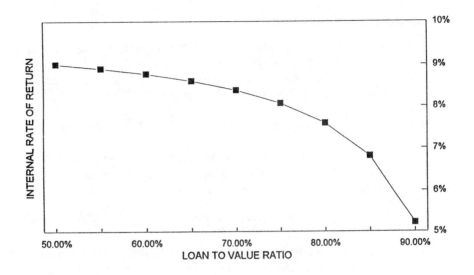

or she is going to use leverage to begin with when purchasing an investment. The expected return must consider the risk that the actual return may be higher or lower depending on what actually happens to market rental rates, vacancy rates, property values, etc. over the investment holding period.

Summary of Leverage Relationships

We can summarize the leverage relationships discussed above as follows:

If $R_O > R_M$ then $R_E > R_O$ positive leverage of equity dividend rate
If $R_O = R_M$ then $R_E = R_O$ neutral leverage of equity dividend rate
If $R_O < R_M$ then $R_E < R_O$ negative leverage of equity dividend rate
If $Y_O > Y_M$ then $Y_E > Y_O$ positive leverage of equity yield rate
If $Y_O = Y_M$ then $Y_E = Y_O$ neutral leverage of equity yield rate
If $Y_O < Y_M$ then $Y_E < Y_O$ negative leverage of equity yield rate

Leverage and Market Value

Note that when we discussed leverage in the examples above we did not suggest that leverage affects the market value of the property. Positive leverage increases the investor's *expected* return but at the same time it increases the riskiness of the investment. With greater amounts of leverage, however, the investor's *actual* rate of return also is more uncertain. This is because any factor that affects Y_O such as an increase in vacancy will have a greater affect on Y_E with higher amounts of leverage. Because risk also increases with financial leverage, the equity investor requires a higher expected rate of return on the investment. Thus, the value of the investment does not necessarily increase. Appraisers must be careful when discounting cash flows to value the equity position to select a discount rate that reflects the risk associated with the level of financial leverage. Otherwise they may over or underestimate the market value of the property.

Loan Amount Determination

Typically, lenders have two methods of selecting the level of funds to be advanced to a property owner. These two so-called *loan constraints* are the *loan-to-value ratio* (*M*) and the first-year debt service coverage ratio (DCR). The *M* for the sample data is calculated as follows:

$$M = \frac{\text{Loan Amount}}{\text{Property Value}} = \frac{\$750,000}{\$1,000,000} = 0.75, \text{ or } 75\%$$

The *debt service coverage ratio* (debt coverage ratio, or DCR for short) is calculated by dividing the first year's NOI by the annual mortgage payment, as shown below.

$$\text{DCR} = \frac{\text{NOI}}{\text{Annual Debt Payment}} = \frac{\$100,000}{\$81,783} = 1.22$$

A ratio greater than 1.00 means that a lender would require that the first-year NOI be greater than the annual debt service payment. In some instances, the maximum a lender can loan on a property is set by law. In other cases, the maximum loan amount is a policy decision of the lending institution. It is possible for the lending constraint to vary by property type, age, location, tenant mix and borrower, especially if any of these result in differences in risk. The formula for finding a loan balance using a DCR is as follows:

$$\text{Mortgage value } (V_M) = \frac{\text{NOI}}{\text{DCR} \times R_M}$$

The NOI equals the first-year NOI, the R_M is the mortgage capitalization rate (see Chapter 4) and the DCR is the first-year ratio required by a lender. Following is an example of the use of the DCR to find the loan amount.

Example 5-4

DCR	1.2
First-year NOI	$200,000
Loan term	9.75% interest; 30 years, monthly payment
Therefore, R_M =	0.103099

$$V_M = \frac{\$200,000}{1.2 \times 0.103099} = \$1,616,569$$

The annual payment for a $1,616,569 loan is $166,666, which indicates a 1.2 ($200,000/$166,666) DCR.

Frequently, lenders look at both the loan-to-value ratio (*M*) and the DCR. It is highly unlikely that a loan amount would exactly satisfy both a specific *M* and a specific DCR. A lender, therefore, picks a controlling restraint and tests to see whether the sister constraint falls within a reasonable range. An example appears on the following page.

In this instance, *M* is exactly 80 percent, but the DCR is only 1.174, which is less than the required rate. The loan as structured, therefore, would not meet the lender's constraints.

Example 5-5

Lender Constraints DCR = 1.20 – 1.30

Given: Value $2,000,000
Loan amount $1,600,000 @ 10.5% interest
20 years (monthly payments)
First year NOI $225,000

$$M = \frac{\$1,600,000}{\$2,000,000} = 0.80, \text{ or } 80\%$$

$$DCR = \frac{\$225,000}{\$191,689} = 1.174$$

Loan Types

The loan used in the examples in this chapter is a level-payment, fully amortized loan. Loans of this type are prevalent in the marketplace. Other loan types, however, exist and are currently available from lenders active in the marketplace. The predominant loan types are

- Interest only mortgage;
- Adjustable rate mortgage;
- Negative amortization mortgage; and
- Loan participation.

Interest Only Mortgages. *Interest only mortgages* are structured so that the entire annual payment just covers the interest; this results in no amortization (repayment) of the mortgage (principal), which remains constant. The lender receives the entire principal at the expiration of the loan. Payment of this balance is referred to as a *balloon payment*. Interest only mortgages typically have shorter amortizing periods than level-payment, self-amortizing loans. Example 5-6 features an interest only loan for $750,000 at 10 percent interest for 10 years, using the sample data.

The before-tax yield rate is slightly higher with the interest only loan, which suggests that the equity investor would prefer an interest only loan to a level amortizing loan at the same rate. The interest only loan, however, is due in ten years, which would probably increase the risk to the equity, thus offsetting any benefits from the interest only structuring of the payment.

Adjustable Rate Mortgages. *Adjustable rate mortgages* are structured so that payments vary over time, either contractually or as a result of general interest rate changes. These loans can be structured on an interest only basis or can have gradual amortization built in. Example 5-7 shows a variable rate loan structured on an interest only basis for ten years. In this case the interest rate for each year is given. In practice, however, the interest rate for each year would be calculated after comparison with some index specified in the loan contract. Under these circumstances, an appraiser would not know the future interest rate and would therefore need to forecast rates to analyze the impact of the loan.

The before-tax Y_E for a variable rate loan is higher than that for an interest only loan, assuming payments at a 10 percent rate. The variable nature of the loan payments, if not specifically set by contract, results in a riskier situation

Example 5-6

Interest Only Mortgage

Given:

Value	$1,000,000
Loan amount	$750,000 interest only @ 10%
Equity value	$250,000
Resale (tenth year)	$1,200,000

Year	1	2	3	4	5
NOI	$100,000	$102,000	$104,000	$106,000	$108,000
Annual debt payment	− 75,000	− 75,000	− 75,000	− 75,000	− 75,000
BTCF	$ 25,000	$ 27,000	$ 29,000	$ 31,000	$ 33,000

Year	6	7	8	9	10
NOI	$110,000	$112,000	$114,000	$116,000	$118,000
Annual debt payment	− 75,000	− 75,000	− 75,000	− 75,000	− 75,000
BTCF	$ 35,000	$ 37,000	$ 39,000	$ 41,000	$ 43,000

Resale price	$1,200,000
Loan balance	− 750,000
Before-tax reversion	$ 450,000

Year	BTCF
0	($250,000)
1	25,000
2	27,000
3	29,000
4	31,000
5	33,000
6	35,000
7	37,000
8	39,000
9	41,000
10	493,000

IRR = Y_E = 0.1633, or 16.33%

for the equity investor. This type of loan, however, would probably represent a lower risk to the lender if payments depend on future market conditions, because of the opportunity to increase payments if interest rates increase.

Negative Amortization Mortgages. *Negative amortization mortgages* are structured so that early payments are below the level needed to meet the interest payments fully. Therefore, the loan balance increases in early years. Loans structured in this manner help investors during periods of temporary high interest rates or during early rent-up of a new project. The mathematics of calculating the interest and principal payment in any year may be complicated, and for this reason, an example of a negative amortization loan is not given in this book.

Loan Participation. *Loan participation* mortgages are structured to include both a constant payment over time and additional payments based on a property's performance over time. The additional income can come from resale

Example 5-7

Adjustable Rate Mortgage

Given:

Value	$1,000,000
Loan amount	$750,000 interest only with variable interest rate
Equity value	$250,000
Resale (tenth year)	$1,200,000

Year:	1	2	3	4	5	6	7	8	9	10
Interest, %	9%	9%	9.5%	10%	10%	11%	11%	10%	10%	10%

Year	1	2	3	4	5
NOI	$100,000	$102,000	$104,000	$106,000	$108,000
Annual debt payment	− 67,500	− 67,500	− 71,250	− 75,000	− 75,000
BTCF	$ 32,500	$ 34,500	$ 32,750	$ 31,000	$ 33,000

Year	6	7	8	9	10
NOI	$110,000	$112,000	$114,000	$116,000	$118,000
Annual debt payment	− 82,500	− 82,500	− 75,000	− 75,000	− 75,000
BTCF	$ 27,500	$ 29,500	$ 39,000	$ 41,000	$ 43,000

Resale price	$1,200,000
Loan balance	− 750,000
Before-tax reversion	$ 450,000

Year	BTCF
0	($250,000)
1	32,500
2	34,500
3	32,750
4	31,000
5	33,000
6	27,500
7	29,500
8	39,000
9	41,000
10	493,000

$$\text{IRR} = Y_E = 0.1694, \text{ or } 16.94\%$$

proceeds, as well as from annual operating income. A multitude of methods are used to calculate additional payments, including percentages of

- gross income;
- gross income above a threshold amount;
- NOI;
- NOI above a threshold amount;
- BTCF (after regular debt service but before the participation);
- BTCF above a threshold amount;
- resale proceeds;
- gain at resale (over the original purchase price); and
- cash flow at resale (sales price less mortgage balance).

Example 5-8

Loan Participation Mortgage

Given:

Value	$1,000,000
Loan amount	$750,000 (@ 9.5% interest for 25 years; monthly payments)
Equity value	$250,000
Resale (tenth year)	$1,200,000
Participation	25% of NOI increase

Year	1	2	3	4	5
NOI	$100,000	$102,000	$104,000	$106,000	$108,000
Annual debt payment	– 78,633	– 78,633	– 78,633	– 78,633	– 78,633
Participation payment	– 0	– 500	– 1,000	– 1,500	– 2,000
BTCF	$ 21,367	$ 22,867	$ 24,367	$ 25,867	$ 27,367

Year	6	7	8	9	10
NOI	$110,000	$112,000	$114,000	$116,000	$118,000
Annual debt payment	– 78,633	– 78,633	– 78,633	– 78,633	– 78,633
Participation payment	– 2,500	– 3,000	– 3,500	– 4,000	– 4,500
BTCF	$ 28,867	$ 30,367	$ 31,867	$ 33,367	$ 34,867

Resale price	$1,200,000
Loan balance	– 627,521
Before-tax reversion	$ 572,479

Year	BTCF
0	($250,000)
1	21,367
2	22,867
3	24,367
4	25,867
5	27,367
6	28,867
7	30,367
8	31,867
9	33,367
10	607,346

IRR = Y_E = 0.1644, or 16.44%

Typically, these loans initially are structured with lower interest rates because of the potential for increased returns to the lender. Example 5-8 shows a loan participation, assuming a $750,000 loan at 9.5 percent interest for 25 years (monthly payments) with an additional income participation based on 25 percent of any NOI above $100,000.

Other Types of Financing

A multitude of other mortgage types exist, including fixed principal repayment loans, convertible mortgages, mortgages that are of one type for a certain period and change to another type later, and various types of joint venture arrangements. Each financing alternative should be judged based on the potential risks to the lender and to the equity holder.

SUMMARY

The use of debt to finance real estate creates both a mortgage and an equity interest in the property. Each of these interests can be analyzed separately, and a market value is associated with each interest. The total value of the property equals the total values of these interests.

The investment return calculations for evaluating the entire property (before considering financing) can also be applied to analysis of the equity interest. Typical measures include the payback period, the equity capitalization rate, the equity yield rate, the net present value of the cash flows to the equity investor, and the adjusted rate of return. These measures usually differ from those for the entire property because of the impact that debt has on cash flows to the equity position.

The concept of financial leverage deals specifically with the impact of debt on the equity investor's cash flow and rate of return. Leverage can either be favorable or unfavorable, depending on the cost of the debt. Conditions for either favorable or unfavorable leverage to be favorable were discussed in terms of the effects on both equity yield rates and equity dividend rates.

The amount of debt that can be obtained for real estate income property is often limited by either a maximum loan-to-value ratio or a minimum debt coverage ratio. A maximum loan-to-value ratio ensures a minimum initial equity investment, whereas a minimum debt coverage ratio ensures that net operating income is sufficient to cover the mortgage payment during the first year of the investment.

A variety of different types of mortgages, in addition to fully amortized fixed rate mortgages, are available to finance real estate income property. These include interest only mortgages, adjustable rate mortgages, negative amortization mortgages and mortgages with participation.

KEY TERMS

adjustable rate mortgage
adjusted internal rate of return
  (AIRR)
amortization term
balloon payment
before-tax cash flow (BTCF)
before-tax equity yield rate
cash throw off (CTO)
debt coverage ratio (DCR)
equity capitalization rate (R_E)
equity dividend
equity dividend rate
equity interest

equity yield rate (Y_E)
financial leverage
interest only mortgage
loan constraints
loan participation
loan-to-value ratio
mortgage interest
negative amortization
negative leverage
net present value
payback period
positive leverage
profitability index

QUESTIONS

1. What is the difference between an equity capitalization rate and an overall capitalization rate?
2. What is the difference between an equity yield rate and an equity capitalization rate?
3. What factors would tend to cause expected equity yield rates to differ for different properties?
4. What is meant by financial leverage? What causes leverage to be positive?
5. Can leverage be evaluated by considering the effect on first-year cash flows?
6. Suppose a property is projected to have a first-year net operating income of $250,000. The lender requires a 1.25 debt coverage ratio. The loan would have a 10 percent interest rate and be amortized over 25 years with monthly payments. How large a loan can be obtained?
7. What is meant by a negative amortization mortgage?
8. What is meant by a loan participation? What is the participation based on?
9. What is meant by a balloon payment?
10. An investor is considering purchasing a property for $2.5 million by obtaining a loan for 80 percent of the purchase price at a 9 percent interest rate with monthly payments over 30 years. The net operating income is expected to be $200,000 the first year and then increase by 4 percent per year until the property is sold. The investor expects to sell the property for $3 million at the end of the fifth year.
    a. What is the debt coverage ratio?
    b. What is the equity capitalization rate?
    c. What is the equity yield rate?
    d. What is the net present value of the cash flows to the equity investor using a 12 percent equity discount rate?

END NOTE

1. In this case the payback of capital was received by the tenth year without considering any cash flow from resale (reversion). If the property was sold before year 10, the payback period would be the same as the holding period, assuming sufficient funds were received from its sale to return any capital not yet received through cash flow from operations.

CHAPTER 6	# Risk Analysis

Risk can be defined as the probability that events will not occur as expected. For example, vacancy rates may be higher than anticipated, market rental rates at the time of lease renewals may be lower than predicted, terminal capitalization rates at the time of resale may be higher than expected. Because actual events in the market can differ from what the investor contemplated at the time the property was purchased, the investor's actual rate of return can differ from the return hoped for when the property was purchased. Thus, we can view risk as the probability that the actual rate of return earned by the investor will differ from the return that was expected when the investment was made.

Risk is important for several reasons. First, the investor's desired rate of return depends on the degree of risk. Second, comparable sales should have the same degree of risk for extraction of capitalization rates or rates must be adjusted for differences in risk. Third, discount rates used to calculate the present value of cash flows must be commensurate with the level of risk.

TYPES OF RISK

There are a number of different types of risk that can affect real estate investors. Knowing the sources of risk that can affect a particular real estate investment is the first step in risk analysis. Following is a discussion of the main types of risk.[1]

Space Market Risk

Space market risk is the risk that changes in the market for real estate space will affect market rents, vacancy rates and net operating income (NOI). This can result from either changes in the demand for space by users or changes in the supply of space from new construction. Space market risk is affected by the type of property (office, retail, residential, etc.) and the location of the property. Space market risk deals with uncertainty in the market for the space provided by real estate to potential tenants.

Capital Market Risk

Capital market risk is the risk that changes in the market for capital will affect the value of the real estate. Note that this differs from changes in the market for space (see previous page). Changes in the capital market can be caused by changes in mortgage interest rates (Y_M) or changes in equity yield rates (Y_E). A change in either of these rates will also result in a change in overall yield rates (Y_O). Overall capitalization rates (R_O) may also be affected because they are related to overall yield rates. Capital market risk is affected by changes in the level of interest rates, changes in the availability of mortgage and equity capital and changes in the rate of return for alternative investment opportunities. Capital market risk affects investors regardless of whether they use debt to finance the investment.

Financial Risk

Financial risk results from use of debt to finance an investment. We saw in Chapter 5 that the use of leverage can increase an investor's return on equity if the leverage is positive, but it will decrease the return on equity if the leverage is negative. Investors normally expect leverage to be positive when they purchase and finance property. Due to unexpected changes in market conditions, however, the leverage may turn out to be negative. The impact of space market risk (discussed above) on the investor's overall return on the property (Y_O) is magnified by the use of financial leverage. This is illustrated later in the chapter after we discuss ways of measuring risk. The use of debt also increases the risk of default on mortgage from use of debt. The degree of financial risk increases with the amount of debt. This is illustrated later in this chapter.

Liquidity Risk

Liquidity risk refers to the difficulty of converting an investment into cash at a price close to market value in a reasonable time. Real estate has a relatively high degree of liquidity risk because there are few potential buyers for a particular type of property at any given point in time. Also, real estate is not publicly traded like stocks and bonds.

Inflation Risk

Inflation risk is the risk that unexpected inflation will cause future income from operations and reversion to lose purchasing power, owing due to the probability that actual inflation will differ from the amount of inflation that was expected when the investment was made. Historically, there has been a relatively low level of inflation risk for real estate investments because inflation tends to increase the replacement cost of properties. For example, construction costs tend to increase with inflation. This puts upward pressure on market values. Because real estate is not a fixed income investment (like a bond), market rents can often increase if inflation is greater than expected. Furthermore, lease provisions like CPI adjustments and expense passthrough provisions in office building leases allow the rental income to increase with inflation. In a weak market, however, building owners may not be able to raise rents to match inflation, and property values may not keep up with replacement costs. This is especially true when vacancy rates are high and new construction is not feasible.

Environmental Risk

Environmental risk is the risk that the value of a property will be affected by environmental factors that affect the owner's ability to develop or lease the space. Examples include properties that contain asbestos or that are exposed to toxic waste. Environmental risk is often difficult to measure and the costs associated with curing the problem can exceed the value of the property.

Legislative Risk

Legislative risk is the risk that changes in laws and regulations and will affect the market value of the property. Examples of legislative risk include

- Federal income tax law changes,
- Environmental regulations,
- Changes in zoning,
- Change in land-use regulations and
- Building codes.

Legislative risk increases when changes in legislation are unexpected, especially when they have an unfavorable effect on real estate investments.

Management Risk

Income producing real estate investments require property management. *Management risk* exists because management can affect the performance of the property. Some properties require more specialized management than others, e.g., convention hotels and regional malls. These properties have greater management risk.

SENSITIVITY ANALYSIS

Sensitivity analysis measures how a change in one of the assumptions affects the performance of the property. Examples of assumptions to vary in sensitivity analysis include projected market rental rates, vacancy rates at lease renewals, expense ratios and price appreciation (or depreciation). *Scenarios* are alternative assumptions about how the property might perform. It is an extension of sensitivity analysis that recognizes if a change occurs in one variable, other variables are also likely to be affected, e.g., if the market softens, rents may decline and vacancy rates may increase. Three alternative scenarios are usually considered, e.g., a pessimistic scenario, a most likely scenario, and an optimistic scenario. This captures the range of alternatives.

EXPECTED RETURN

A range of possible outcomes such as the equity dividend rate or equity yield rate can be identified from the analysis of scenarios. Each scenario can then be assigned a probability of occurrence based on the appraiser's judgment. The expected rate of return is found by weighing each possible return according to its probability. For example, suppose that the probabilities of occurrence of each scenario are estimated as follows:

Scenario	Overall Yield (Y_0)	Probability
Pessimistic	5	.30
Most likely	10	.40
Optimistic	20	.30

What is the expected return (overall yield rate)?

Solution:

$$\text{Expected return} = 0.05(0.30) + 0.10(0.40) + 0.20(0.30)$$
$$= 0.1150, \text{ or } 11.5\%$$

Note that the expected return is not necessarily the same as the most likely return.

VARIANCE AND STANDARD DEVIATION

Variance is a measure of the uncertainty or risk associated with an investment. It measures the tendency of individual returns to vary from the expected return. The variance is calculated as the mean of the squares of the deviations from the mean of the frequency distribution. The *standard deviation* (SD) is the square root of the variance. The larger the SD or variance, the greater the risk. For a normal distribution, there is about a 68 percent chance that the outcome will fall within plus or minus one SD from what was expected. There is about a 95 percent chance that the outcome will fall within two SDs and there is a greater than 99 percent chance that the outcome will fall within three SDs. (The relationships are discussed in statistics books.) Using the previous example, the variance is calculated as follows:

$$\text{Variance} = 0.30(0.05 - 0.1150)^2 + 0.40(0.10 - 0.1150)^2 +$$
$$0.30(0.20 - 0.1150)^2$$
$$= 0.003525$$

The standard deviation is found by taking the square root of the variance, e.g., $\sqrt{0.003525} = 0.05937$ or 5.937%.

The expected (mean) return is 11.50 percent, and the calculated SD is about 6 percent. Thus, assuming the returns are normally distributed, there is about a 68 percent probability that the overall yield will fall within the range of 11.50 percent $\pm$ 6 percent, or between 5.5 percent and 17.5 percent.

The mean and variance also can be calculated for equity yield rates (Y_E) and other measures of investment performance.

Ranking Investments

The expected return and standard deviation (of returns) can be used to compare investment alternatives. This is illustrated in an example.

Example 6-1

How would you rank the following properties in terms of risk and return?

	Expected Return	*Standard Deviation*
Property A	9%	4.0%
Property B	9	2.0
Property C	10	4.0

Solution: A and B have the same expected return, but A has a higher standard deviation. Thus, B is better than A. C has the same standard deviation as A but has a higher expected return. Thus, C also is better than A.

Because C has a higher return but more risk than B, it is not possible to say whether B or C is more desirable. This decision depends on the amount of risk the investor is willing to incur for the increase in the expected return. Given the standard deviations, property C could do worse than B.

EXPECTED PRESENT VALUE

We can also identify scenarios for the cash flows for a property and calculate the expected value of the property. This is illustrated in the following example.

Example 6-2

A property is projected to have an NOI of $100,000 in year 1.

	Pessimistic	*Most Likely*	*Optimistic*
Increase in NOI	0	2%	4%
Resale in year 5	$1,000,000	$1,200,000	$1,400,000
Probability	20%	50%	30%

Do the following exercises, using the assumptions in pessimistic, most likely and optimistic scenarios.

1. Using an overall yield rate (Y_o) of 10 percent to discount the cash flows, calculate the present value of the property for each scenario.

Scenario	Year 1 Cash Flows	Year 2	Year 3	Year 4	Year 5
Pessimistic	$100,000	$100,000	$100,000	$100,000	$100,000 + $1,000,000
Most likely	100,000	102,000	104,040	106,120	108,243 + 1,200,000
Optimistic	100,000	104,000	108,160	112,486	116,986 + 1,400,000

PV @ 10%

Pessimistic	$1,000,000
Most likely	1,138,171
Optimistic	1,276,880

2. Considering the likelihood that each scenario will occur, what is the expected present value?

$$\text{Expected PV} = 0.20(\$1,000,000) + 0.50(\$1,138,171) +$$
$$0.30(\$1,276,880) = \$1,152,150$$

3. Calculate the variance and standard deviation for the present values calculated in exercise 2.

$$\text{Variance} = 0.20(1,000,000 - 1,152,150)^2 + 0.50(1,138,171 - 1,152,150)^2 + 0.30(1,276,880 - 1,152,150)^2 = \$9,394,902,591$$

$$\text{Standard deviation} = \sqrt{9,394,902,591} = \$96,927$$

4. Within what range of values could you predict the true value to fall with 95 percent accuracy?

$$\$1,152,150 \pm 2 \times \$96,927 \text{ or } \$958,296 \text{ to } \$1,346,004$$

The above analysis indicates the degree of precision of the estimated value. Most appraisers report a single value estimate, e.g., $1,152,150. Based on this analysis, however, we see that this is the midpoint of a range of values that may be correct.

PARTITIONING THE IRR

The expected cash flow from a real estate investment comes from different sources that do not necessarily have the same degree of risk.

Partitioning the IRR is a method of calculating the relative contribution of different components of cash flow to the expected IRR. For example, IRR for a real estate investment can be broken down into the following components:

1. Net operating income
   a. Income from existing leases
   b. Income from expected lease renewals
2. Reversion
   a. Cash flow from recapture of original investment (i.e., purchase price)
   b. Cash flow from expected price appreciation

Partitioning also can be used to break down the cash flows that contribute to the equity yield rate (Y_E). For example, how much of the value comes from the pre-tax cash flow (NOI – debt service) versus the reversion to the equity investor? Partitioning uses the IRR as a discount rate to calculate the present value of each component of cash flow that is partitioned. By the original amount of the investment (e.g., equity investment or purchase price). The relative contribution of each component provides insight into the riskiness of the investment. (See Example 6-3.)

DISCOUNTING NOI AND REVERSION AT DIFFERENT RATES

Rather than use a single discount rate, it is appropriate to discount sources of cash flow with different degrees of risk at a different discount rate. The NOI is often considered less risky than cash flow from reversion. NOI is more dependent on income from existing leases than the reversion that depends on future lease renewals. Therefore, the NOI could be discounted at a lower rate than the reversion. (See Example 6-4).

Example 6-3

An investor considers purchasing one of the following properties. Each can be purchased for $500,000 and would have NOI and an expected sale price after 5 years as follows:

Property	Purchase Price	NOI	Sale Price
A	$500,000	$50,000	$500,000
B	500,000	10,000	744,204

Calculate the IRR, *and partition the IRR for each property.*

Solution:

Property	Year 0	Year 1–5	Year 5	IRR
A	($500,000)	$50,000	$500,000	10%
B	(500,000)	10,000	744,204	10

Partitioning the IRR using a 10% discount rate

Property	PV of NOI	%	PV of Sale Price	%	Total PV	%
A	$189,539	38	$310,461	62	$500,000	100
B	37,908	8	462,092	92	500,000	100

Property *B* could be considered riskier than property A. A greater proportion of its value depends on the cash flow from the sale in year 5 that relies on price appreciation.

It is insightful to note that the adjusted IRR for property B is higher than that of property A, which is consistent with the differences in risk. Using a 5 percent reinvestment rate, for example, the adjusted IRRs are 9.2 percent and 9.8 percent for properties A and B, respectively.

Example 6-4

A property is leased for five years with a net lease at $90,000 per year. It is expected to sell for $1.2 million in five years, when the lease expires. The discount rate for the leased portion of the cash flow is 9 percent and the discount rate for the reversion is 12 percent. What is the indicated value?

PV of $90,000 for 5 years at 9% = $350,069
PV of $1,200,000 at the end of 5 years at 12 percent = $680,912
$350,069 + $680,912 = $1,030,981

The value of the property is $1,030,981. Assuming the property is purchased for this amount, what is the IRR?

Year 0	Year 1–5	Year 5
($1,030,981)	$90,000	$1,200,000

IRR = 11.34%

NOTE: In Example 6-4, the IRR falls between the discount rate of 9 percent used for the NOI and the discount rate of 12 percent used for the reversion. Conceptually the IRR of 11.34 percent is a weighted average of the 9 percent discount rate for the NOI and the 12 percent discount rate for the reversion. To arrive at the same present value either the NOI and reversion must be discounted at 9 percent and 12 percent respectively, or all the cash flow (income and reversion) must be discounted at 11.34 percent.

EFFECT OF LEVERAGE ON FINANCIAL RISK

This use of debt can result in positive financial leverage as illustrated in Chapter 5. The use of leverage also increases financial risk, however, as illustrated in the following example.

Example 6-5

Consider the following assumptions about a proposed investment:

Purchase price = $100,000
Debt financing: 10% interest; 30 year amortization

Scenario	NOI	Resale	Probability
Pessimistic	$10,000 per year	$ 90,000	.30
Most likely	12,000 per year	100,000	.60
Optimistic	14,000 per year	110,000	.10

Calculate Y_E at loan-to-value ratios of 0 percent, 30 percent, 60 percent, and 90 percent. How does risk change with different levels of financing?

Loan/value (%)	Pessimistic Return (%)	Most Likely Return (%)	Optimistic Return (%)	Expected Return (%)	Standard Deviation (%)
0	8.31	12.00	15.47	11.24	2.17
30	7.57	12.86	17.70	11.76	3.09
60	5.66	14.97	23.02	12.98	5.34
90	−12.54	28.72	54.38	18.91	21.92

As the loan/value ratio increases, so does the expected return. Thus, there is positive financial leverage. The SD also increases, however, due to an increase in financial risk. An investor choosing no debt can expect no more than an 11.24 percent return, but that investor's pessimistic return is 8.31 percent. An investor who used 90 percent debt would have an expected return of 18.91 percent but could have a negative return of −12.54 percent under the pessimistic scenario.

Financial leverage clearly magnifies the risk in this example. The SD increases from 2.17 percent with no debt to 21.92 percent with 90 percent debt.

SUMMARY

Although difficult to quantify, risk must be considered when doing investment analysis or appraisal. Investors cannot interpret expected returns without considering risk. Appraisers should not select discount rates (Y_O or Y_E) or capitalization rates (R_O or R_E) without considering the riskiness of the interest being valued. In highest-and-best-use analysis of a site, the riskiness of each possible use must be considered when selecting a discount rate or a capitalization rate.

This chapter discussed the different sources of risk that may affect a real estate investment. These risks are interrelated. For example, higher than expected inflation (inflation risk) can also cause interest rates and equity yield rates to increase (capital market risk). Changes in federal income tax laws (legislative risk) can lead to changes in the required before-tax equity yield rate (capital market risk). A decrease in the availability of capital for real estate (capital market risk) can make it more difficult to sell the property (liquidity risk). Environmental problem (environmental risk) can lead to new environmental laws (legislative risk). Alternative ways of measuring the risk include sensitivity analysis, calculating the mean and variance, and partitioning the IRR.

KEY TERMS

capital market risk	partitioning the IRR
environmental risk	risk
expected return	scenarios
financial risk	sensitivity analysis
inflation risk	space market risk
legislative risk	standard deviation
liquidity risk	variance
management risk	

QUESTIONS

1. In the context of real estate investment, what do we mean by risk?
2. What is the difference between space market risk and capital market risk?
3. a. What is the purpose of sensitivity analysis?
   b. How does the use of scenarios improve on sensitivity analysis?
4. A property is projected to have NOI as shown below. Partition the IRR based on NOI and reversion.

	Year 1	Year 2	Year 3	Year 4	Year 5
NOI	$75,000	$80,000	$85,000	$88,000	$90,000
Reversion (after Year 5)			$1,000,000		

Assume that the property can be purchased for $800,000.

5. The distribution of expected cash flow from a subject property produces an expected value of $100,000, with a standard deviation of $2,000. What does this suggest about the precision of the value estimate?
6. Would capital market risk affect an investor who does not have a mortgage on the property?
7. A single-use property is leased absolute net for $200,000 per year for the next ten years to a tenant with an excellent credit rating. The appraiser has applied a terminal capitalization rate to the estimated NOI in year 11 and arrived at an estimated resale price of $2.5 million when the lease expires at the end of year 10. Based on the yield currently quoted for the tenant's corporate bonds, the appraiser believes that if the income stream were discounted separately from the reversion, it would be discounted at a 9 percent rate. Due to

uncertainty about the NOI after the lease expires, the appraiser believes the reversion should be discounted at a 12 percent rate.

    a.   What is the value of the property?

    b.   What single discount rate would result in the same value?

8.   An investor has projected three possible scenarios for a project:

Pessimistic: NOI will be $500,000 the first year and decrease 3 percent per year over a 5-year holding period. The property will sell for $4.5 million after five years.

Most likely: NOI will be level at $500,000 per year for the next five years. The property will sell for $5 million.

Optimistic: NOI will be $500,000 the first year and increase 3 percent per year over a 5-year holding period. The property then will sell for $5.5 million.

    The asking price is $5 million.

    The investor thinks there is about a 20 percent probability for the pessimistic scenario, a 40 percent probability for the most likely scenario, and a 40 percent probability for the optimistic scenario.

    a.   Compute the IRR *for each scenario.*

    b.   Compute the expected IRR.

    c.   Compute the variance and standard deviation of the IRRs.

    d.   Would this project be better than one with a 13 percent expected return and a standard deviation of 4 percent?

9.   Refer to question 8. Assume a loan for $4 million is obtained at a 10 percent interest rate and a 20-year term.

    a.   Calculate the expected IRR on equity and the standard deviation of the return on equity.

    b.   Contrast the results of question 9 with those of question 8. Has the loan increased the risk?

END NOTE

1.   The types of risk discussed in this section are fairly standard in the finance literature. There are some differences, however, to capture that unique nature of real estate, e.g., the term "space market risk." The discussion of sources of risk in this chapter was influenced by the discussion found in Course 510, Advanced Income Capitalization, published by the Appraisal Institute, 1993.

CHAPTER 7	# Tax Considerations in Investment Analysis

Income from the operation and sale of real estate income property is subject to federal income taxes. Federal income taxes affect the after-tax cash flow and after-tax rate of return available to investors. Thus, investors are concerned about how taxes affect real estate as well as other investment alternatives. This affects the investment value of real estate because the price that investors are willing to pay for a property depends in part on how that property is taxed. All else being equal, investors will pay a higher price for investments that receive a more favorable tax treatment and vice versa. Historically real estate investors received favorable tax treatment, although this has diminished substantially since the Tax Reform Act of 1986.

It is often argued that taxes affect only the investment value of a property because the amount of taxes depends on the particular investor's tax status. Market value does reflect the price that a typical investor is willing to pay. Thus, if the typical investor is concerned about the after-tax IRR, the taxes ultimately affect market value.

This chapter provides an overview of tax considerations that are important to real estate investors. Investment analysis calculations from previous chapters are then extended to show how taxes affect the investor's rate of return and other investment performance measures. The implications for valuation of real estate income property are then discussed.

TAXABLE INCOME FROM OPERATION OF REAL ESTATE

Recall that the calculation of net operating income (NOI) involved deducting expenses associated with operating a property, such as property taxes, insurance, maintenance, management and utilities. After subtracting the mortgage payment from the NOI, before-tax cash flow from operating the property results. Taxable income from operating real estate income property differs from before-tax cash flow derived from operations for two main reasons:

1. Only the interest portion of a loan payment, not the total payment, is deductible from NOI for tax purposes.
2. The tax code allows owners to deduct an allowance for depreciation from NOI.

Thus, taxable income from operating a real estate income property can be stated as follows:

$$
\begin{array}{l}
\text{NOI} \\
-\text{ Interest} \\
\underline{-\text{ Depreciation allowance}} \\
=\text{ Taxable income}
\end{array}
$$

The amount of interest deductible in a given taxable year is equal to the total interest paid to the lender during that year.

Depreciation Allowances

Physical assets such as buildings suffer from physical depreciation over time, which reduces their economic value. Because buildings must eventually be replaced and because investment in improvements is allowed to be recovered before income produced from the improvement is taxed, a deduction for depreciation is allowed prior to the determination of taxable income. Otherwise, taxable income would be overstated. Tax laws have historically allowed investors to write off buildings for tax purposes at a rate that exceeds the actual loss in value. Even under the current tax law, buildings can be depreciated on a straight-line basis over a period of either 27½ years for residential properties or 39 years for nonresidential properties.

Depreciation of Personal Property

When investors acquire real estate income property, they also often purchase furniture and fixtures in addition to the land and building. For example, apartments may include stoves and refrigerators, and hotels and motels usually include beds, tables, lobby furniture, kitchen equipment and so on. Furniture and fixtures are categorized as personal property, not real property and may be depreciated over seven years, using the double-declining balance method. The following table shows the percent of the depreciable basis that would apply for personal property.

Year	Depreciation %
1	14.286
2	24.490
3	17.493
4	12.495
5	8.925
6	8.925
7	8.925
8	4.461
Total	100.000

The first-year depreciation allowance is lower than the second year because the tables assume that the property is purchased in the middle of the tax year. This is also why the property is not fully depreciated until the eighth year.

Loan Points

Points paid in connection with obtaining a loan to purchase, refinance or operate a real estate income property investment must be deducted ratably over the term of the loan. For example, suppose a loan for $1 million is made to purchase an office building. The loan is to be amortized over a 25-year term. Suppose two points, or $20,000, are paid on the loan. For tax purposes, the $20,000 would have to be amortized over 25 years, or $800 per year. If the property is sold before the points are completely amortized, the balance can be expensed in the year of sale. Thus, in the above example, if the property is sold and the loan is repaid after five years, $16,000 could be expensed.

The deductibility of points is based on the *term* of the loan, not the amortization period. If the loan in our example had a balloon payment due in the tenth year, then the points could be deducted over ten years, even though the loan payments are based on a 25-year amortization.

TAXABLE INCOME FROM SALE OF DEPRECIABLE REAL PROPERTY

To determine whether a taxable gain or loss has occurred when a property is sold, the gross sales price must first be established. The gross sales price is equal to any cash or other property received in payment for the property sold, plus any liabilities against the property assumed by the buyer. Any selling expenses, e.g., legal fees, recording fees and brokerage fees, may then be deducted to establish net sales proceeds. To determine gain or loss, the adjusted basis of the property is subtracted from net sales proceeds. The adjusted basis of a property is its original basis (cost of land and improvements) plus the cost of any capital improvements, made during the period of ownership, less accumulated depreciation taken to date. Any excess of net sales proceeds over the adjusted basis results in a taxable gain, and any deficit results in a taxable loss.

Calculations of taxable income from the operation and disposition of real estate are illustrated in the following section.

AFTER-TAX INVESTMENT ANALYSIS

Let us consider the effect of federal income taxes on the investment analysis example from the beginning of Chapter 5, "Investment Measures with Mortgage Financing." Our example applies to a depreciable property held by an individual to produce income in a trade or business. We assume that the property is an apartment building. As a starting point for our discussion, Table 7-1 shows the summary calculation of before-tax cash flow from that example.

Table 7-1
Estimates of Cash Flow from Operations

			Year		
	1	2	3	4	5
A. Before-tax cash flow					
NOI	$100,000	$102,000	$104,000	$106,000	$108,000
Less: debt service	81,783	81,783	81,783	81,783	81,783
Before-tax cash flow	$ 18,217	$ 20,217	$ 22,217	$ 24,217	$ 26,217

			Year		
	6	7	8	9	10
NOI	$110,000	$112,000	$114,000	$116,000	$118,000
Less: debt service	81,783	81,783	81,783	81,783	81,783
Before-tax cash flow	$ 28,217	$ 30,217	$ 32,217	$ 34,217	$ 36,217

After-Tax Cash Flow from Operation

We have estimated before-tax cash flows from the investment. Now we must determine the increase or decrease in the investor's taxable income as a result of undertaking this investment. The investor's federal income tax will either increase or decrease as a result of the investment. We must consider how much taxable income is produced each year from operations and then consider taxes in the year that the property is sold. Table 7-2 shows the calculation of taxable income and after-tax cash flow from operating the property.

Table 7-2
Taxable Income and After-Tax Cash Flow from Operations

			Year		
	1	*2*	*3*	*4*	*5*
B. Taxable income or loss					
NOI	$100,000	$102,000	$104,000	$106,000	$108,000
Less: Interest	74,680	73,937	73,115	72,207	71,205
Depreciation	30,909	30,909	30,909	30,909	30,909
Taxable income (loss)	(5,589)	(2,846)	(24)	2,884	5,886
Tax or (savings)	(1,565)	(797)	(7)	807	1,648
C. After-tax cash flow					
Before-tax cash flow	$ 18,217	$ 20,217	$ 22,217	$ 24,217	$ 26,217
Less tax or add (savings)	(1,565)	(797)	(7)	807	1,648
After-tax cash flow	$ 19,782	$ 21,014	$ 22,224	$ 23,410	$ 24,569

			Year		
	6	*7*	*8*	*9*	*10*
B. Taxable income or loss					
NOI	$110,000	$112,000	$114,000	$116,000	$118,000
Less: Interest	70,097	68,873	67,521	66,028	64,378
Depreciation	30,909	30,909	30,909	30,909	30,909
Taxable income (loss)	8,994	12,218	15,570	19,063	22,713
Tax or (savings)	2,518	3,421	4,359	5,338	6,360
C. After-tax cash flow					
Before-tax cash flow	$ 28,217	$ 30,217	$ 32,217	$ 34,217	$ 36,217
Less tax or add (savings)	2,518	3,421	4,359	5,338	6,360
After-tax cash flow	$ 25,699	$ 26,796	$ 27,857	$ 28,879	$ 29,857

In Table 7-2, we see that taxable income is found by subtracting interest and depreciation from the NOI. Note that only the interest, not the total loan payment, is tax deductible. In our example, interest was based on having a $750,000 loan amortized over a 25-year term with monthly payments based on a 10 percent interest rate. Table 7-3 shows a summary loan schedule for the property.

Table 7-3
Summary Loan Information

End of year	*1*	*2*	*3*	*4*	*5*
Payment	$ 81,783	$ 81,783	$ 81,783	$ 81,783	$ 81,783
Mortgage balance	742,897	735,051	726,383	716,807	706,228
Interest	74,680	73,937	73,115	72,207	71,205
Principal	7,103	7,847	8,668	9,576	10,579

End of year	*6*	*7*	*8*	*9*	*10*
Payment	$ 81,783	$ 81,783	$ 81,783	$ 81,783	$ 81,783
Mortgage balance	694,542	681,632	667,370	651,615	634,210
Interest	70,097	68,873	67,521	66,028	64,378
Principal	11,686	12,910	14,262	15,755	17,405

Depreciation

Taxable income is also affected by an allowance for depreciation. As discussed earlier in the chapter, residential properties may be depreciated over 27½ years and nonresidential real property must be depreciated over 39 years. Both must be depreciated in a straight-line basis. Also recall that only the improvements, not the land, can be depreciated. Thus, we need to know what portion of the $1 million purchase price of the office building represents building improvements. For our case example, we assume that expenditures for land are 15 percent of the purchase price, or $150,000, leaving improvements of $850,000. Dividing improvement cost by 27½ results in an annual depreciation deduction of $30,909.09.[1]

Depreciation allowances do not represent an actual cash outflow for the investor. The deduction only affects taxable income and after tax cash flows. In our example, taxable income is –$5,589 in year 1. Assuming the investor is in a 28 percent tax bracket and can use this loss to offset other income,[2] the decrease in tax liability as a result of owning the property will be .28 × $5,589 = $1,565. Adding this to before-tax cash flow results in after-tax cash flow of $19,782 in year 1.

After the third year the taxable income is positive, and additional taxes must be paid as a result of this investment. Note, however, that the taxable income is still much less than the before-tax cash flow.

After-Tax Cash Flow from Sale

Table 7-4 illustrates how sale of the property affects the investor's taxable income.

Table 7-4
After-Tax Cash Flow from Sale

Estimates of Cash Flows from Sale in Year 10

Sales price			$1,200,000
Mortgage balance			634,210
Before-tax cash flow (BTCF)			$ 565,790
Sales price		$1,200,000	
Original cost basis1	$1,000,000		
Accumulated depreciation	309,091		
Adjusted basis		$ 690,909	
Capital gain		$ 509,091	
Tax from sale ($509,091 × 0.28)*			142,545
After-tax cash flow from sale			$ 423,244

*Assumes investor is in the 28 percent tax bracket.

In our example, depreciation was $30,909.09 per year for 10 years, resulting in accumulated depreciation of $309,091. Subtracting the accumulated depreciation from the original cost basis of the property (cost of the land and improvements) results in an adjusted basis of $690,909. The difference between the adjusted basis ($690,909) and the sale price ($1.2 million) is the capital gain, which is $509,091. As discussed earlier, under current tax law the entire taxable gain is taxed at the same rate as ordinary income. Thus, assuming the investor is still in the 28 percent tax bracket upon sale of the property (and assuming tax laws haven't changed again), taxes resulting from sale of the property would be $142,545. Subtracting the tax from the before-tax cash flow results in after-tax cash flow of $423,244.

After-Tax IRR

Using the information from Tables 7-2 and 7-4 we may now calculate the after-tax internal rate of return (IRR). The cash flows are summarized in Table 7-5, along with the before-tax cash flows for comparison.

Table 7-5
Cash-Flow Summary

Cash-flow (CF) summary:

End of year	0	1	2	3	4	5
Before-tax CF	($250,000)	$18,217	$20,217	$ 22,217	$24,217	$26,217
After-tax CF	(250,000)	19,782	21,014	22,224	23,410	24,569

End of year	6	7	8	9	10
Before-tax CF	$28,217	$30,217	$32,217	$34,217	$602,007
After-tax CF	25,699	26,796	27,857	28,879	453,101

Before-tax IRR	15.90%
After-tax IRR	13.27
Effective tax rate	16.57

The after-tax IRR is lower than the before-tax IRR. However, although the investor's tax rate was 28 percent, the after-tax IRR is about 16.5 percent lower than the before-tax IRR. That is,

$$1 - (13.27/15.90) = 16.54\%$$

Thus, the *effective tax rate* for this investment is 16.54 percent.

CLASSIFICATION OF INCOME

The current tax law requires that income and loss from all sources, including real estate, be divided into three categories.[3]

1. Passive income (loss): Income or loss from a trade or business where the investor does not materially participate in the management or operation of the property. Material participation is defined as "involvement in the operations of the activity on a regular, continuous and substantial basis." Real estate investment is considered to be a passive activity. Hence, unless an investor materially participates in the operation of the property, income and losses earned from such activity are categorized as passive income or loss. Income (or loss) received by a limited partner in a partnership is considered passive by definition.

2. Active income (loss): Salaries, wages, fees for services and income from a trade or business in which the investor materially participates. Even if a taxpayer materially participates, however, income or loss from "rental activity" is not considered active income. Thus, income from rental housing, office buildings, shopping centers and other real estate activities in which a taxpayer is a landlord are not classified as active income (or loss). They are classified as passive income. The operation of a hotel, other transient lodging or a nursing home, however, is not a rental activity; therefore, its owners will have active income if they materially participate.

3. Portfolio income (loss): Interest and dividend income from stocks, bonds and some categories of real estate that are classified as capital assets. Examples of portfolio income from real estate activity are (1) dividends received on shares in a Real Estate Investment Trust (REIT) or (2) income

received on long-term land leases or net leases on real estate where the owner does not materially participate in its operation.

In general, passive losses cannot be used to offset income from another category. This is referred to as the "passive activity loss limitation". Passive losses produced from real estate investments and other passive activities must be used to offset passive income earned during the tax year. Any remaining, or unused, passive losses must be "suspended" and carried forward to offset any passive income earned in future years.

When an investment producing passive income is sold and a capital gain occurs, any unused or "suspended" losses from that activity may be

- used to offset any capital gain from the sale of that activity;
- then used to offset any other passive income produced from other passive activities during that year; and
- then used to offset any income, including active and portfolio income, earned during that year.

To the extent that unused losses remain, they may be carried forward into succeeding years as capital losses, not subject to passive loss rules.

Special Exceptions: Loss Allowances for Rental Real Estate

One special exception to the passive activity loss limitation applies to individual rental property owners (other than limited partners). These investors are allowed to offset active income with up to $25,000 of passive activity losses (to the extent they exceed income from passive activities) from rental real estate activities in which the individual "actively" participates. Active participation is less restrictive than the material participation standard referred to earlier and requires less personal involvement. In general, the individual must own a 10 percent or greater interest in the activity and must either be involved in management decisions, selection of tenants and determination of rents or arrange for others to provide services (e.g., a property manager to manage the property on a day-to-day basis).

This special rule is phased out for individuals with adjusted gross incomes between $100,000 and $150,000. When an individual's adjusted gross income for the taxable year exceeds $100,000, the $25,000 loss allowance is reduced by 50 percent of the amount of the excess. Thus, individuals with an adjusted gross income of $120,000 would only be allowed to use up to $15,000 of any passive losses to reduce active income.* An individual with adjusted gross income in excess of $150,000 receives no loss allowance.[4]

Conclusion

The above analysis is rather cumbersome. We could have arrived at the same answer, however, with a computer program. For example, we could have used a trial-and-error process to estimate the price that would result in the same 12 percent after-tax IRR with the same assumptions about financing, depreciation, taxes, etc. The computer can be programmed to do this very quickly, eliminating the need to use any special equations. The approach above was used to illustrate the technique of after-tax valuation.

---

*The $25,000 loss allowance would be reduced by $10,000 which is 50 percent of the $20,000 when the adjusted gross income exceeds $100,000.

SUMMARY

Federal income tax laws affect the after-tax cash flows that are available from a real estate income property investment. The taxation of real estate differs from many other investments such as stocks and bonds. Therefore, many investors believe that they must compare the after-tax cash flows and after-tax IRRs when evaluating different investment alternatives.

Because taxes can affect investment decisions, it is useful for appraisers to be able to calculate the after-tax IRR for a real estate investment. If the typical investor for a property being appraised is a taxable investor, then the expected after-tax IRR must be sufficient to attract investment capital.

This chapter discussed the key tax considerations that affect real estate income property and illustrated the calculation of the after-tax IRR. An optional technique for estimating the value of a property on an after-tax basis was also demonstrated. In practice, the same answer can be obtained by using a discounted cash-flow computer program to determine the purchase price that results in a specified after-tax IRR.

The purpose of this chapter was to provide a general overview of how federal income taxes might affect the price a typical investor might pay for a real estate income property. The purpose was not to provide sufficient information to allow tax planning for a particular individual. This is not within the purview of a real estate appraiser. Investors should consult their tax accountant for advice as to the tax consequences of their specific investments.

KEY TERMS

accumulated depreciation
active income
adjusted basis
after-tax cash flow
after-tax IRR
capital gain
depreciation allowance

effective tax rate
gross sale price
net sale proceeds
passive income
portfolio income
taxable income

QUESTIONS

1. Why should appraisers be concerned about the effect of federal income taxes on real estate returns?
2. What is meant by "passive income"? Why is this important to real estate investors?
3. How is the gain from the sale of real estate taxed?
4. What is meant by an "effective tax rate"? What does it measure?
5. Do you think taxes affect the value of real estate versus that of other investments?
6. A property is projected to have NOI of $100,000 per year for the next five years. It can be purchased for $1 million and financed with a $750,000 loan at a 10 percent interest rate with monthly payments over a 25-year term. For tax purposes, 15 percent of the purchase price would be considered land and the rest would be considered improvements that would be depreciated over 27½ years using straight-line depreciation. The property is expected to be sold

for $1.2 million at the end of a five-year holding period. The investor is in a 30 percent tax bracket and can use any tax losses from this investment to offset other income.

a. Calculate the after-tax cash flow from operations and reversion.
b. What is the after-tax IRR?
c. What is the effective tax rate?
d. Suppose an appraiser is asked to value this property and believes that the investor described above is typical except that the appraiser thinks the after-tax discount rate should be 12 percent. Does this imply that the property value would be higher or lower than $1 million? Explain but do not calculate.

END NOTES

1. The IRS publishes tables that taxpayers must use to calculate depreciation deductions. The tables assume that the investor purchases the property in the middle of the month and prorate the first-year depreciation according to the actual month of the year the property is purchased. We are simply dividing by 27½ years.

2. As discussed later in this chapter, there are severe limits on the ability of real estate investors to use tax losses to offset income from other investments.

3. The following tax rules are based on the Tax Reform Act of 1986. Refer to Chapter 11 of *Real Estate Finance and Investments* by William B. Brueggeman and Jeffrey D. Fisher, ninth edition (Chicago: Richard D. Irwin, Inc., 1993), for a further discussion and numerical examples of the effect of tax rules on real estate investors.

4. For further discussion see P. Fass, R. Haft, L. Loffman and S. Presant, *Tax Reform Act of 1986* (New York: Clark Boardman Co., Ltd., 1986).

Glossary of Terms

absolute net lease. A lease in which the tenant pays all operating expenses usually with the exception of management fees.

absorption period. An estimate of the total time period over which a property can be successfully sold, leased, put into use or traded in its market area at prevailing prices or rentals.

accrued depreciation. The total deduction from cost new due to physical deterioration, functional obsolescence and/or external obsolescence. Accrued depreciation represents the total difference between an improvement's reproduction cost or replacement cost and its contributing value in the cost approach.

accumulated depreciation. The sum of the annual depreciation deductions taken by the investor to reduce taxable income.

accumulation of $1 per period. *See* future value annuity of $1 per period.

active income. Salaries, wages or fees for services and income from a trade or business in which the investor materially participates, by being involved in the operations of the activity on a regular, continuous and substantial basis. Rental real estate is *not* usually considered active income even if the investor materially participates in its operation.

adjustable rate mortgage (ARM). A mortgage loan in which the interest rate is adjusted periodically based on a specified index or formula. ARMs may include a limit on the amount that the interest rate can rise or fall in a given year as well as a limit on the total amount the rate can

rise or fall over the life of the loan. Adjustable rate mortgages often have an initial interest rate that is lower than fixed rate mortgages because the risk of interest rate change is partially borne by the borrower with an adjustable rate loan. *See also* fixed rate mortgage.

adjusted basis. The original cost or purchase price of an investment (including land and improvements) plus any capital improvements made to the property less any accumulated depreciation taken to date. *See also* capital gain, accumulated depreciation.

adjusted internal rate of return (AIRR). An internal rate of return analysis in which different reinvestment and discount rates for both positive and negative cash flows have been specified. The adjusted internal rate applies a "safe rate" to all negative cash flows, discounts them to time period zero and adds them to the initial investment. The safe rate is the rate that could be earned on the funds until needed to cover negative cash flows. A market rate is applied to all positive cash flows, which are carried forward to the end of the investment holding period. The market rate is the rate that can be earned by investing the positive cash flows in other investments. The AIRR equals the internal rate of return (IRR) that equates the present value figure to the future value figure. The AIRR is usually less than the IRR for the same property because funds are assumed to be reinvested at a lower rate. Also called the modified internal rate of return. *See also* financial management rate of return, internal rate of return.

adjusted sales price. The estimated sales price of a comparable property after additions and/or subtractions have been made to the actual sales price to allow for differences between the comparable and the subject property transaction. This is what the comparable would have sold for if it had possessed all the characteristics of the subject property as of the effective date of the appraisal. *See also* adjustments, sales adjustment grid, direct sales comparison approach.

after-tax cash flow (ATCF). The cash flow (either from operations or at resale) that remains from net operating income and net resale proceeds after deduction for annual debt service, loan repayment and all ordinary income taxes applicable to each period. *See also* before-tax cash flow, debt service, net operating income, tax liability, taxable income.

after-tax equity yield rate. The annualized rate of return that discounts all expected after-tax cash flows (from operations and resale) to a present value equal to the original equity investment in the property. It represents the internal rate of return on equity after taxes. *See also* before-tax equity yield rate, equity yield rate.

after-tax IRR. *See* after-tax equity yield rate.

amortization. (1) The process of retiring a debt through repayment of principal. It occurs when the payment on the debt exceeds the required interest payment for a particular time period. (2) Annual deductions allowed in the calculation of federal income taxes. For example, points paid on a loan on income property are amortized over the loan term.

amortization schedule. A table that shows the allocation of payments for principal and interest on a debt. Also referred to as a loan schedule. *See also* amortization.

amortization term. The length of time over which the periodic principal repayments are made to pay off a loan in its entirety. *See also* amortization, amortization schedule.

amount of $1 at compound interest. *See* future value of $1.

annualizer (*a*). A factor used in yield capitalization formulas to convert the total change in property value over a time period to an annual rate of change; the value of (*a*) varies depending on the pattern of income flow. *See* yield capitalization formulas, sinking fund factor.

annuity in advance. A series of payments that occur at the beginning of each period. Also called an annuity due. *See also* ordinary annuity.

appraisal. According to the Uniform Standards of Professional Appraisal Practice, (1) The act or process of estimating value; an estimate of value.

(2) Pertains to appraising and related functions, e.g., appraisal practice, appraisal services. *See also* direct sales comparison approach, income capitalization approach, cost approach.

appraisal report. *See* report.

ATCF. *See* after-tax cash flow.

balloon payment. The remaining balance that is due at the end of a balloon mortgage. The final or balloon payment is substantially larger than the previous periodic payments. A balloon payment is necessary in mortgages in which the periodic payment does not fully amortize the principal balance over the life of the loan. Also called lump-sum payment.

before-tax cash flow (BTCF). Income that remains from net operating income (NOI) after debt service is paid but before ordinary income tax on operations is deducted. Also called equity dividend or pre-tax cash flow. *See also* after-tax cash flow (ATCF), net operating income (NOI).

before-tax equity yield rate. The annualized rate of return that discounts all expected before-tax cash flows (either from operations or at resale) to a present value equal to the original equity investment in the property. It represents the internal rate of return on equity before taxes. *See also* after-tax equity yield rate, equity yield rate.

book value. The capital amount at which property is carried on the books of a company. It usually equals the original cost less reserves for depreciation plus any additions to capital. *See also* adjusted basis.

building capitalization rate (*R_B*). The capitalization rate that reflects the ratio of annual building income divided by the building value. Historically, the building capitalization rate was used to estimate building value in the building and land residual techniques.

bundle of rights. An ownership concept that describes real property by the legal rights associated with owning the property. It specifies rights such as the rights to sell, lease, use, occupy, mortgage and trade the property, among others. These rights are typically purchased by the buyer in a sales transaction unless specifically noted or limited in the sale.

business value. The value resulting from business organization including such things as management skills, assembled work force, working capital, trade names, franchises, patents, trademarks, contracts, leases and operating agreements. Business value is an intangible asset that is distinct from the real property and tangible personal property. It is also referred to as enterprise value or business enterprise value. *See also* going-concern value.

capital gain. The amount of taxable gain that results from sale or disposition of an investment. A capital gain results from the sale of real estate if the net sale proceeds is greater than the property's adjusted basis. *See also* capital loss, adjusted basis.

capital loss. The amount of taxable loss that results from sale or disposition of an investment. A capital gain results from the sale of real estate if the net sale proceeds is less than the property's adjusted basis. *See also* capital gain, adjusted basis.

capital market. The market in which long-term or intermediate-term money instruments are traded by buyers and sellers.

capitalization. Any process of converting income into an estimate of value. *See also* capitalization rate, direct capitalization, ground rent capitalization, income capitalization approach, yield capitalization, yield capitalization formulas.

capitalization in perpetuity. A capitalization procedure used to determine the value of a project in which an endless time period is considered. It provides for a return *on* investment, but not a return *of* investment.

capitalization of ground rental. *See* ground rent capitalization.

capitalization rate. A ratio that represents the relationship between a particular year's cash flow and the present value or the interest applicable to the cash flow. It is usually assumed to be an overall capitalization rate unless stated otherwise. In appraisal, the term is typically preceded by a description that identifies the applicable interest. For example, the capitalization rate found by dividing first-year net operating income by the overall property value is called the overall capitalization rate. Also called cap rate. *See also* building capitalization rate, equity capitalization rate, going-in capitalization rate, land capitalization rate, terminal capitalization rate, direct capitalization, yield capitalization, band-of-investment technique, mortgage capitalization rate.

capital market risk. Uncertainty due to changes in the market for debt or equity capital used to finance real estate investments.

cash flow. The periodic income or loss arising from the operation and ultimate resale of an income-producing property. The cash flow could further be classified as either before-tax or after-tax cash flow and could also reflect the impact of financing. *See also* before-tax cash flow, after-tax cash flow, net operating income.

cash-flow ratio. *See* capitalization rate.

cash throw-off. *See* cash flow.

compound interest. Continuous and systematic additions to a principal sum over a series of time periods. The additions are based on a specific periodic interest rate with additions based on the total prior accumulation of interest and principal. *See also* amortization schedule, simple interest.

compound interest factor. *See* future value of $1.

cost-benefit study. An analysis of the cost of creating an improvement versus the benefits that will be created by the improvement, including nonmonetary issues. A cost-benefit study is typically used by public agencies to make decisions concerning capital improvements.

debt coverage ratio (DCR). The ratio of annual net operating income (NOI) divided by the annual debt service. Lenders usually specify a minimum DCR (e.g., 1.2) that they require the property to meet during the first year of a loan term.

debt financing. The use of borrowed funds to acquire a capital investment, as opposed to investing one's own funds. In real estate, the property itself usually serves as the security for the debt.

debt service. The periodic payment specified in a loan contract that covers the repayment needed to amortize the outstanding debt. *See also* amortization.

depreciation. The loss in property value due to age, wear and tear, any negative functional superadequacy or deficiencies and/or external forces. Also called cost recovery. *See also* accrued depreciation.

depreciation allowance. The amount of tax depreciation that is allowed by federal income tax law to be deducted as an expense in the calculation of taxable income. This is *not* related to any loss in property value due to physical depreciation, functional obsolescence or economic obsolescence.

discount rate. A general term representing a compound interest rate used to convert expected future cash flow into a present value estimate. In appraisal practice, the discount rate is the competitive rate of return applicable to the interest and cash flows analyzed and is identified by adding a descriptor to the rate. For example, the mortgage interest rate is the mortgage discount rate. *See also* yield rate.

discounted cash-flow analysis (DCF). In appraisal, any method whereby an appraiser prepares a cash-flow forecast (including income from operations and resale) for the interests appraised, selects a discount rate that reflects the return expected for the interest and uses the rate to calculate the present value of each of the cash-flows. The total present value of the cash becomes the value estimate for that interest. Sometimes the cash-flow forecast is based on an assumed pattern of change, e.g., compound growth. Also referred to as discounted cash flow. *See also* income capitalization approach, internal rate of return, net present value, present value, profitability index, yield capitalization.

discounting. The process of converting future income to a present value by mathematically reducing future cash flow by the implied interest that would have been earned assuming an initial investment, an interest rate and a specified period (possibly divided into shorter equal periodic increments). *See also* future value, income capitalization approach, present value.

disposition costs. The costs associated with selling a property. Selling costs must be subtracted from sales proceeds to determine the resale price when using the discounted cash-flow analysis or the yield capitalization analysis. *See also* discounted cash-flow analysis, yield capitalization analysis.

distressed property. A property that has problems due to factors such as an oversupplied market, poor design or improper location of the improvements, inadequate maintenance and poor management decisions.

effective gross income (EGI). The anticipated income from the operation of a project after adjustment for vacancy and credit loss. The effective income can be further classified as actual, market and/or economic effective gross income depending on which rent levels were considered when making the calculation. *See also* effective gross income multiplier, net operating income, potential gross income.

effective gross income multiplier (EGIM). The ratio of the sales price, after adjustment for nonrealty interests and favorable financing divided by the projected first-year effective gross income. For income-producing properties, the EGIM can be derived from comparable sales as one method of estimating a property value in the direct sales comparison approach. *See also* effective gross income, potential gross income multiplier.

effective tax rate. (1) The ratio between a property's annual property tax and its market value; the tax rate times the assessed value divided by the market value; and the official tax rate times the assessment ratio. (2) A measure of the amount that the before-tax IRR is reduced due to the effect of federal income taxes. The effective tax rate is calculated by subtracting the after-tax IRR from the before-tax IRR and dividing the remainder by the before-tax IRR.

environmental impact study (EIS). An analysis of the impact of a proposed land use on its environment, including the direct and indirect effects of the project during all phases of use and their long-run implications.

environmental risk. Uncertainty due to changes in the property's environment that may affect the value of a property.

equity. The owner's capital investment in a property; the property value less the balance of any debt as of a particular point in time. Equity is equal to the property value if there is no debt on the property.

equity capitalization rate (R_E). The capitalization rate that reflects the relationship between a single year's before-tax cash flow and the equity investment in the property. The before-tax cash flow in this instance is the net operating income less the annual debt service payment, and the equity is the property value less any outstanding loan balance. The equity capitalization rate, when divided into the before-tax cash flows, gives an indication of the value of the equity. Also called cash-flow rate, cash on cash rate or equity dividend rate.

equity discount rate. *See* equity yield rate.

equity dividend. *See* before-tax cash flow.

equity dividend rate. *See* equity capitalization rate.

equity interest. *See* equity.

equity participation. An agreement by which a lender receives some share of the income and/or cash flow of a property based on the performance of that property. The participation might be based on a percentage of the net operating income, cash flow from operations and/or the gain from sale of the property. The equity participation results in an additional return to the lender above the interest rate charged on the loan.

equity yield rate (Y_E). A rate of return on the equity capital; the equity investor's internal rate of return based on expected before-tax cash flows and the investor's original equity; used as the discount rate in a discounted cash-flow analysis to estimate the present value of the before-tax cash flows (from operation and resale) to arrive at a value estimate for the equity. The equity yield rate reflects the effect of financing on the investor's rate of return. *See also* after-tax equity yield rate, before-tax equity yield rate, yield capitalization.

expected return. The return found by weighing possible returns by their respective probabilities.

expense passthrough. *See* passthrough.

expense ratio. *See* operating expense ratio.

expense stop. In a lease, a dollar amount (usually expressed on a per square foot basis) above which the tenant agrees to pay operating expenses. An expense stop is used to help protect the lessor from unexpected increases in expenses from inflation or other factors. The amount paid by the tenant is said to "pass through" to the tenant. *See also* passthrough.

feasibility analysis. According to the Uniform Standards of Professional Appraisal Practice, a study of the cost-benefit relationship of an economic endeavor. *See also* marketability study, market analysis.

feasibility rent. The level of rent that is necessary for it to be feasible to construct a new building.

feasibility study. *See* feasibility analysis.

fee simple estate. Absolute ownership of real estate that is unencumbered by any other interest or estate and is subject to the limitations of eminent domain, escheat, police power and taxation. A fee simple estate can be valuated by the present value of market rents. *See also* leased fee estate, leasehold estate.

fee simple interest. *See* fee simple estate.

fee simple value. The value of a fee simple estate. *See* fee simple estate.

financial leverage. *See* leverage, positive leverage, negative leverage, zero leverage.

financial management rate of return (FMRR). Similar in concept to the adjusted internal rate of return. Negative cash flows are discounted at a safe rate, and positive cash flows are compounded forward to the end of the holding period at a reinvestment rate. If negative cash flows occur after a positive cash flow, the negative cash flow is discounted back and netted against the positive cash flow. The net remaining is either discounted back (if negative) or compounded forward (if positive). *See also* adjusted internal rate of return, internal rate of return.

financial risk. Uncertainty that results from the use of debt to finance an investment.

fixed expense. An operating expense that does not vary with the occupancy level of a property, e.g., property taxes, insurance, repairs and maintenance, advertising and promotions. *See also* variable expense.

fixed rate mortgage. A loan in which the interest rate is constant over the term of the loan. *See also* adjustable rate mortgage.

forecasting. The process of assimilating past information and compiling the data for the purpose of drawing conclusions as to the probable happenings or conditions in the future.

future value. The worth of a property at some later date. See also future value of $1, future value annuity of $1 per period.

future value annuity of $1 per period ($S_n$). A compound interest factor that represents the sum to which a constant periodic investment of $1 per period will grow, assuming compound growth at a specific rate of return for a specific number of compounding periods. It is shown in column two of the compound interest tables. In an appraisal, these payments are generally assumed to be made at the end of each period. Also called accumulation of $1 per period. *See also* six functions of $1.

future value of $1 ($S^n$). The amount to which an investment of $1 grows with compound interest after a specified number of years at a specified interest rate. It is shown in column one of the compound interest tables. Also called the amount of $1, future value interest factor, future worth of one dollar. *See also* six functions of $1.

future worth of $1 per period. *See* future value annuity of $1 per period.

general market area. A geographic area or political jurisdiction in which similar property types compete on an economic basis for potential buyers, users or patrons.

going-concern value. The value of a property that includes the value due to a successful operating business enterprise that is expected to continue. Going-concern value results from the process of assembling the land, building, labor, equipment and marketing operation and includes consideration of the efficiency of plant, the know-how of management and the sufficiency of capital. The portion of going-concern value that exceeds that of the real property and tangible personal property is an intangible value that is referred to as business value. *See also* business value.

going-in capitalization rate. The overall capitalization rate found by dividing first year's net operating income by the present value of the property. When the term capitalization rate is used without a prefix, it is assumed to be a going-in capitalization rate. *See also* capitalization rate, terminal capitalization rate.

governmental forces. In appraisal theory, one of four forces thought to affect real estate value, e.g., governmental controls and regulations, public services, fiscal policies, and zoning and building codes. *See also* forces.

government regulations. *See* governmental forces.

gross building area (GBA). The total floor area of a building measured in square feet from the external walls, excluding unenclosed areas. Unlike gross living area measurements, GBA does include basement areas.

gross lease. A lease that specifies that the landlord is responsible for the payment of all operating expenses. The lease, however, may contain expense increase passthrough provisions. *See also* expense stop, net lease.

gross sale price. Cash or other property received in payment for the property sold plus any liabilities against the property assumed by the buyer. *See also* net sale proceeds.

ground lease. A lease for the use and occupancy of land only. Also called land lease.

ground rent. Rent paid for the right to use and occupy land; a percentage of total rent designated for land use and occupancy.

heating, ventilation and air-conditioning system (HVAC). A system that provides consistent regulation and distribution of heat and fresh air throughout a building.

highest and best use (HBU). The reasonable and probable use that results in the highest present value of the land after considering all legally permissible, physically possible and economically feasible uses. Capitalization rates or discount rates for each feasible use should reflect typical returns expected in the market. Highest and best use is usually determined under two different premises: as if the site was vacant and could be improved in the optimal manner or as the site is currently improved.

In the latter premise, the highest and best use of the site will either be to keep the existing building or demolish the building and develop a building that is the highest and best use. In general, it is not feasible to demolish an existing building as long as it contributes to the value of the site.

highest and best use of land. *See* highest and best use.

highest and best use of improved site. *See* highest and best use.

holding period. The term of ownership or expected ownership of an investment. In appraisal, the holding period used reflects the appraiser's estimate as to what the typical expected holding period would be for a particular property.

improvements. Structures or buildings that are permanently attached to the land.

income approach. *See* income capitalization approach.

income capitalization approach. One of the three traditional appraisal approaches to estimat-ing value. In this approach, value is based on the present value of future benefits of property ownership. In direct capitalization, a single year's income is converted to a value indication using a capitalization rate. In yield capitalization, future cash flows are estimated and discounted to a present value using a capitalization rate. *See also* appraisal, capitalization rate, yield rate.

income multiplier. First-year ratios calculated by dividing the value of the property by either the potential gross income, effective gross income or net operating income. *See also* after-tax cash flow, effective gross income, net operating income, potential gross income.

income. *See* net operating income.

income property. A property that is held in anticipation of receiving income; e.g., residential properties that are typically rented, such as apartments, and nonresidential properties that are typically leased, such as office buildings, shopping centers and hotels.

income rate. *See* capitalization rate.

inflation risk. Uncertainty due to unexpected inflation that could cause cash flows from a property to lose purchasing power.

installment to amortize $1. *See* payment to amortize $1.

insulation. In construction, material such as plasterboard, asbestos, compressed wood-wool or fiberboard placed between inner and outer surfaces that reduces the transfer of heat, cold or sound by dissipating air currents.

insurable value. The value of the destructible parts of a property. This value is used to determine the amount of insurance carried on the property.

interest. Money paid for the use of money over time; a return on capital. Interest payments are deductible for income tax purposes, although payments of principal are not. *See also* amortization schedule, effective annual rate.

interest rate. The ratio of the cost of using money divided by the money advanced. *See also* interest.

interest only mortgage. A nonamortizing loan in which payments of interest are made at specified times throughout the life of the loan and the principal is paid in a lump sum at the maturity of the loan.

internal rate of return (IRR). A rate of return that discounts all expected future cash flows to a present value that is equal to the original investment. An IRR can be calculated for any defined cash flows, e.g., for the whole property or for just the equity position. Also called yield rate. *See* *also* adjusted internal rate of return, discounted cash-flow analysis.

investment analysis. According to the Uniform Standards of Professional Appraisal Practice, a study that reflects the relationship between acquisition price and anticipated future benefits of a real estate investment.

investment value. The value of a property to a particular investor. *See also* investment analysis.

Inwood annuity factor. *See* present value annuity of $1 per period.

Inwood premise. An appraisal theory used to value an income stream of equal payments in which the present value of the income stream is based on a single discount figure; the basis for the present value of an ordinary annuity factor in compound interest tables. *See* present value annuity of $1 per period.

land. The earth's surface including the solid surface of the earth, water and anything attached to it; natural resources in their original state, e.g., mineral deposits, timber, soil. In law, land is considered to be the solid surface of the earth and does not include water.

land capitalization rate (R_L). The rate that reflects the first-year land lease payment divided by the value of the land. *See also* band-of-investment technique, building residual technique, land residual technique.

land density. The ratio of building units or occupants divided by a unit of land area (acre, square mile).

land lease. *See* ground lease.

land utilization study. An analysis of the potential uses of a parcel of land and a determination of the highest and best use for that parcel; a complete inventory of the parcels in a given community or other area classified by type of use, plus (in some cases) an analysis of the spatial patterns of use revealed by this inventory. Land utilization studies do not embody the viewpoint of any particular investor nor do they focus on any one parcel. Furthermore, no consideration of markets and feasibility is normally included.

leased fee estate. An ownership interest in the real estate held by a landlord who has transferred the right of occupancy to a property through the execution of a lease. The leased fee estate can be valued as the present value of the lease income plus the right to the reversion at the end of the lease. *See also* fee simple estate, leasehold estate.

leased fee interest. *See* leased fee estate.

leased fee value. The value of a leased fee estate. *See* leased fee estate.

leasehold estate. An ownership interest in real estate held by a tenant during the term of a lease. The leasehold estate can be valued as the present value of the difference between the market rent and the rent specified by the lease. *See also* fee simple estate, leased fee estate.

leasehold interest. *See* leasehold estate.

leasehold value. The value of a leasehold estate. *See* leasehold estate.

legislative risk. Uncertainty due to changes in laws and regulations.

lender participation. *See* equity participation.

lessee. A person or entity that has been granted the right to use and occupy a property as the result of the execution of a lease agreement; a tenant. *See also* leasehold estate.

lessor. The owner of a property who transfers the right to use and occupy the property to a tenant as the result of the execution of a lease agreement; a landlord. *See also* leased fee estate.

level-payment mortgage. A mortgage in which equal, periodic payments are made over the life of the loan that cover both interest and principal. Payments are credited first against interest on the declining balance and then against principal, so that the amount of money credited to principal gradually increases over the life of the loan, while that credited to interest gradually decreases.

leverage. The use of borrowed funds in the purchase of an investment. If the addition of the mortgage increases the return to the equity (equity dividend rate or equity yield rate), the addition of the mortgage has resulted in positive leverage. If the addition of the mortgage decreases the return to the equity, the addition of the mortgage has resulted in negative leverage. *See also* negative leverage, positive leverage, zero leverage.

liquidity. The ease with which an asset may be sold for cash at a price close to its true value.

liquidity risk. Uncertainty caused by the lack of a ready, organized real estate market and the length of time required to find a buyer. *See also* risk.

loan constant. *See* mortgage capitalization rate.

loan constraints. Typically, one of two methods of selecting the level of funds to be advanced to a property owner. The methods are loan-to-value ratio (M) or the first-year debt service coverage ratio (DCR). *See also* debt coverage ratio, loan-to-value ratio.

loan participation. *See* equity participation.

loan-to-value ratio (M). The ratio of the outstanding loan balance divided by the total property value.

management risk. Uncertainty caused by the quality of the management operating the property. *See also* risk.

market analysis. According to the Uniform Standards of Professional Appraisal Practice, a study of real estate market conditions for a specific type of property.

market area. *See* general market area.

market price. The amount actually paid, or to be paid, for a property in a particular transaction. Market price differs from market value; it is an accomplished historical fact, whereas market value is and remains an estimate. Market price involves no assumption of information or prudent conduct by the parties or absence of undue stimulus or of any other condition basic to the market value concept. *See also* market value.

market rent. The rental income that a property would command if exposed for lease in a competitive market.

market segmentation. (1) The process of classifying consumers or buyers into relatively homogeneous groups based on their economic, demographic and/or psychographic characteristics (such as attitudes, habits and lifestyles). (2) The process of differentiating the potential users of the subject property from the general population, according to defined consumer characteristics.

market study. *See* market analysis.

market value. According to the Uniform Standards of Professional Appraisal Practice, market value is the major focus of most real property appraisal assignments. Both economic and legal definitions of market value have been developed and refined. A current economic definition agreed upon by federal financial institutions in the United States is:

The most probable price a property should bring in a competitive and open market under all conditions requisite to a fair sale, the buyer and seller each acting prudently and knowledgeably, and assuming the price is not affected by undue stimulus. Implicit in this definition is the consummation of a sale as of a specified date and the passing of title from seller to buyer under conditions whereby:

1. buyer and seller are typically motivated;
2. both parties are well informed or well advised, and acting in what they consider their best interests;
3. a reasonable time is allowed for exposure in the open market;
4. payment is made in terms of cash in United States dollars or in terms of financial arrangements comparable thereto; and

5. the price represents the normal consideration for the property sold unaffected by special or creative financing or sales concessions granted by anyone associated with the sale.

Substitution of another currency for United States dollars in the fourth condition is appropriate in other countries or in reports addressed to clients from other countries.

Persons performing appraisal services that may be subject to litigation are cautioned to seek the exact legal definition of market value in the jurisdiction in which the services are being performed.

marketability study. A real estate analysis of a specific property that addresses the ability of the property to be absorbed, sold or leased under current and anticipated market conditions.

marketing period. The time period beginning when an owner decides to begin actively selling a property to when the sale is actually closed. The marketing period is typically an observable fact. If a marketing period that is shorter than typical is assumed in an analysis, the value found would be considered a forced, or liquidation, value rather than market value.

minimum rent. *See* base rent.

modified internal rate of return. *See* adjusted internal rate of return.

mortgage. A legal document in which real estate is named under certain conditions as the security or collateral for the repayment of a loan.

mortgage capitalization rate (R_M). The mortgage capitalization rate that is the ratio of the first-year debt payment divided by the beginning loan balance. In some instances, the ratio may be calculated using one month's payment, but typically it is the total of the loan payment for an entire year. Also called mortgage constant.

mortgage constant. *See* mortgage capitalization rate.

mortgage interest. Money paid for the use of borrowed money through a mortgage. The rate can be fixed or variable.

mortgage loan value (V_M). The benchmark on which lenders base mortgage investments in real estate. Typically, market value and mortgage value would be identical. A lender, however, may introduce restrictions in underwriting policy that may alter this relationship.

mortgage yield rate (R_M). The discount rate that equates the present value of the loan payments with the principal borrowed. *See also* effective annual rate, mortgage interest.

negative amortization. The difference between the loan payment and the amount of interest charged when the loan payment is less than the interest charged per period. In effect, the loan balance increases each period by the amount of interest unpaid. This generally occurs in mortgages with initially low payments that increase at some point in time. Mortgages with negative amortization usually require higher interest rates or larger down payments. *See also* amortization schedule.

negative leverage. A situation in which the rate paid on a mortgage is greater than the rate generated by an investment on an unleveraged basis. *See also* leverage, positive leverage, zero leverage.

net income multiplier (NIM). The ratio of the price or value of a property divided by its net operating income; the reciprocal of the overall rate.

net leasable area. Floor space that can be rented to tenants; may include common areas.

net lease. A lease in which the tenant pays expenses such as property taxes, insurance and maintenance. Sometimes referred to as a net-net-net lease. *See also* gross lease.

net operating income (NOI). The actual or anticipated income remaining during a year after deducting operating expenses from effective gross income but before any deductions for debt service payment or income taxes.

net present value (NPV). The discounted value of all future cash flows minus the initial cash outlay. A net present value greater than or equal to zero is acceptable. *See also* discounted cash-flow analysis, internal rate of return, present value.

net sale proceeds. The gross sale price less selling expenses, e.g., legal fees, recording fees, brokerage fees.

net usable area. Floor space that can be occupied by tenants. *See also* net leasable area.

nonrealty interests. Property rights that might be purchased with real estate, land, buildings and fixtures that are either tangible or intangible personal property such as furniture in a hotel or the franchise (business) value of the hotel.

nonresidential property. Property that is not used as a permanent dwelling, including property types such as office, industrial, retail, hotel and special purpose properties.

operating expense ratio (OER). The ratio of total operating expenses divided by effective gross income.

operating expenses. Expenditures necessary to maintain the real property and continue the production of income. Includes both fixed expenses and variable expenses, but does not include debt service, depreciation or capital expenditures. *See also* fixed expense, variable expense.

ordinary annuity. A series of level payments that are made at the end of a series of equal time periods; the type of annuity assumed in compound interest tables. *See also* annuity in advance.

overall capitalization rate (R_O). A single year's cash-flow ratio that is calculated by dividing the net operating income (NOI) by the total value of the property. When calculated, using NOI for the first year of operations, it is sometimes referred to as a "current yield." However, it is *not* a yield rate that considers NOI over the entire holding period, nor does it consider resale proceeds. Thus it should not be confused with an overall yield rate. Frequently used to find the value of a property by dividing the first year's net operating income by the overall capitalization rate. The inverse of the overall capitalization rate is the net income multiplier. Also called overall cap rate. *See also* band-of-investment technique, yield capitalization formulas, capitalization rate, direct capitalization, income capitalization approach, net income multiplier and overall yield rate.

overall yield rate (Y_O). The discount rate that equates the present value of the net operating income and resale proceeds with the purchase price. Sometimes referred to as a free and clear yield because it does not consider financing. *See also* internal rate of return, equity yield rate.

ownership interest. *See* fee simple estate, leased fee estate, leasehold estate.

partitioning the IRR. Using the internal rate of return for an investment to determine the proportion of the present value that comes from different sources of cash flow.

passive income. Income or loss from a trade or business where the investor does not materially participate in the management or operation of the property by being involved in the operations of the activity on a regular, continuous and substantial basis. Income from real estate investment is generally classified as passive income.

passthrough. Expenses charged to a tenant as a result of expense stop provisions in a lease. *See also* expense stop.

payback period. The time required for cumulative income from an investment to equal the amount initially invested. Usually calculated to the next whole year. It does not consider the time value of money and, therefore, is not a discounted cash-flow analysis technique. *See also* discounted cash-flow analysis.

payment to amortize \$1 ($1/a_n$). The periodic payment necessary to repay a \$1 loan with interest paid at a specified rate over a specified time on the outstanding loan balance; column six of the compound interest tables. *See also* six functions of $1.

percentage rent. A type of rent that is based on a percentage of sales from the property, usually associated with a guaranteed base rent. *See also* base rent, overage rent.

perpetuity. (1) The state of existing forever. (2) An ordinary annuity that continues forever. *See also* capitalization in perpetuity.

personal property. According to the Uniform Standards of Professional Appraisal Practice, identifiable, portable and tangible objects that are considered by the general public as being personal, e.g., furnishings, artwork, antiques, gems and jewelry, collectibles, machinery and equipment; all property that is not classified as real estate.

portfolio income. Interest and dividend income from stocks, bonds and some categories of real estate that are classified as capital assets.

positive leverage. A situation in which the rate paid on a mortgage is less than the rate generated by an investment on an unleveraged basis. *See also* leverage, negative leverage, zero leverage.

potential gross income (PGI). The amount of theoretical income a property could potentially generate assuming 100% occupancy at market rental rates. *See also* after-tax cash flow, before-tax cash flow, effective gross income, net operating income.

potential gross income multiplier (PGIM). The ratio calculated by dividing the sales price of a property by its potential gross income. *See also* potential gross income.

present value (PV). The current value of a payment or series of future payments found by discounting the expected payments by a desired rate of return in order to compensate for the time value of money. *See also* discounted cash-flow analysis, internal rate of return, net present value, yield capitalization.

present value annuity of $1 per period ($a_n$). A compound interest factor typically calculated for an annual interest rate that is used to discount a series of equal future cash flows in order to arrive at a current present value of the total stream of income; column five of the compound interest tables. *See also* six functions of $1.

present value of $1 ($1/S^n$). A compound interest factor typically calculated for an annual interest rate that is used to discount an expected future cash flow in order to arrive at its current present value. It is found in column four of the compound interest tables. Also called present value of one dollar, present value of one factor, present

value interest factor, present worth of $1. *See also* six functions of $1.

preservation of capital. *See* return of capital.

pre-tax cash flow (PTCF). *See* before-tax cash flow.

price per square foot. A unit of comparison in the direct sales comparison approach. Gives a good indication of the value of a subject property only after ensuring that each sale represents the same ownership interests and that adjustments have been made for differences in the locational and physical characteristics of the subject and the comparable properties. *See also* direct sales comparison approach, sales adjustment grid, units of comparison.

primary mortgage market. The interaction of lenders who originate loans with borrowers seeking mortgage loans to purchase or refinance a property. *See also* secondary mortgage market.

principal (loan). The amount of capital borrowed or remaining to be paid on an investment. Also refers to that portion of a loan payment that reduces the balance of the loan.

proceeds of resale. *See* reversion.

profitability index (PI). The ratio of the present value of future cash flows at a specified discount rate divided by the initial cash outlay. It is similar to the net present value except that the initial cash outlay is divided into the present value of future cash flows instead of subtracted from the present value of future cash flows. A profitability index greater than one is acceptable. *See also* net present value, discounted cash-flow analysis.

property tax. An ad valorem levy issued by the government based on the assessed value of privately owned property.

property value (V). The monetary worth of interests held in real estate arising from property ownership. A property may have several different values depending on the interest or use involved. Common methods of estimating property value include the cost approach, direct sales comparison approach and income approach.

property yield rate. *See* overall yield rate.

real estate. According to the Uniform Standards of Professional Appraisal Practice, an identified parcel or tract of land, including improvements, if any. *See also* real property, personal property.

real property. According to the Uniform Standards of Professional Appraisal Practice, the interests, benefits and rights inherent in the ownership of real estate. *See also* real estate, personal property.

Comment: In some jurisdictions, the terms *real estate* and *real property* have the same legal meaning. The separate definitions recognize the traditional distinction between the two concepts in appraisal theory.

reinvestment rate. An interest rate used to modify interim cash flows in a cash-flow analysis to arrive at a future value estimate when calculating an adjusted interest rate of return. *See* adjusted internal rate of return, financial management rate of return.

resale. Sale of a property at the termination of the holding period. The resale price can be estimated by a growth rate or by a terminal cap rate applied to the net operating income occurring the year following the holding period.

resale proceeds. *See* reversionary value.

resale value. *See* reversionary value.

reserve for replacement. *See* allowance for replacements.

residential property. Vacant sites or land improved with buildings devoted to or available for use for human habitation, e.g., single-family houses, rental apartments, residential condominium units and rooming houses, but not hotels or motels.

residual techniques. Valuation techniques in which one component of value (e.g., land or mortgage) is assumed to be known. Income is estimated for the known component and subtracted from net operating income to estimate values for the unknown component.

See also building residual technique, equity residual technique, land residual technique, mortgage residual technique.

return of capital. The recovery of the original investment either through operating income cash flows or proceeds from resale. Also called capital recovery.

return on capital. An annual rate of return that results when income received is greater than the invested capital.

reversion. The lump-sum payment received by an investor at resale of the investment. *See also* after-tax cash flow, before-tax cash flow.

reversionary value (V_R). The value of a property at resale. Also called resale value. *See also* resale.

risk. Uncertainty arising from the probability that events will not occur as expected. *See also* financial risk, liquidity risk, management risk, capital market risk, space market risk, environmental risk, inflation risk, legislative risk.

safe rate. The rate of return that can be obtained on a risk-free or relatively risk-free investment, e.g., the rate on U.S. treasury bills. *See also* adjusted internal rate of return, financial management rate of return, speculative rate.

scenarios. Alternative assumptions as to how a property may perform in the future.

secondary mortgage market. The interaction of buyers and sellers of existing mortgages. Created by government and private agencies, the secondary mortgage market provides greater liquidity for the mortgage market. *See also* Federal National Mortgage Association, Federal Home Loan Mortgage Corporation.

segmented market. *See* market segmentation.

sensitivity analysis. Evaluating how a change in assumptions affects the performance of a property.

simple interest. Interest that is based only on the principal amount and not on accrued interest. *See also* compound interest.

sinking fund factor ($1/S_n$). A compound interest factor that represents the level payment percentage required to be periodically invested and compounded at a specific interest rate in order to grow to an amount equal to $1 over a specified time period; column three of the compound interest tables. *See also* six functions of $1.

site. A plot of land improved for a specific purpose.

site improvements. *See* on-site improvements.

six functions of $1. The six compound interest factors that are used in the mathematics of finance in order to adjust present or future payments for the time value of money. Includes future value of $1 ($S^n$), future value annuity of $1 per period ($S_n$), sinking fund factor ($1/S_n$), present value of $1 ($1/S^n$), present value annuity of $1 per period ($a_n$) and the payment to amortize $1 ($1/a_n$).

space market risk. Uncertainty arising from changes in the market for space that is leased to tenants.

speculative rate. The rate that typically could be earned on comparable real estate investments. *See also* adjusted internal rate of return, financial management rate of return, safe rate.

standard deviation. The square root of the variance. *See also* variance.

tax liability. The dollar amount of taxes owed for a specific time period. The tax liability from operations equals the taxable income multiplied by the appropriate marginal ordinary income tax rate. The tax liability from sale of a property equals the capital gain multiplied by the appropriate marginal ordinary income tax rate. *See also* after-tax cash flow, taxable income.

taxable income. Income that is taxable by law; calculated as the net operating income minus interest and depreciation. Taxable income from sale of a property equals the capital gain. *See also* after-tax cash flow.

taxation. A governmental right to raise income for use of public property and projects by assessing goods and services.

terminal capitalization rate. An overall capitalization rate used to forecast a reversionary value in a discounted cash-flow analysis. It is calculated by dividing the projected net operating income (NOI) for the year of sale by the selected rate. Sometimes the projected NOI for the year *after* the sale is used because this is the NOI that the buyer will receive for the first year. The terminal capitalization rate is typically forecast to be higher than the going-in cap rate due to a higher risk associated with estimating NOI at the time of the sale. *See also* capitalization rate, going-in capitalization rate.

time value of money. A financial principle based on the assumption that a positive interest can be earned on an investment and, therefore, that money received today is more valuable than money received in the future. *See also* discounted cash-flow analysis.

units of comparison. A physical or economic measure that can be divided into the property's price to provide a more standardized comparison of the properties. The measure should be one that accounts for differences in the price typically paid for the properties such as price per square foot (office building), price per seat (theater) or price per gallon of gas pumped (gas station). Income can also be a unit of comparison such as when price is divided by effective gross income to obtain an effective gross income multiplier.

See also elements of comparison, direct sales comparison approach.

usable area. *See* net leasable area.

vacancy allowance. In the income approach, a deduction from potential income for current or expected future space not rented due to tenant turnover. *See also* collection loss, potential gross income, effective gross income.

vacancy and collection loss. *See* vacancy allowance, collection loss.

value as is. The value of a property based on the land and any existing improvements on the site at the date of the appraisal. *See also* prospective value.

variable expense. An operating expense that varies with the occupancy level or intensity of use of a property, e.g., utilities, management, and maintenance. *See also* fixed expense.

variable interest rate. An interest rate on a mortgage that changes throughout the term of the mortgage and is usually tied to an index, e.g., treasury bills, prime rate.

variable rate mortgage. *See* adjustable rate mortgage.

variance. A measure of the uncertainty or risk associated with an investment.

yield rate (Y). The return on an investment, which considers income received over time; the discount rate that equates the present value of future cash flows with the initial investment. Same as internal rate of return. *See also* equity yield rate, overall yield rate.

zero leverage. The use of borrowed funds at a rate equal to the equity yield rate. *See also* leverage.

Annual Compound Interest Tables

IRV

$V \times R = I$

$\dfrac{R}{I} = V$

$\dfrac{I}{V} = R$

ANNUAL COMPOUND INTEREST TABLES

6.00% ANNUAL INTEREST RATE

	1 FUTURE VALUE OF $1	2 FUTURE VALUE ANNUITY OF $1 PER YEAR	3 SINKING FUND FACTOR	4 PRESENT VALUE OF $1 (REVERSION)	5 PRESENT VALUE ANNUITY OF $1 PER YEAR	6 PAYMENT TO AMORTIZE $1	
YEARS							YEARS
1	1.060000	1.000000	1.000000	0.943396	0.943396	1.060000	1
2	1.123600	2.060000	0.485437	0.889996	1.833393	0.545437	2
3	1.191016	3.183600	0.314110	0.839619	2.673012	0.374110	3
4	1.262477	4.374616	0.228591	0.792094	3.465106	0.288591	4
5	1.338226	5.637093	0.177396	0.747258	4.212364	0.237396	5
6	1.418519	6.975319	0.143363	0.704961	4.917324	0.203363	6
7	1.503630	8.393838	0.119135	0.665057	5.582381	0.179135	7
8	1.593848	9.897468	0.101036	0.627412	6.209794	0.161036	8
9	1.689479	11.491316	0.087022	0.591898	6.801692	0.147022	9
10	1.790848	13.180795	0.075868	0.558395	7.360087	0.135868	10
11	1.898299	14.971643	0.066793	0.526788	7.886875	0.126793	11
12	2.012196	16.869941	0.059277	0.496969	8.383844	0.119277	12
13	2.132928	18.882138	0.052960	0.468839	8.852683	0.112960	13
14	2.260904	21.015066	0.047585	0.442301	9.294984	0.107585	14
15	2.396558	23.275970	0.042963	0.417265	9.712249	0.102963	15
16	2.540352	25.672528	0.038952	0.393646	10.105895	0.098952	16
17	2.692773	28.212880	0.035445	0.371364	10.477260	0.095445	17
18	2.854339	30.905653	0.032357	0.350344	10.827603	0.092357	18
19	3.025600	33.759992	0.029621	0.330513	11.158116	0.089621	19
20	3.207135	36.785591	0.027185	0.311805	11.469921	0.087185	20
21	3.399564	39.992727	0.025005	0.294155	11.764077	0.085005	21
22	3.603537	43.392290	0.023046	0.277505	12.041582	0.083046	22
23	3.819750	46.995828	0.021278	0.261797	12.303379	0.081278	23
24	4.048935	50.815577	0.019679	0.246967	12.550358	0.079679	24
25	4.291871	54.864512	0.018227	0.232999	12.783356	0.078227	25
26	4.549383	59.156383	0.016904	0.219810	13.003166	0.076904	26
27	4.822346	63.705766	0.015697	0.207368	13.210534	0.075697	27
28	5.111687	68.528112	0.014593	0.195630	13.406164	0.074593	28
29	5.418388	73.639798	0.013580	0.184557	13.590721	0.073580	29
30	5.743491	79.058186	0.012649	0.174110	13.764831	0.072649	30
31	6.088101	84.801677	0.011792	0.164255	13.929086	0.071792	31
32	6.453387	90.889778	0.011002	0.154957	14.084043	0.071002	32
33	6.840590	97.343165	0.010273	0.146186	14.230230	0.070273	33
34	7.251025	104.183755	0.009598	0.137912	14.368141	0.069598	34
35	7.686087	111.434780	0.008974	0.130105	14.498246	0.068974	35
36	8.147252	119.120867	0.008395	0.122741	14.620987	0.068395	36
37	8.636087	127.268119	0.007857	0.115793	14.736780	0.067857	37
38	9.154252	135.904206	0.007358	0.109239	14.846019	0.067358	38
39	9.703507	145.058458	0.006894	0.103056	14.949075	0.066894	39
40	10.285718	154.761966	0.006462	0.097222	15.046297	0.066462	40
41	10.902861	165.047684	0.006059	0.091719	15.138016	0.066059	41
42	11.557033	175.950545	0.005683	0.086527	15.224543	0.065683	42
43	12.250455	187.507577	0.005333	0.081630	15.306173	0.065333	43
44	12.985482	199.758032	0.005006	0.077009	15.383182	0.065006	44
45	13.764611	212.743514	0.004700	0.072650	15.455832	0.064700	45
46	14.590487	226.508125	0.004415	0.068538	15.524370	0.064415	46
47	15.465917	241.098612	0.004148	0.064658	15.589028	0.064148	47
48	16.393872	256.564529	0.003898	0.060998	15.650027	0.063898	48
49	17.377504	272.958401	0.003664	0.057546	15.707572	0.063664	49
50	18.420154	290.335905	0.003444	0.054288	15.761861	0.063444	50

①   COLUMN
FUTURE VALUE
I RV

8 I

I N
___
FV

②   COLUMN
FUTUR VALUE ANNUITY
OF $1 PER YEAR
I PMT

I

N

FV

114   Appendix A

ANNUAL COMPOUND INTEREST TABLES

8.00% ANNUAL INTEREST RATE

	1 FUTURE VALUE OF $1	2 FUTURE VALUE ANNUITY OF $1 PER YEAR	3 SINKING FUND FACTOR	4 PRESENT VALUE OF $1 (REVERSION)	5 PRESENT VALUE ANNUITY OF $1 PER YEAR	6 PAYMENT TO AMORTIZE $1	
YEARS							YEARS
1	1.080000	1.000000	1.000000	0.925926	0.925926	1.080000	1
2	1.166400	2.080000	0.480769	0.857339	1.783265	0.560769	2
3	1.259712	3.246400	0.308034	0.793832	2.577097	0.388034	3
4	1.360489	4.506112	0.221921	0.735030	3.312127	0.301921	4
5	1.469328	5.866601	0.170456	0.680583	3.992710	0.250456	5
6	1.586874	7.335929	0.136315	0.630170	4.622880	0.216315	6
7	1.713824	8.922803	0.112072	0.583490	5.206370	0.192072	7
8	1.850930	10.636628	0.094015	0.540269	5.746639	0.174015	8
9	1.999005	12.487558	0.080080	0.500249	6.246888	0.160080	9
10	2.158925	14.486562	0.069029	0.463193	6.710081	0.149029	10
11	2.331639	16.645487	0.060076	0.428883	7.138964	0.140076	11
12	2.518170	18.977126	0.052695	0.397114	7.536078	0.132695	12
13	2.719624	21.495297	0.046522	0.367698	7.903776	0.126522	13
14	2.937194	24.214920	0.041297	0.340461	8.244237	0.121297	14
15	3.172169	27.152114	0.036830	0.315242	8.559479	0.116830	15
16	3.425943	30.324283	0.032977	0.291890	8.851369	0.112977	16
17	3.700018	33.750226	0.029629	0.270269	9.121638	0.109629	17
18	3.996019	37.450244	0.026702	0.250249	9.371887	0.106702	18
19	4.315701	41.446263	0.024128	0.231712	9.603599	0.104128	19
20	4.660957	45.761964	0.021852	0.214548	9.818147	0.101852	20
21	5.033834	50.422921	0.019832	0.198656	10.016803	0.099832	21
22	5.436540	55.456755	0.018032	0.183941	10.200744	0.098032	22
23	5.871464	60.893296	0.016422	0.170315	10.371059	0.096422	23
24	6.341181	66.764759	0.014978	0.157699	10.528758	0.094978	24
25	6.848475	73.105940	0.013679	0.146018	10.674776	0.093679	25
26	7.396353	79.954415	0.012507	0.135202	10.809978	0.092507	26
27	7.988061	87.350768	0.011448	0.125187	10.935165	0.091448	27
28	8.627106	95.338830	0.010489	0.115914	11.051078	0.090489	28
29	9.317275	103.965936	0.009619	0.107328	11.158406	0.089619	29
30	10.062657	113.283211	0.008827	0.099377	11.257783	0.088827	30
31	10.867669	123.345868	0.008107	0.092016	11.349799	0.088107	31
32	11.737083	134.213537	0.007451	0.085200	11.434999	0.087451	32
33	12.676050	145.950620	0.006852	0.078889	11.513888	0.086852	33
34	13.690134	158.626670	0.006304	0.073045	11.586934	0.086304	34
35	14.785344	172.316804	0.005803	0.067635	11.654568	0.085803	35
36	15.968172	187.102148	0.005345	0.062625	11.717193	0.085345	36
37	17.245626	203.070320	0.004924	0.057986	11.775179	0.084924	37
38	18.625276	220.315945	0.004539	0.053690	11.828869	0.084539	38
39	20.115298	238.941221	0.004185	0.049713	11.878582	0.084185	39
40	21.724521	259.056519	0.003860	0.046031	11.924613	0.083860	40
41	23.462483	280.781040	0.003561	0.042621	11.967235	0.083561	41
42	25.339482	304.243523	0.003287	0.039464	12.006699	0.083287	42
43	27.366640	329.583005	0.003034	0.036541	12.043240	0.083034	43
44	29.555972	356.949646	0.002802	0.033834	12.077074	0.082802	44
45	31.920449	386.505617	0.002587	0.031328	12.108402	0.082587	45
46	34.474085	418.426067	0.002390	0.029007	12.137409	0.082390	46
47	37.232012	452.900152	0.002208	0.026859	12.164267	0.082208	47
48	40.210573	490.132164	0.002040	0.024869	12.189136	0.082040	48
49	43.427419	530.342737	0.001886	0.023027	12.212163	0.081886	49
50	46.901613	573.770156	0.001743	0.021321	12.233485	0.081743	50

ANNUAL COMPOUND INTEREST TABLES

9.00% ANNUAL INTEREST RATE

	1 FUTURE VALUE OF $1	2 FUTURE VALUE ANNUITY OF $1 PER YEAR	3 SINKING FUND FACTOR	4 PRESENT VALUE OF $1 (REVERSION)	5 PRESENT VALUE ANNUITY OF $1 PER YEAR	6 PAYMENT TO AMORTIZE $1	
YEARS							YEARS
1	1.090000	1.000000	1.000000	0.917431	0.917431	1.090000	1
2	1.188100	2.090000	0.478469	0.841680	1.759111	0.568469	2
3	1.295029	3.278100	0.305055	0.772183	2.531295	0.395055	3
4	1.411582	4.573129	0.218669	0.708425	3.239720	0.308669	4
5	1.538624	5.984711	0.167092	0.649931	3.889651	0.257092	5
6	1.677100	7.523335	0.132920	0.596267	4.485919	0.222920	6
7	1.828039	9.200435	0.108691	0.547034	5.032953	0.198691	7
8	1.992563	11.028474	0.090674	0.501866	5.534819	0.180674	8
9	2.171893	13.021036	0.076799	0.460428	5.995247	0.166799	9
10	2.367364	15.192930	0.065820	0.422411	6.417658	0.155820	10
11	2.580426	17.560293	0.056947	0.387533	6.805191	0.146947	11
12	2.812665	20.140720	0.049651	0.355535	7.160725	0.139651	12
13	3.065805	22.953385	0.043567	0.326179	7.486904	0.133567	13
14	3.341727	26.019189	0.038433	0.299246	7.786150	0.128433	14
15	3.642482	29.360916	0.034059	0.274538	8.060688	0.124059	15
16	3.970306	33.003399	0.030300	0.251870	8.312558	0.120300	16
17	4.327633	36.973705	0.027046	0.231073	8.543631	0.117046	17
18	4.717120	41.301338	0.024212	0.211994	8.755625	0.114212	18
19	5.141661	46.018458	0.021730	0.194490	8.950115	0.111730	19
20	5.604411	51.160120	0.019546	0.178431	9.128546	0.109546	20
21	6.108808	56.764530	0.017617	0.163698	9.292244	0.107617	21
22	6.658600	62.873338	0.015905	0.150182	9.442425	0.105905	22
23	7.257874	69.531939	0.014382	0.137781	9.580207	0.104382	23
24	7.911083	76.789813	0.013023	0.126405	9.706612	0.103023	24
25	8.623081	84.700896	0.011806	0.115968	9.822580	0.101806	25
26	9.399158	93.323977	0.010715	0.106393	9.928972	0.100715	26
27	10.245082	102.723135	0.009735	0.097608	10.026580	0.099735	27
28	11.167140	112.968217	0.008852	0.089548	10.116128	0.098852	28
29	12.172182	124.135356	0.008056	0.082155	10.198283	0.098056	29
30	13.267678	136.307539	0.007336	0.075371	10.273654	0.097336	30
31	14.461770	149.575217	0.006686	0.069148	10.342802	0.096686	31
32	15.763329	164.036987	0.006096	0.063438	10.406240	0.096096	32
33	17.182028	179.800315	0.005562	0.058200	10.464441	0.095562	33
34	18.728411	196.982344	0.005077	0.053395	10.517835	0.095077	34
35	20.413968	215.710755	0.004636	0.048986	10.566821	0.094636	35
36	22.251225	236.124723	0.004235	0.044941	10.611763	0.094235	36
37	24.253835	258.375948	0.003870	0.041231	10.652993	0.093870	37
38	26.436680	282.629783	0.003538	0.037826	10.690820	0.093538	38
39	28.815982	309.066463	0.003236	0.034703	10.725523	0.093236	39
40	31.409420	337.882445	0.002960	0.031838	10.757360	0.092960	40
41	34.236268	369.291865	0.002708	0.029209	10.786569	0.092708	41
42	37.317532	403.528133	0.002478	0.026797	10.813366	0.092478	42
43	40.676110	440.845665	0.002268	0.024584	10.837950	0.092268	43
44	44.336960	481.521775	0.002077	0.022555	10.860505	0.092077	44
45	48.327286	525.858734	0.001902	0.020692	10.881197	0.091902	45
46	52.676742	574.186021	0.001742	0.018984	10.900181	0.091742	46
47	57.417649	626.862762	0.001595	0.017416	10.917597	0.091595	47
48	62.585237	684.280411	0.001461	0.015978	10.933575	0.091461	48
49	68.217908	746.865648	0.001339	0.014659	10.948234	0.091339	49
50	74.357520	815.083556	0.001227	0.013449	10.961683	0.091227	50

ANNUAL COMPOUND INTEREST TABLES

10.00% ANNUAL INTEREST RATE

	1 FUTURE VALUE OF $1	2 FUTURE VALUE ANNUITY OF $1 PER YEAR	3 SINKING FUND FACTOR	4 PRESENT VALUE OF $1 (REVERSION)	5 PRESENT VALUE ANNUITY OF $1 PER YEAR	6 PAYMENT TO AMORTIZE $1	
YEARS							YEARS
1	1.100000	1.000000	1.000000	0.909091	0.909091	1.100000	1
2	1.210000	2.100000	0.476190	0.826446	1.735537	0.576190	2
3	1.331000	3.310000	0.302115	0.751315	2.486852	0.402115	3
4	1.464100	4.641000	0.215471	0.683013	3.169865	0.315471	4
5	1.610510	6.105100	0.163797	0.620921	3.790787	0.263797	5
6	1.771561	7.715610	0.129607	0.564474	4.355261	0.229607	6
7	1.948717	9.487171	0.105405	0.513158	4.868419	0.205405	7
8	2.143589	11.435888	0.087444	0.466507	5.334926	0.187444	8
9	2.357948	13.579477	0.073641	0.424098	5.759024	0.173641	9
10	2.593742	15.937425	0.062745	0.385543	6.144567	0.162745	10
11	2.853117	18.531167	0.053963	0.350494	6.495061	0.153963	11
12	3.138428	21.384284	0.046763	0.318631	6.813692	0.146763	12
13	3.452271	24.522712	0.040779	0.289664	7.103356	0.140779	13
14	3.797498	27.974983	0.035746	0.263331	7.366687	0.135746	14
15	4.177248	31.772482	0.031474	0.239392	7.606080	0.131474	15
16	4.594973	35.949730	0.027817	0.217629	7.823709	0.127817	16
17	5.054470	40.544703	0.024664	0.197845	8.021553	0.124664	17
18	5.559917	45.599173	0.021930	0.179859	8.201412	0.121930	18
19	6.115909	51.159090	0.019547	0.163508	8.364920	0.119547	19
20	6.727500	57.274999	0.017460	0.148644	8.513564	0.117460	20
21	7.400250	64.002499	0.015624	0.135131	8.648694	0.115624	21
22	8.140275	71.402749	0.014005	0.122846	8.771540	0.114005	22
23	8.954302	79.543024	0.012572	0.111678	8.883218	0.112572	23
24	9.849733	88.497327	0.011300	0.101526	8.984744	0.111300	24
25	10.834706	98.347059	0.010168	0.092296	9.077040	0.110168	25
26	11.918177	109.181765	0.009159	0.083905	9.160945	0.109159	26
27	13.109994	121.099942	0.008258	0.076278	9.237223	0.108258	27
28	14.420994	134.209936	0.007451	0.069343	9.306567	0.107451	28
29	15.863093	148.630930	0.006728	0.063039	9.369606	0.106728	29
30	17.449402	164.494023	0.006079	0.057309	9.426914	0.106079	30
31	19.194342	181.943425	0.005496	0.052099	9.479013	0.105496	31
32	21.113777	201.137767	0.004972	0.047362	9.526376	0.104972	32
33	23.225154	222.251544	0.004499	0.043057	9.569432	0.104499	33
34	25.547670	245.476699	0.004074	0.039143	9.608575	0.104074	34
35	28.102437	271.024368	0.003690	0.035584	9.644159	0.103690	35
36	30.912681	299.126805	0.003343	0.032349	9.676508	0.103343	36
37	34.003949	330.039486	0.003030	0.029408	9.705917	0.103030	37
38	37.404343	364.043434	0.002747	0.026735	9.732651	0.102747	38
39	41.144778	401.447778	0.002491	0.024304	9.756956	0.102491	39
40	45.259256	442.592556	0.002259	0.022095	9.779051	0.102259	40
41	49.785181	487.851811	0.002050	0.020086	9.799137	0.102050	41
42	54.763699	537.636992	0.001860	0.018260	9.817397	0.101860	42
43	60.240069	592.400692	0.001688	0.016600	9.833998	0.101688	43
44	66.264076	652.640761	0.001532	0.015091	9.849089	0.101532	44
45	72.890484	718.904837	0.001391	0.013719	9.862808	0.101391	45
46	80.179532	791.795321	0.001263	0.012472	9.875280	0.101263	46
47	88.197485	871.974853	0.001147	0.011338	9.886618	0.101147	47
48	97.017234	960.172338	0.001041	0.010307	9.896926	0.101041	48
49	106.718957	1057.189572	0.000946	0.009370	9.906296	0.100946	49
50	117.390853	1163.908529	0.000859	0.008519	9.914814	0.100859	50

ANNUAL COMPOUND INTEREST TABLES

11.00% ANNUAL INTEREST RATE

	1 FUTURE VALUE OF $1	2 FUTURE VALUE ANNUITY OF $1 PER YEAR	3 SINKING FUND FACTOR	4 PRESENT VALUE OF $1 (REVERSION)	5 PRESENT VALUE ANNUITY OF $1 PER YEAR	6 PAYMENT TO AMORTIZE $1	
YEARS							YEARS
1	1.110000	1.000000	1.000000	0.900901	0.900901	1.110000	1
2	1.232100	2.110000	0.473934	0.811622	1.712523	0.583934	2
3	1.367631	3.342100	0.299213	0.731191	2.443715	0.409213	3
4	1.518070	4.709731	0.212326	0.658731	3.102446	0.322326	4
5	1.685058	6.227801	0.160570	0.593451	3.695897	0.270570	5
6	1.870415	7.912860	0.126377	0.534641	4.230538	0.236377	6
7	2.076160	9.783274	0.102215	0.481658	4.712196	0.212215	7
8	2.304538	11.859434	0.084321	0.433926	5.146123	0.194321	8
9	2.558037	14.163972	0.070602	0.390925	5.537048	0.180602	9
10	2.839421	16.722009	0.059801	0.352184	5.889232	0.169801	10
11	3.151757	19.561430	0.051121	0.317283	6.206515	0.161121	11
12	3.498451	22.713187	0.044027	0.285841	6.492356	0.154027	12
13	3.883280	26.211638	0.038151	0.257514	6.749870	0.148151	13
14	4.310441	30.094918	0.033228	0.231995	6.981865	0.143228	14
15	4.784589	34.405359	0.029065	0.209004	7.190870	0.139065	15
16	5.310894	39.189948	0.025517	0.188292	7.379162	0.135517	16
17	5.895093	44.500843	0.022471	0.169633	7.548794	0.132471	17
18	6.543553	50.395936	0.019843	0.152822	7.701617	0.129843	18
19	7.263344	56.939488	0.017563	0.137678	7.839294	0.127563	19
20	8.062312	64.202832	0.015576	0.124034	7.963328	0.125576	20
21	8.949166	72.265144	0.013838	0.111742	8.075070	0.123838	21
22	9.933574	81.214309	0.012313	0.100669	8.175739	0.122313	22
23	11.026267	91.147884	0.010971	0.090693	8.266432	0.120971	23
24	12.239157	102.174151	0.009787	0.081705	8.348137	0.119787	24
25	13.585464	114.413307	0.008740	0.073608	8.421745	0.118740	25
26	15.079865	127.998771	0.007813	0.066314	8.488058	0.117813	26
27	16.738650	143.078636	0.006989	0.059742	8.547800	0.116989	27
28	18.579901	159.817286	0.006257	0.053822	8.601622	0.116257	28
29	20.623691	178.397187	0.005605	0.048488	8.650110	0.115605	29
30	22.892297	199.020878	0.005025	0.043683	8.693793	0.115025	30
31	25.410449	221.913174	0.004506	0.039354	8.733146	0.114506	31
32	28.205599	247.323624	0.004043	0.035454	8.768600	0.114043	32
33	31.308214	275.529222	0.003629	0.031940	8.800541	0.113629	33
34	34.752118	306.837437	0.003259	0.028775	8.829316	0.113259	34
35	38.574851	341.589555	0.002927	0.025924	8.855240	0.112927	35
36	42.818085	380.164406	0.002630	0.023355	8.878594	0.112630	36
37	47.528074	422.982490	0.002364	0.021040	8.899635	0.112364	37
38	52.756162	470.510564	0.002125	0.018955	8.918590	0.112125	38
39	58.559340	523.266726	0.001911	0.017077	8.935666	0.111911	39
40	65.000867	581.826066	0.001719	0.015384	8.951051	0.111719	40
41	72.150963	646.826934	0.001546	0.013860	8.964911	0.111546	41
42	80.087569	718.977896	0.001391	0.012486	8.977397	0.111391	42
43	88.897201	799.065465	0.001251	0.011249	8.988646	0.111251	43
44	98.675893	887.962666	0.001126	0.010134	8.998780	0.111126	44
45	109.530242	986.638559	0.001014	0.009130	9.007910	0.111014	45
46	121.578568	1096.168801	0.000912	0.008225	9.016135	0.110912	46
47	134.952211	1217.747369	0.000821	0.007410	9.023545	0.110821	47
48	149.796954	1352.699580	0.000739	0.006676	9.030221	0.110739	48
49	166.274619	1502.496533	0.000666	0.006014	9.036235	0.110666	49
50	184.564827	1668.771152	0.000599	0.005418	9.041653	0.110599	50

ANNUAL COMPOUND INTEREST TABLES

12.00% ANNUAL INTEREST RATE

YEARS	1 FUTURE VALUE OF $1	2 FUTURE VALUE ANNUITY OF $1 PER YEAR	3 SINKING FUND FACTOR	4 PRESENT VALUE OF $1 (REVERSION)	5 PRESENT VALUE ANNUITY OF $1 PER YEAR	6 PAYMENT TO AMORTIZE $1	YEARS
1	1.120000	1.000000	1.000000	0.892857	0.892857	1.120000	1
2	1.254400	2.120000	0.471698	0.797194	1.690051	0.591698	2
3	1.404928	3.374400	0.296349	0.711780	2.401831	0.416349	3
4	1.573519	4.779328	0.209234	0.635518	3.037349	0.329234	4
5	1.762342	6.352847	0.157410	0.567427	3.604776	0.277410	5
6	1.973823	8.115189	0.123226	0.506631	4.111407	0.243226	6
7	2.210681	10.089012	0.099118	0.452349	4.563757	0.219118	7
8	2.475963	12.299693	0.081303	0.403883	4.967640	0.201303	8
9	2.773079	14.775656	0.067679	0.360610	5.328250	0.187679	9
10	3.105848	17.548735	0.056984	0.321973	5.650223	0.176984	10
11	3.478550	20.654583	0.048415	0.287476	5.937699	0.168415	11
12	3.895976	24.133133	0.041437	0.256675	6.194374	0.161437	12
13	4.363493	28.029109	0.035677	0.229174	6.423548	0.155677	13
14	4.887112	32.392602	0.030871	0.204620	6.628168	0.150871	14
15	5.473566	37.279715	0.026824	0.182696	6.810864	0.146824	15
16	6.130394	42.753280	0.023390	0.163122	6.973986	0.143390	16
17	6.866041	48.883674	0.020457	0.145644	7.119630	0.140457	17
18	7.689966	55.749715	0.017937	0.130040	7.249670	0.137937	18
19	8.612762	63.439681	0.015763	0.116107	7.365777	0.135763	19
20	9.646293	72.052442	0.013879	0.103667	7.469444	0.133879	20
21	10.803848	81.698736	0.012240	0.092560	7.562003	0.132240	21
22	12.100310	92.502584	0.010811	0.082643	7.644646	0.130811	22
23	13.552347	104.602894	0.009560	0.073788	7.718434	0.129560	23
24	15.178629	118.155241	0.008463	0.065882	7.784316	0.128463	24
25	17.000064	133.333870	0.007500	0.058823	7.843139	0.127500	25
26	19.040072	150.333934	0.006652	0.052521	7.895660	0.126652	26
27	21.324881	169.374007	0.005904	0.046894	7.942554	0.125904	27
28	23.883866	190.698887	0.005244	0.041869	7.984423	0.125244	28
29	26.749930	214.582754	0.004660	0.037383	8.021806	0.124660	29
30	29.959922	241.332684	0.004144	0.033378	8.055184	0.124144	30
31	33.555113	271.292606	0.003686	0.029802	8.084986	0.123686	31
32	37.581726	304.847719	0.003280	0.026609	8.111594	0.123280	32
33	42.091533	342.429446	0.002920	0.023758	8.135352	0.122920	33
34	47.142517	384.520979	0.002601	0.021212	8.156564	0.122601	34
35	52.799620	431.663496	0.002317	0.018940	8.175504	0.122317	35
36	59.135574	484.463116	0.002064	0.016910	8.192414	0.122064	36
37	66.231843	543.598690	0.001840	0.015098	8.207513	0.121840	37
38	74.179664	609.830533	0.001640	0.013481	8.220993	0.121640	38
39	83.081224	684.010197	0.001462	0.012036	8.233030	0.121462	39
40	93.050970	767.091420	0.001304	0.010747	8.243777	0.121304	40
41	104.217087	860.142391	0.001163	0.009595	8.253372	0.121163	41
42	116.723137	964.359478	0.001037	0.008567	8.261939	0.121037	42
43	130.729914	1081.082615	0.000925	0.007649	8.269589	0.120925	43
44	146.417503	1211.812529	0.000825	0.006830	8.276418	0.120825	44
45	163.987604	1358.230032	0.000736	0.006098	8.282516	0.120736	45
46	183.666116	1522.217636	0.000657	0.005445	8.287961	0.120657	46
47	205.706050	1705.883752	0.000586	0.004861	8.292822	0.120586	47
48	230.390776	1911.589803	0.000523	0.004340	8.297163	0.120523	48
49	258.037669	2141.980579	0.000467	0.003875	8.301038	0.120467	49
50	289.002190	2400.018249	0.000417	0.003460	8.304498	0.120417	50

ANNUAL COMPOUND INTEREST TABLES

13.00% ANNUAL INTEREST RATE

	1 FUTURE VALUE OF $1	2 FUTURE VALUE ANNUITY OF $1 PER YEAR	3 SINKING FUND FACTOR	4 PRESENT VALUE OF $1 (REVERSION)	5 PRESENT VALUE ANNUITY OF $1 PER YEAR	6 PAYMENT TO AMORTIZE $1	
YEARS							YEARS
1	1.130000	1.000000	1.000000	0.884956	0.884956	1.130000	1
2	1.276900	2.130000	0.469484	0.783147	1.668102	0.599484	2
3	1.442897	3.406900	0.293522	0.693050	2.361153	0.423522	3
4	1.630474	4.849797	0.206194	0.613319	2.974471	0.336194	4
5	1.842435	6.480271	0.154315	0.542760	3.517231	0.284315	5
6	2.081952	8.322706	0.120153	0.480319	3.997550	0.250153	6
7	2.352605	10.404658	0.096111	0.425061	4.422610	0.226111	7
8	2.658444	12.757263	0.078387	0.376160	4.798770	0.208387	8
9	3.004042	15.415707	0.064869	0.332885	5.131655	0.194869	9
10	3.394567	18.419749	0.054290	0.294588	5.426243	0.184290	10
11	3.835861	21.814317	0.045841	0.260698	5.686941	0.175841	11
12	4.334523	25.650178	0.038986	0.230706	5.917647	0.168986	12
13	4.898011	29.984701	0.033350	0.204165	6.121812	0.163350	13
14	5.534753	34.882712	0.028667	0.180677	6.302488	0.158667	14
15	6.254270	40.417464	0.024742	0.159891	6.462379	0.154742	15
16	7.067326	46.671735	0.021426	0.141496	6.603875	0.151426	16
17	7.986078	53.739060	0.018608	0.125218	6.729093	0.148608	17
18	9.024268	61.725138	0.016201	0.110812	6.839905	0.146201	18
19	10.197423	70.749406	0.014134	0.098064	6.937969	0.144134	19
20	11.523088	80.946829	0.012354	0.086782	7.024752	0.142354	20
21	13.021089	92.469917	0.010814	0.076798	7.101550	0.140814	21
22	14.713831	105.491006	0.009479	0.067963	7.169513	0.139479	22
23	16.626629	120.204837	0.008319	0.060144	7.229658	0.138319	23
24	18.788091	136.831465	0.007308	0.053225	7.282883	0.137308	24
25	21.230542	155.619556	0.006426	0.047102	7.329985	0.136426	25
26	23.990513	176.850098	0.005655	0.041683	7.371668	0.135655	26
27	27.109279	200.840611	0.004979	0.036888	7.408556	0.134979	27
28	30.633486	227.949890	0.004387	0.032644	7.441200	0.134387	28
29	34.615839	258.583376	0.003867	0.028889	7.470088	0.133867	29
30	39.115898	293.199215	0.003411	0.025565	7.495653	0.133411	30
31	44.200965	332.315113	0.003009	0.022624	7.518277	0.133009	31
32	49.947090	376.516078	0.002656	0.020021	7.538299	0.132656	32
33	56.440212	426.463168	0.002345	0.017718	7.556016	0.132345	33
34	63.777439	482.903380	0.002071	0.015680	7.571696	0.132071	34
35	72.068506	546.680819	0.001829	0.013876	7.585572	0.131829	35
36	81.437412	618.749325	0.001616	0.012279	7.597851	0.131616	36
37	92.024276	700.186738	0.001428	0.010867	7.608718	0.131428	37
38	103.987432	792.211014	0.001262	0.009617	7.618334	0.131262	38
39	117.505798	896.198445	0.001116	0.008510	7.626844	0.131116	39
40	132.781552	1013.704243	0.000986	0.007531	7.634376	0.130986	40
41	150.043153	1146.485795	0.000872	0.006665	7.641040	0.130872	41
42	169.548763	1296.528948	0.000771	0.005898	7.646938	0.130771	42
43	191.590103	1466.077712	0.000682	0.005219	7.652158	0.130682	43
44	216.496816	1657.667814	0.000603	0.004619	7.656777	0.130603	44
45	244.641402	1874.164630	0.000534	0.004088	7.660864	0.130534	45
46	276.444784	2118.806032	0.000472	0.003617	7.664482	0.130472	46
47	312.382606	2395.250816	0.000417	0.003201	7.667683	0.130417	47
48	352.992345	2707.633422	0.000369	0.002833	7.670516	0.130369	48
49	398.881350	3060.625767	0.000327	0.002507	7.673023	0.130327	49
50	450.735925	3459.507117	0.000289	0.002219	7.675242	0.130289	50

ANNUAL COMPOUND INTEREST TABLES

14.00% ANNUAL INTEREST RATE

	1 FUTURE VALUE OF $1	2 FUTURE VALUE ANNUITY OF $1 PER YEAR	3 SINKING FUND FACTOR	4 PRESENT VALUE OF $1 (REVERSION)	5 PRESENT VALUE ANNUITY OF $1 PER YEAR	6 PAYMENT TO AMORTIZE $1	
YEARS							YEARS
1	1.140000	1.000000	1.000000	0.877193	0.877193	1.140000	1
2	1.299600	2.140000	0.467290	0.769468	1.646661	0.607290	2
3	1.481544	3.439600	0.290731	0.674972	2.321632	0.430731	3
4	1.688960	4.921144	0.203205	0.592080	2.913712	0.343205	4
5	1.925415	6.610104	0.151284	0.519369	3.433081	0.291284	5
6	2.194973	8.535519	0.117157	0.455587	3.888668	0.257157	6
7	2.502269	10.730491	0.093192	0.399637	4.288305	0.233192	7
8	2.852586	13.232760	0.075570	0.350559	4.638864	0.215570	8
9	3.251949	16.085347	0.062168	0.307508	4.946372	0.202168	9
10	3.707221	19.337295	0.051714	0.269744	5.216116	0.191714	10
11	4.226232	23.044516	0.043394	0.236617	5.452733	0.183394	11
12	4.817905	27.270749	0.036669	0.207559	5.660292	0.176669	12
13	5.492411	32.088654	0.031164	0.182069	5.842362	0.171164	13
14	6.261349	37.581065	0.026609	0.159710	6.002072	0.166609	14
15	7.137938	43.842414	0.022809	0.140096	6.142168	0.162809	15
16	8.137249	50.980352	0.019615	0.122892	6.265060	0.159615	16
17	9.276464	59.117601	0.016915	0.107800	6.372859	0.156915	17
18	10.575169	68.394066	0.014621	0.094561	6.467420	0.154621	18
19	12.055693	78.969235	0.012663	0.082948	6.550369	0.152663	19
20	13.743490	91.024928	0.010986	0.072762	6.623131	0.150986	20
21	15.667578	104.768418	0.009545	0.063826	6.686957	0.149545	21
22	17.861039	120.435996	0.008303	0.055988	6.742944	0.148303	22
23	20.361585	138.297035	0.007231	0.049112	6.792056	0.147231	23
24	23.212207	158.658620	0.006303	0.043081	6.835137	0.146303	24
25	26.461916	181.870827	0.005498	0.037790	6.872927	0.145498	25
26	30.166584	208.332743	0.004800	0.033149	6.906077	0.144800	26
27	34.389906	238.499327	0.004193	0.029078	6.935155	0.144193	27
28	39.204493	272.889233	0.003664	0.025507	6.960662	0.143664	28
29	44.693122	312.093725	0.003204	0.022375	6.983037	0.143204	29
30	50.950159	356.786847	0.002803	0.019627	7.002664	0.142803	30
31	58.083181	407.737006	0.002453	0.017217	7.019881	0.142453	31
32	66.214826	465.820186	0.002147	0.015102	7.034983	0.142147	32
33	75.484902	532.035012	0.001880	0.013248	7.048231	0.141880	33
34	86.052788	607.519914	0.001646	0.011621	7.059852	0.141646	34
35	98.100178	693.572702	0.001442	0.010194	7.070045	0.141442	35
36	111.834203	791.672881	0.001263	0.008942	7.078987	0.141263	36
37	127.490992	903.507084	0.001107	0.007844	7.086831	0.141107	37
38	145.339731	1030.998076	0.000970	0.006880	7.093711	0.140970	38
39	165.687293	1176.337806	0.000850	0.006035	7.099747	0.140850	39
40	188.883514	1342.025099	0.000745	0.005294	7.105041	0.140745	40
41	215.327206	1530.908613	0.000653	0.004644	7.109685	0.140653	41
42	245.473015	1746.235819	0.000573	0.004074	7.113759	0.140573	42
43	279.839237	1991.708833	0.000502	0.003573	7.117332	0.140502	43
44	319.016730	2271.548070	0.000440	0.003135	7.120467	0.140440	44
45	363.679072	2590.564800	0.000386	0.002750	7.123217	0.140386	45
46	414.594142	2954.243872	0.000338	0.002412	7.125629	0.140338	46
47	472.637322	3368.838014	0.000297	0.002116	7.127744	0.140297	47
48	538.806547	3841.475336	0.000260	0.001856	7.129600	0.140260	48
49	614.239464	4380.281883	0.000228	0.001628	7.131228	0.140228	49
50	700.232988	4994.521346	0.000200	0.001428	7.132656	0.140200	50

ANNUAL COMPOUND INTEREST TABLES

15.00% ANNUAL INTEREST RATE

YEARS	1 FUTURE VALUE OF $1	2 FUTURE VALUE ANNUITY OF $1 PER YEAR	3 SINKING FUND FACTOR	4 PRESENT VALUE OF $1 (REVERSION)	5 PRESENT VALUE ANNUITY OF $1 PER YEAR	6 PAYMENT TO AMORTIZE $1	YEARS
1	1.150000	1.000000	1.000000	0.869565	0.869565	1.150000	1
2	1.322500	2.150000	0.465116	0.756144	1.625709	0.615116	2
3	1.520875	3.472500	0.287977	0.657516	2.283225	0.437977	3
4	1.749006	4.993375	0.200265	0.571753	2.854978	0.350265	4
5	2.011357	6.742381	0.148316	0.497177	3.352155	0.298316	5
6	2.313061	8.753738	0.114237	0.432328	3.784483	0.264237	6
7	2.660020	11.066799	0.090360	0.375937	4.160420	0.240360	7
8	3.059023	13.726819	0.072850	0.326902	4.487322	0.222850	8
9	3.517876	16.785842	0.059574	0.284262	4.771584	0.209574	9
10	4.045558	20.303718	0.049252	0.247185	5.018769	0.199252	10
11	4.652391	24.349276	0.041069	0.214943	5.233712	0.191069	11
12	5.350250	29.001667	0.034481	0.186907	5.420619	0.184481	12
13	6.152788	34.351917	0.029110	0.162528	5.583147	0.179110	13
14	7.075706	40.504705	0.024688	0.141329	5.724476	0.174688	14
15	8.137062	47.580411	0.021017	0.122894	5.847370	0.171017	15
16	9.357621	55.717472	0.017948	0.106865	5.954235	0.167948	16
17	10.761264	65.075093	0.015367	0.092926	6.047161	0.165367	17
18	12.375454	75.836357	0.013186	0.080805	6.127966	0.163186	18
19	14.231772	88.211811	0.011336	0.070265	6.198231	0.161336	19
20	16.366537	102.443583	0.009761	0.061100	6.259331	0.159761	20
21	18.821518	118.810120	0.008417	0.053131	6.312462	0.158417	21
22	21.644746	137.631638	0.007266	0.046201	6.358663	0.157266	22
23	24.891458	159.276384	0.006278	0.040174	6.398837	0.156278	23
24	28.625176	184.167841	0.005430	0.034934	6.433771	0.155430	24
25	32.918953	212.793017	0.004699	0.030378	6.464149	0.154699	25
26	37.856796	245.711970	0.004070	0.026415	6.490564	0.154070	26
27	43.535315	283.568766	0.003526	0.022970	6.513534	0.153526	27
28	50.065612	327.104080	0.003057	0.019974	6.533508	0.153057	28
29	57.575454	377.169693	0.002651	0.017369	6.550877	0.152651	29
30	66.211772	434.745146	0.002300	0.015103	6.565980	0.152300	30
31	76.143538	500.956918	0.001996	0.013133	6.579113	0.151996	31
32	87.565068	577.100456	0.001733	0.011420	6.590533	0.151733	32
33	100.699829	664.665524	0.001505	0.009931	6.600463	0.151505	33
34	115.804803	765.365353	0.001307	0.008635	6.609099	0.151307	34
35	133.175523	881.170156	0.001135	0.007509	6.616607	0.151135	35
36	153.151852	1014.345680	0.000986	0.006529	6.623137	0.150986	36
37	176.124630	1167.497532	0.000857	0.005678	6.628815	0.150857	37
38	202.543324	1343.622161	0.000744	0.004937	6.633752	0.150744	38
39	232.924823	1546.165485	0.000647	0.004293	6.638045	0.150647	39
40	267.863546	1779.090308	0.000562	0.003733	6.641778	0.150562	40
41	308.043078	2046.953854	0.000489	0.003246	6.645025	0.150489	41
42	354.249540	2354.996933	0.000425	0.002823	6.647848	0.150425	42
43	407.386971	2709.246473	0.000369	0.002455	6.650302	0.150369	43
44	468.495017	3116.633443	0.000321	0.002134	6.652437	0.150321	44
45	538.769269	3585.128460	0.000279	0.001856	6.654293	0.150279	45
46	619.584659	4123.897729	0.000242	0.001614	6.655907	0.150242	46
47	712.522358	4743.482388	0.000211	0.001403	6.657310	0.150211	47
48	819.400712	5456.004746	0.000183	0.001220	6.658531	0.150183	48
49	942.310819	6275.405458	0.000159	0.001061	6.659592	0.150159	49
50	1083.657442	7217.716277	0.000139	0.000923	6.660515	0.150139	50

ANNUAL COMPOUND INTEREST TABLES

16.00% ANNUAL INTEREST RATE

YEARS	1 FUTURE VALUE OF $1	2 FUTURE VALUE ANNUITY OF $1 PER YEAR	3 SINKING FUND FACTOR	4 PRESENT VALUE OF $1 (REVERSION)	5 PRESENT VALUE ANNUITY OF $1 PER YEAR	6 PAYMENT TO AMORTIZE $1	YEARS
1	1.160000	1.000000	1.000000	0.862069	0.862069	1.160000	1
2	1.345600	2.160000	0.462963	0.743163	1.605232	0.622963	2
3	1.560896	3.505600	0.285258	0.640658	2.245890	0.445258	3
4	1.810639	5.066496	0.197375	0.552291	2.798181	0.357375	4
5	2.100342	6.877135	0.145409	0.476113	3.274294	0.305409	5
6	2.436396	8.977477	0.111390	0.410442	3.684736	0.271390	6
7	2.826220	11.413873	0.087613	0.353840	4.038565	0.247613	7
8	3.278415	14.240093	0.070224	0.305025	4.343591	0.230224	8
9	3.802961	17.518508	0.057082	0.262953	4.606544	0.217082	9
10	4.411435	21.321469	0.046901	0.226684	4.833227	0.206901	10
11	5.117265	25.732904	0.038861	0.195417	5.028644	0.198861	11
12	5.936027	30.850169	0.032415	0.168463	5.197107	0.192415	12
13	6.885791	36.786196	0.027184	0.145227	5.342334	0.187184	13
14	7.987518	43.671987	0.022898	0.125195	5.467529	0.182898	14
15	9.265521	51.659505	0.019358	0.107927	5.575456	0.179358	15
16	10.748004	60.925026	0.016414	0.093041	5.668497	0.176414	16
17	12.467685	71.673030	0.013952	0.080207	5.748704	0.173952	17
18	14.462514	84.140715	0.011885	0.069144	5.817848	0.171885	18
19	16.776517	98.603230	0.010142	0.059607	5.877455	0.170142	19
20	19.460759	115.379747	0.008667	0.051385	5.928841	0.168667	20
21	22.574481	134.840506	0.007416	0.044298	5.973139	0.167416	21
22	26.186398	157.414987	0.006353	0.038188	6.011326	0.166353	22
23	30.376222	183.601385	0.005447	0.032920	6.044247	0.165447	23
24	35.236417	213.977607	0.004673	0.028380	6.072627	0.164673	24
25	40.874244	249.214024	0.004013	0.024465	6.097092	0.164013	25
26	47.414123	290.088267	0.003447	0.021091	6.118183	0.163447	26
27	55.000382	337.502390	0.002963	0.018182	6.136364	0.162963	27
28	63.800444	392.502773	0.002548	0.015674	6.152038	0.162548	28
29	74.008515	456.303216	0.002192	0.013512	6.165550	0.162192	29
30	85.849877	530.311731	0.001886	0.011648	6.177198	0.161886	30
31	99.585857	616.161608	0.001623	0.010042	6.187240	0.161623	31
32	115.519594	715.747465	0.001397	0.008657	6.195897	0.161397	32
33	134.002729	831.267059	0.001203	0.007463	6.203359	0.161203	33
34	155.443166	965.269789	0.001036	0.006433	6.209792	0.161036	34
35	180.314073	1120.712955	0.000892	0.005546	6.215338	0.160892	35
36	209.164324	1301.027028	0.000769	0.004781	6.220119	0.160769	36
37	242.630616	1510.191352	0.000662	0.004121	6.224241	0.160662	37
38	281.451515	1752.821968	0.000571	0.003553	6.227794	0.160571	38
39	326.483757	2034.273483	0.000492	0.003063	6.230857	0.160492	39
40	378.721158	2360.757241	0.000424	0.002640	6.233497	0.160424	40
41	439.316544	2739.478399	0.000365	0.002276	6.235773	0.160365	41
42	509.607191	3178.794943	0.000315	0.001962	6.237736	0.160315	42
43	591.144341	3688.402134	0.000271	0.001692	6.239427	0.160271	43
44	685.727436	4279.546475	0.000234	0.001458	6.240886	0.160234	44
45	795.443826	4965.273911	0.000201	0.001257	6.242143	0.160201	45
46	922.714838	5760.717737	0.000174	0.001084	6.243227	0.160174	46
47	1070.349212	6683.432575	0.000150	0.000934	6.244161	0.160150	47
48	1241.605086	7753.781787	0.000129	0.000805	6.244966	0.160129	48
49	1440.261900	8995.386873	0.000111	0.000694	6.245661	0.160111	49
50	1670.703804	10435.648773	0.000096	0.000599	6.246259	0.160096	50

ANNUAL COMPOUND INTEREST TABLES

17.00% ANNUAL INTEREST RATE

	1 FUTURE VALUE OF $1	2 FUTURE VALUE ANNUITY OF $1 PER YEAR	3 SINKING FUND FACTOR	4 PRESENT VALUE OF $1 (REVERSION)	5 PRESENT VALUE ANNUITY OF $1 PER YEAR	6 PAYMENT TO AMORTIZE $1	
YEARS							YEARS
1	1.170000	1.000000	1.000000	0.854701	0.854701	1.170000	1
2	1.368900	2.170000	0.460829	0.730514	1.585214	0.630829	2
3	1.601613	3.538900	0.282574	0.624371	2.209585	0.452574	3
4	1.873887	5.140513	0.194533	0.533650	2.743235	0.364533	4
5	2.192448	7.014400	0.142564	0.456111	3.199346	0.312564	5
6	2.565164	9.206848	0.108615	0.389839	3.589185	0.278615	6
7	3.001242	11.772012	0.084947	0.333195	3.922380	0.254947	7
8	3.511453	14.773255	0.067690	0.284782	4.207163	0.237690	8
9	4.108400	18.284708	0.054691	0.243404	4.450566	0.224691	9
10	4.806828	22.393108	0.044657	0.208037	4.658604	0.214657	10
11	5.623989	27.199937	0.036765	0.177810	4.836413	0.206765	11
12	6.580067	32.823926	0.030466	0.151974	4.988387	0.200466	12
13	7.698679	39.403993	0.025378	0.129892	5.118280	0.195378	13
14	9.007454	47.102672	0.021230	0.111019	5.229299	0.191230	14
15	10.538721	56.110126	0.017822	0.094888	5.324187	0.187822	15
16	12.330304	66.648848	0.015004	0.081101	5.405288	0.185004	16
17	14.426456	78.979152	0.012662	0.069317	5.474605	0.182662	17
18	16.878953	93.405608	0.010706	0.059245	5.533851	0.180706	18
19	19.748375	110.284561	0.009067	0.050637	5.584488	0.179067	19
20	23.105599	130.032936	0.007690	0.043280	5.627767	0.177690	20
21	27.033551	153.138535	0.006530	0.036991	5.664758	0.176530	21
22	31.629255	180.172086	0.005550	0.031616	5.696375	0.175550	22
23	37.006228	211.801341	0.004721	0.027022	5.723397	0.174721	23
24	43.297287	248.807569	0.004019	0.023096	5.746493	0.174019	24
25	50.657826	292.104856	0.003423	0.019740	5.766234	0.173423	25
26	59.269656	342.762681	0.002917	0.016872	5.783106	0.172917	26
27	69.345497	402.032337	0.002487	0.014421	5.797526	0.172487	27
28	81.134232	471.377835	0.002121	0.012325	5.809851	0.172121	28
29	94.927051	552.512066	0.001810	0.010534	5.820386	0.171810	29
30	111.064650	647.439118	0.001545	0.009004	5.829390	0.171545	30
31	129.945641	758.503768	0.001318	0.007696	5.837085	0.171318	31
32	152.036399	888.449408	0.001126	0.006577	5.843663	0.171126	32
33	177.882587	1040.485808	0.000961	0.005622	5.849284	0.170961	33
34	208.122627	1218.368395	0.000821	0.004805	5.854089	0.170821	34
35	243.503474	1426.491022	0.000701	0.004107	5.858196	0.170701	35
36	284.899064	1669.994496	0.000599	0.003510	5.861706	0.170599	36
37	333.331905	1954.893560	0.000512	0.003000	5.864706	0.170512	37
38	389.998329	2288.225465	0.000437	0.002564	5.867270	0.170437	38
39	456.298045	2678.223794	0.000373	0.002192	5.869461	0.170373	39
40	533.868713	3134.521839	0.000319	0.001873	5.871335	0.170319	40
41	624.626394	3668.390552	0.000273	0.001601	5.872936	0.170273	41
42	730.812881	4293.016946	0.000233	0.001368	5.874304	0.170233	42
43	855.051071	5023.829827	0.000199	0.001170	5.875473	0.170199	43
44	1000.409753	5878.880897	0.000170	0.001000	5.876473	0.170170	44
45	1170.479411	6879.290650	0.000145	0.000854	5.877327	0.170145	45
46	1369.460910	8049.770061	0.000124	0.000730	5.878058	0.170124	46
47	1602.269265	9419.230971	0.000106	0.000624	5.878682	0.170106	47
48	1874.655040	11021.500236	0.000091	0.000533	5.879215	0.170091	48
49	2193.346397	12896.155276	0.000078	0.000456	5.879671	0.170078	49
50	2566.215284	15089.501673	0.000066	0.000390	5.880061	0.170066	50

ANNUAL COMPOUND INTEREST TABLES

18.00% ANNUAL INTEREST RATE

	1 FUTURE VALUE OF $1	2 FUTURE VALUE ANNUITY OF $1 PER YEAR	3 SINKING FUND FACTOR	4 PRESENT VALUE OF $1 (REVERSION)	5 PRESENT VALUE ANNUITY OF $1 PER YEAR	6 PAYMENT TO AMORTIZE $1	
YEARS							YEARS
1	1.180000	1.000000	1.000000	0.847458	0.847458	1.180000	1
2	1.392400	2.180000	0.458716	0.718184	1.565642	0.638716	2
3	1.643032	3.572400	0.279924	0.608631	2.174273	0.459924	3
4	1.938778	5.215432	0.191739	0.515789	2.690062	0.371739	4
5	2.287758	7.154210	0.139778	0.437109	3.127171	0.319778	5
6	2.699554	9.441968	0.105910	0.370432	3.497603	0.285910	6
7	3.185474	12.141522	0.082362	0.313925	3.811528	0.262362	7
8	3.758859	15.326996	0.065244	0.266038	4.077566	0.245244	8
9	4.435454	19.085855	0.052395	0.225456	4.303022	0.232395	9
10	5.233836	23.521309	0.042515	0.191064	4.494086	0.222515	10
11	6.175926	28.755144	0.034776	0.161919	4.656005	0.214776	11
12	7.287593	34.931070	0.028628	0.137220	4.793225	0.208628	12
13	8.599359	42.218663	0.023686	0.116288	4.909513	0.203686	13
14	10.147244	50.818022	0.019678	0.098549	5.008062	0.199678	14
15	11.973748	60.965266	0.016403	0.083516	5.091578	0.196403	15
16	14.129023	72.939014	0.013710	0.070776	5.162354	0.193710	16
17	16.672247	87.068036	0.011485	0.059980	5.222334	0.191485	17
18	19.673251	103.740283	0.009639	0.050830	5.273164	0.189639	18
19	23.214436	123.413534	0.008103	0.043077	5.316241	0.188103	19
20	27.393035	146.627970	0.006820	0.036506	5.352746	0.186820	20
21	32.323781	174.021005	0.005746	0.030937	5.383683	0.185746	21
22	38.142061	206.344785	0.004846	0.026218	5.409901	0.184846	22
23	45.007632	244.486847	0.004090	0.022218	5.432120	0.184090	23
24	53.109006	289.494479	0.003454	0.018829	5.450949	0.183454	24
25	62.668627	342.603486	0.002919	0.015957	5.466906	0.182919	25
26	73.948980	405.272113	0.002467	0.013523	5.480429	0.182467	26
27	87.259797	479.221093	0.002087	0.011460	5.491889	0.182087	27
28	102.966560	566.480890	0.001765	0.009712	5.501601	0.181765	28
29	121.500541	669.447450	0.001494	0.008230	5.509831	0.181494	29
30	143.370638	790.947991	0.001264	0.006975	5.516806	0.181264	30
31	169.177353	934.318630	0.001070	0.005911	5.522717	0.181070	31
32	199.629277	1103.495983	0.000906	0.005009	5.527726	0.180906	32
33	235.562547	1303.125260	0.000767	0.004245	5.531971	0.180767	33
34	277.963805	1538.687807	0.000650	0.003598	5.535569	0.180650	34
35	327.997290	1816.651612	0.000550	0.003049	5.538618	0.180550	35
36	387.036802	2144.648902	0.000466	0.002584	5.541201	0.180466	36
37	456.703427	2531.685705	0.000395	0.002190	5.543391	0.180395	37
38	538.910044	2988.389132	0.000335	0.001856	5.545247	0.180335	38
39	635.913852	3527.299175	0.000284	0.001573	5.546819	0.180284	39
40	750.378345	4163.213027	0.000240	0.001333	5.548152	0.180240	40
41	885.446447	4913.591372	0.000204	0.001129	5.549281	0.180204	41
42	1044.826807	5799.037819	0.000172	0.000957	5.550238	0.180172	42
43	1232.895633	6843.864626	0.000146	0.000811	5.551049	0.180146	43
44	1454.816847	8076.760259	0.000124	0.000687	5.551737	0.180124	44
45	1716.683879	9531.577105	0.000105	0.000583	5.552319	0.180105	45
46	2025.686977	11248.260984	0.000089	0.000494	5.552813	0.180089	46
47	2390.310633	13273.947961	0.000075	0.000418	5.553231	0.180075	47
48	2820.566547	15664.258594	0.000064	0.000355	5.553586	0.180064	48
49	3328.268525	18484.825141	0.000054	0.000300	5.553886	0.180054	49
50	3927.356860	21813.093666	0.000046	0.000255	5.554141	0.180046	50

ANNUAL COMPOUND INTEREST TABLES

19.00% ANNUAL INTEREST RATE

	1 FUTURE VALUE OF $1	2 FUTURE VALUE ANNUITY OF $1 PER YEAR	3 SINKING FUND FACTOR	4 PRESENT VALUE OF $1 (REVERSION)	5 PRESENT VALUE ANNUITY OF $1 PER YEAR	6 PAYMENT TO AMORTIZE $1	
YEARS							YEARS
1	1.190000	1.000000	1.000000	0.840336	0.840336	1.190000	1
2	1.416100	2.190000	0.456621	0.706165	1.546501	0.646621	2
3	1.685159	3.606100	0.277308	0.593416	2.139917	0.467308	3
4	2.005339	5.291259	0.188991	0.498669	2.638586	0.378991	4
5	2.386354	7.296598	0.137050	0.419049	3.057635	0.327050	5
6	2.839761	9.682952	0.103274	0.352142	3.409777	0.293274	6
7	3.379315	12.522713	0.079855	0.295918	3.705695	0.269855	7
8	4.021385	15.902028	0.062885	0.248671	3.954366	0.252885	8
9	4.785449	19.923413	0.050192	0.208967	4.163332	0.240192	9
10	5.694684	24.708862	0.040471	0.175602	4.338935	0.230471	10
11	6.776674	30.403546	0.032891	0.147565	4.486500	0.222891	11
12	8.064242	37.180220	0.026896	0.124004	4.610504	0.216896	12
13	9.596448	45.244461	0.022102	0.104205	4.714709	0.212102	13
14	11.419773	54.840909	0.018235	0.087567	4.802277	0.208235	14
15	13.589530	66.260682	0.015092	0.073586	4.875863	0.205092	15
16	16.171540	79.850211	0.012523	0.061837	4.937700	0.202523	16
17	19.244133	96.021751	0.010414	0.051964	4.989664	0.200414	17
18	22.900518	115.265884	0.008676	0.043667	5.033331	0.198676	18
19	27.251616	138.166402	0.007238	0.036695	5.070026	0.197238	19
20	32.429423	165.418018	0.006045	0.030836	5.100862	0.196045	20
21	38.591014	197.847442	0.005054	0.025913	5.126775	0.195054	21
22	45.923307	236.438456	0.004229	0.021775	5.148550	0.194229	22
23	54.648735	282.361762	0.003542	0.018299	5.166849	0.193542	23
24	65.031994	337.010497	0.002967	0.015377	5.182226	0.192967	24
25	77.388073	402.042491	0.002487	0.012922	5.195148	0.192487	25
26	92.091807	479.430565	0.002086	0.010859	5.206007	0.192086	26
27	109.589251	571.522372	0.001750	0.009125	5.215132	0.191750	27
28	130.411208	681.111623	0.001468	0.007668	5.222800	0.191468	28
29	155.189338	811.522831	0.001232	0.006444	5.229243	0.191232	29
30	184.675312	966.712169	0.001034	0.005415	5.234658	0.191034	30
31	219.763621	1151.387481	0.000869	0.004550	5.239209	0.190869	31
32	261.518710	1371.151103	0.000729	0.003824	5.243033	0.190729	32
33	311.207264	1632.669812	0.000612	0.003213	5.246246	0.190612	33
34	370.336645	1943.877077	0.000514	0.002700	5.248946	0.190514	34
35	440.700607	2314.213721	0.000432	0.002269	5.251215	0.190432	35
36	524.433722	2754.914328	0.000363	0.001907	5.253122	0.190363	36
37	624.076130	3279.348051	0.000305	0.001602	5.254724	0.190305	37
38	742.650594	3903.424180	0.000256	0.001347	5.256071	0.190256	38
39	883.754207	4646.074775	0.000215	0.001132	5.257202	0.190215	39
40	1051.667507	5529.828982	0.000181	0.000951	5.258153	0.190181	40
41	1251.484333	6581.496488	0.000152	0.000799	5.258952	0.190152	41
42	1489.266356	7832.980821	0.000128	0.000671	5.259624	0.190128	42
43	1772.226964	9322.247177	0.000107	0.000564	5.260188	0.190107	43
44	2108.950087	11094.474141	0.000090	0.000474	5.260662	0.190090	44
45	2509.650603	13203.424228	0.000076	0.000398	5.261061	0.190076	45
46	2986.484218	15713.074831	0.000064	0.000335	5.261396	0.190064	46
47	3553.916219	18699.559049	0.000053	0.000281	5.261677	0.190053	47
48	4229.160301	22253.475268	0.000045	0.000236	5.261913	0.190045	48
49	5032.700758	26482.635569	0.000038	0.000199	5.262112	0.190038	49
50	5988.913902	31515.336327	0.000032	0.000167	5.262279	0.190032	50

Monthly Compound
Interest Tables

MONTHLY COMPOUND INTEREST TABLES

6.00% ANNUAL INTEREST RATE   0.5000% MONTHLY EFFECTIVE INTEREST RATE

	1	2 FUTURE VALUE ANNUITY OF $1 MONTH	3	4	5 PRESENT VALUE ANNUITY OF $1 MONTH	6	
	FUTURE VALUE OF $1		SINKING FUND FACTOR	PRESENT VALUE OF $1 (REVERSION)		PAYMENT TO AMORTIZE $1	
MONTHS							MONTHS
1	1.005000	1.000000	1.000000	0.995025	0.995025	1.005000	1
2	1.010025	2.005000	0.498753	0.990075	1.985099	0.503753	2
3	1.015075	3.015025	0.331672	0.985149	2.970248	0.336672	3
4	1.020151	4.030100	0.248133	0.980248	3.950496	0.253133	4
5	1.025251	5.050251	0.198010	0.975371	4.925866	0.203010	5
6	1.030378	6.075502	0.164595	0.970518	5.896384	0.169595	6
7	1.035529	7.105879	0.140729	0.965690	6.862074	0.145729	7
8	1.040707	8.141409	0.122829	0.960885	7.822959	0.127829	8
9	1.045911	9.182116	0.108907	0.956105	8.779064	0.113907	9
10	1.051140	10.228026	0.097771	0.951348	9.730412	0.102771	10
11	1.056396	11.279167	0.088659	0.946615	10.677027	0.093659	11
12	1.061678	12.335562	0.081066	0.941905	11.618932	0.086066	12
YEARS							MONTHS
1	1.061678	12.335562	0.081066	0.941905	11.618932	0.086066	12
2	1.127160	25.431955	0.039321	0.887186	22.562866	0.044321	24
3	1.196681	39.336105	0.025422	0.835645	32.871016	0.030422	36
4	1.270489	54.097832	0.018485	0.787098	42.580318	0.023485	48
5	1.348850	69.770031	0.014333	0.741372	51.725561	0.019333	60
6	1.432044	86.408856	0.011573	0.698302	60.339514	0.016573	72
7	1.520370	104.073927	0.009609	0.657735	68.453042	0.014609	84
8	1.614143	122.828542	0.008141	0.619524	76.095218	0.013141	96
9	1.713699	142.739900	0.007006	0.583533	83.293424	0.012006	108
10	1.819397	163.879347	0.006102	0.549633	90.073453	0.011102	120
11	1.931613	186.322629	0.005367	0.517702	96.459599	0.010367	132
12	2.050751	210.150163	0.004759	0.487626	102.474743	0.009759	144
13	2.177237	235.447328	0.004247	0.459298	108.140440	0.009247	156
14	2.311524	262.304766	0.003812	0.432615	113.476990	0.008812	168
15	2.454094	290.818712	0.003439	0.407482	118.503515	0.008439	180
16	2.605457	321.091337	0.003114	0.383810	123.238025	0.008114	192
17	2.766156	353.231110	0.002831	0.361513	127.697486	0.007831	204
18	2.936766	387.353194	0.002582	0.340511	131.897876	0.007582	216
19	3.117899	423.579854	0.002361	0.320729	135.854246	0.007361	228
20	3.310204	462.040895	0.002164	0.302096	139.580772	0.007164	240
21	3.514371	502.874129	0.001989	0.284546	143.090806	0.006989	252
22	3.731129	546.225867	0.001831	0.268015	146.396927	0.006831	264
23	3.961257	592.251446	0.001688	0.252445	149.510979	0.006688	276
24	4.205759	641.115782	0.001560	0.237779	152.444121	0.006560	288
25	4.464970	692.993962	0.001443	0.223966	155.206864	0.006443	300
26	4.740359	748.071876	0.001337	0.210954	157.809106	0.006337	312
27	5.032734	806.546875	0.001240	0.198699	160.260172	0.006240	324
28	5.343142	868.628484	0.001151	0.187156	162.568844	0.006151	336
29	5.672696	934.539150	0.001070	0.176283	164.743394	0.006070	348
30	6.022575	1004.515042	0.000996	0.166042	166.791614	0.005996	360
31	6.394034	1078.806895	0.000927	0.156396	168.720844	0.005927	372
32	6.788405	1157.680906	0.000864	0.147310	170.537996	0.005864	384
33	7.207098	1241.419693	0.000806	0.138752	172.249581	0.005806	396
34	7.651617	1330.323306	0.000752	0.130691	173.861732	0.005752	408
35	8.123551	1424.710299	0.000702	0.123099	175.380226	0.005702	420
36	8.624594	1524.918875	0.000656	0.115947	176.810504	0.005656	432
37	9.156540	1631.308097	0.000613	0.109212	178.157690	0.005613	444
38	9.721296	1744.259173	0.000573	0.102867	179.426611	0.005573	456
39	10.320884	1864.176824	0.000536	0.096891	180.621815	0.005536	468
40	10.957454	1991.490734	0.000502	0.091262	181.747584	0.005502	480

MONTHLY COMPOUND INTEREST TABLES

8.00% ANNUAL INTEREST RATE   0.6667% MONTHLY EFFECTIVE INTEREST RATE

	1 FUTURE VALUE OF $1	2 FUTURE VALUE ANNUITY OF $1 PER MONTH	3 SINKING FUND FACTOR	4 PRESENT VALUE OF $1 (REVERSION)	5 PRESENT VALUE ANNUITY OF $1 PER MONTH	6 PAYMENT TO AMORTIZE $1	
MONTHS							**MONTHS**
1	1.006667	1.000000	1.000000	0.993377	0.993377	1.006667	1
2	1.013378	2.006667	0.498339	0.986799	1.980176	0.505006	2
3	1.020134	3.020044	0.331121	0.980264	2.960440	0.337788	3
4	1.026935	4.040178	0.247514	0.973772	3.934212	0.254181	4
5	1.033781	5.067113	0.197351	0.967323	4.901535	0.204018	5
6	1.040673	6.100893	0.163910	0.960917	5.862452	0.170577	6
7	1.047610	7.141566	0.140025	0.954553	6.817005	0.146692	7
8	1.054595	8.189176	0.122112	0.948232	7.765237	0.128779	8
9	1.061625	9.243771	0.108181	0.941952	8.707189	0.114848	9
10	1.068703	10.305396	0.097037	0.935714	9.642903	0.103703	10
11	1.075827	11.374099	0.087919	0.929517	10.572420	0.094586	11
12	1.083000	12.449926	0.080322	0.923361	11.495782	0.086988	12
YEARS							**MONTHS**
1	1.083000	12.449926	0.080322	0.923361	11.495782	0.086988	12
2	1.172888	25.933190	0.038561	0.852596	22.110544	0.045227	24
3	1.270237	40.535558	0.024670	0.787255	31.911806	0.031336	36
4	1.375666	56.349915	0.017746	0.726921	40.961913	0.024413	48
5	1.489846	73.476856	0.013610	0.671210	49.318433	0.020276	60
6	1.613502	92.025325	0.010867	0.619770	57.034522	0.017533	72
7	1.747422	112.113308	0.008920	0.572272	64.159261	0.015586	84
8	1.892457	133.868583	0.007470	0.528414	70.737970	0.014137	96
9	2.049530	157.429535	0.006352	0.487917	76.812497	0.013019	108
10	2.219640	182.946035	0.005466	0.450523	82.421481	0.012133	120
11	2.403869	210.580392	0.004749	0.415996	87.600600	0.011415	132
12	2.603389	240.508387	0.004158	0.384115	92.382800	0.010825	144
13	2.819469	272.920390	0.003664	0.354677	96.798498	0.010331	156
14	3.053484	308.022574	0.003247	0.327495	100.875784	0.009913	168
15	3.306921	346.038222	0.002890	0.302396	104.640592	0.009557	180
16	3.581394	387.209149	0.002583	0.279221	108.116871	0.009249	192
17	3.878648	431.797244	0.002316	0.257822	111.326733	0.008983	204
18	4.200574	480.086128	0.002083	0.238063	114.290596	0.008750	216
19	4.549220	532.382966	0.001878	0.219818	117.027313	0.008545	228
20	4.926803	589.020416	0.001698	0.202971	119.554292	0.008364	240
21	5.335725	650.358746	0.001538	0.187416	121.887606	0.008204	252
22	5.778588	716.788127	0.001395	0.173053	124.042099	0.008062	264
23	6.258207	788.731114	0.001268	0.159790	126.031475	0.007935	276
24	6.777636	866.645333	0.001154	0.147544	127.868388	0.007821	288
25	7.340176	951.026395	0.001051	0.136237	129.564523	0.007718	300
26	7.949407	1042.411042	0.000959	0.125796	131.130668	0.007626	312
27	8.609204	1141.380571	0.000876	0.116155	132.576786	0.007543	324
28	9.323763	1248.564521	0.000801	0.107253	133.912076	0.007468	336
29	10.097631	1364.644687	0.000733	0.099033	135.145031	0.007399	348
30	10.935730	1490.359449	0.000671	0.091443	136.283494	0.007338	360
31	11.843390	1626.508474	0.000615	0.084435	137.334707	0.007281	372
32	12.826385	1773.957801	0.000564	0.077964	138.305357	0.007230	384
33	13.890969	1933.645350	0.000517	0.071989	139.201617	0.007184	396
34	15.043913	2106.586886	0.000475	0.066472	140.029190	0.007141	408
35	16.292550	2293.882485	0.000436	0.061378	140.793338	0.007103	420
36	17.644824	2496.723526	0.000401	0.056674	141.498923	0.007067	432
37	19.109335	2716.400273	0.000368	0.052330	142.150433	0.007035	444
38	20.695401	2954.310082	0.000338	0.048320	142.752013	0.007005	456
39	22.413109	3211.966288	0.000311	0.044617	143.307488	0.006978	468
40	24.273386	3491.007831	0.000286	0.041197	143.820392	0.006953	480

MONTHLY COMPOUND INTEREST TABLES

9.00% ANNUAL INTEREST RATE

0.7500% MONTHLY EFFECTIVE INTEREST RATE

	1 FUTURE VALUE OF $1	2 FUTURE VALUE ANNUITY OF $1 PER MONTH	3 SINKING FUND FACTOR	4 PRESENT VALUE OF $1 (REVERSION)	5 PRESENT VALUE ANNUITY OF $1 PER MONTH	6 PAYMENT TO AMORTIZE $1	
MONTHS							**MONTHS**
1	1.007500	1.000000	1.000000	0.992556	0.992556	1.007500	1
2	1.015056	2.007500	0.498132	0.985167	1.977723	0.505632	2
3	1.022669	3.022556	0.330846	0.977833	2.955556	0.338346	3
4	1.030339	4.045225	0.247205	0.970554	3.926110	0.254705	4
5	1.038067	5.075565	0.197022	0.963329	4.889440	0.204522	5
6	1.045852	6.113631	0.163569	0.956158	5.845598	0.171069	6
7	1.053696	7.159484	0.139675	0.949040	6.794638	0.147175	7
8	1.061599	8.213180	0.121756	0.941975	7.736613	0.129256	8
9	1.069561	9.274779	0.107819	0.934963	8.671576	0.115319	9
10	1.077583	10.344339	0.096671	0.928003	9.599580	0.104171	10
11	1.085664	11.421922	0.087551	0.921095	10.520675	0.095051	11
12	1.093807	12.507586	0.079951	0.914238	11.434913	0.087451	12
YEARS							**MONTHS**
1	1.093807	12.507586	0.079951	0.914238	11.434913	0.087451	12
2	1.196414	26.188471	0.038185	0.835831	21.889146	0.045685	24
3	1.308645	41.152716	0.024300	0.764149	31.446805	0.031800	36
4	1.431405	57.520711	0.017385	0.698614	40.184782	0.024885	48
5	1.565681	75.424137	0.013258	0.638700	48.173374	0.020758	60
6	1.712553	95.007028	0.010526	0.583924	55.476849	0.018026	72
7	1.873202	116.426928	0.008589	0.533845	62.153965	0.016089	84
8	2.048921	139.856164	0.007150	0.488062	68.258439	0.014650	96
9	2.241124	165.483223	0.006043	0.446205	73.839382	0.013543	108
10	2.451357	193.514277	0.005168	0.407937	78.941693	0.012668	120
11	2.681311	224.174837	0.004461	0.372952	83.606420	0.011961	132
12	2.932837	257.711570	0.003880	0.340967	87.871092	0.011380	144
13	3.207957	294.394279	0.003397	0.311725	91.770018	0.010897	156
14	3.508886	334.518079	0.002989	0.284991	95.334564	0.010489	168
15	3.838043	378.405769	0.002643	0.260549	98.593409	0.010143	180
16	4.198078	426.410427	0.002345	0.238204	101.572769	0.009845	192
17	4.591887	478.918252	0.002088	0.217775	104.296613	0.009588	204
18	5.022638	536.351674	0.001864	0.199099	106.786856	0.009364	216
19	5.493796	599.172747	0.001669	0.182024	109.063531	0.009169	228
20	6.009152	667.886870	0.001497	0.166413	111.144954	0.008997	240
21	6.572851	743.046852	0.001346	0.152141	113.047870	0.008846	252
22	7.189430	825.257358	0.001212	0.139093	114.787589	0.008712	264
23	7.863848	915.179777	0.001093	0.127164	116.378106	0.008593	276
24	8.601532	1013.537539	0.000987	0.116258	117.832218	0.008487	288
25	9.408415	1121.121937	0.000892	0.106288	119.161622	0.008392	300
26	10.290989	1238.798495	0.000807	0.097172	120.377014	0.008307	312
27	11.256354	1367.513924	0.000731	0.088839	121.488172	0.008231	324
28	12.312278	1508.303750	0.000663	0.081220	122.504035	0.008163	336
29	13.467255	1662.300631	0.000602	0.074254	123.432776	0.008102	348
30	14.730576	1830.743483	0.000546	0.067886	124.281866	0.008046	360
31	16.112406	2014.987436	0.000496	0.062064	125.058136	0.007996	372
32	17.623861	2216.514743	0.000451	0.056741	125.767832	0.007951	384
33	19.277100	2436.946701	0.000410	0.051875	126.416664	0.007910	396
34	21.085425	2678.056697	0.000373	0.047426	127.009850	0.007873	408
35	23.063384	2941.784474	0.000340	0.043359	127.552164	0.007840	420
36	25.226888	3230.251735	0.000310	0.039640	128.047967	0.007810	432
37	27.593344	3545.779215	0.000282	0.036241	128.501250	0.007782	444
38	30.181790	3890.905350	0.000257	0.033133	128.915659	0.007757	456
39	33.013050	4268.406696	0.000234	0.030291	129.294526	0.007734	468
40	36.109902	4681.320273	0.000214	0.027693	129.640902	0.007714	480

MONTHLY COMPOUND INTEREST TABLES

10.00% ANNUAL INTEREST RATE   0.8333% MONTHLY EFFECTIVE INTEREST RATE

	1 FUTURE VALUE OF $1	2 FUTURE VALUE ANNUITY OF $1 PER MONTH	3 SINKING FUND FACTOR	4 PRESENT VALUE OF $1 (REVERSION)	5 PRESENT VALUE ANNUITY OF $1 PER MONTH	6 PAYMENT TO AMORTIZE $1	
MONTHS							**MONTHS**
1	1.008333	1.000000	1.000000	0.991736	0.991736	1.008333	1
2	1.016736	2.008333	0.497925	0.983539	1.975275	0.506259	2
3	1.025209	3.025069	0.330571	0.975411	2.950686	0.338904	3
4	1.033752	4.050278	0.246897	0.967350	3.918036	0.255230	4
5	1.042367	5.084031	0.196694	0.959355	4.877391	0.205028	5
6	1.051053	6.126398	0.163228	0.951427	5.828817	0.171561	6
7	1.059812	7.177451	0.139325	0.943563	6.772381	0.147659	7
8	1.068644	8.237263	0.121400	0.935765	7.708146	0.129733	8
9	1.077549	9.305907	0.107459	0.928032	8.636178	0.115792	9
10	1.086529	10.383456	0.096307	0.920362	9.556540	0.104640	10
11	1.095583	11.469985	0.087184	0.912756	10.469296	0.095517	11
12	1.104713	12.565568	0.079583	0.905212	11.374508	0.087916	12
YEARS							**MONTHS**
1	1.104713	12.565568	0.079583	0.905212	11.374508	0.087916	12
2	1.220391	26.446915	0.037812	0.819410	21.670855	0.046145	24
3	1.348182	41.781821	0.023934	0.741740	30.991236	0.032267	36
4	1.489354	58.722492	0.017029	0.671432	39.428160	0.025363	48
5	1.645309	77.437072	0.012914	0.607789	47.065369	0.021247	60
6	1.817594	98.111314	0.010193	0.550178	53.978665	0.018526	72
7	2.007920	120.950418	0.008268	0.498028	60.236667	0.016601	84
8	2.218176	146.181076	0.006841	0.450821	65.901488	0.015174	96
9	2.450448	174.053713	0.005745	0.408089	71.029355	0.014079	108
10	2.707041	204.844979	0.004882	0.369407	75.671163	0.013215	120
11	2.990504	238.860493	0.004187	0.334392	79.872986	0.012520	132
12	3.303649	276.437876	0.003617	0.302696	83.676528	0.011951	144
13	3.649584	317.950102	0.003145	0.274004	87.119542	0.011478	156
14	4.031743	363.809201	0.002749	0.248032	90.236201	0.011082	168
15	4.453920	414.470346	0.002413	0.224521	93.057439	0.010746	180
16	4.920303	470.436376	0.002126	0.203240	95.611259	0.010459	192
17	5.435523	532.262780	0.001879	0.183975	97.923008	0.010212	204
18	6.004693	600.563216	0.001665	0.166536	100.015633	0.009998	216
19	6.633463	676.015601	0.001479	0.150751	101.909902	0.009813	228
20	7.328074	759.368836	0.001317	0.136462	103.624619	0.009650	240
21	8.095419	851.450244	0.001174	0.123527	105.176801	0.009508	252
22	8.943115	953.173779	0.001049	0.111818	106.581856	0.009382	264
23	9.879576	1065.549097	0.000938	0.101219	107.853730	0.009272	276
24	10.914097	1189.691580	0.000841	0.091625	109.005045	0.009174	288
25	12.056945	1326.833403	0.000754	0.082940	110.047230	0.009087	300
26	13.319465	1478.335767	0.000676	0.075078	110.990629	0.009010	312
27	14.714187	1645.702407	0.000608	0.067962	111.844605	0.008941	324
28	16.254954	1830.594523	0.000546	0.061520	112.617635	0.008880	336
29	17.957060	2034.847258	0.000491	0.055688	113.317392	0.008825	348
30	19.837399	2260.487925	0.000442	0.050410	113.950820	0.008776	360
31	21.914634	2509.756117	0.000398	0.045632	114.524207	0.008732	372
32	24.209383	2785.125947	0.000359	0.041306	115.043244	0.008692	384
33	26.744422	3089.330596	0.000324	0.037391	115.513083	0.008657	396
34	29.544912	3425.389447	0.000292	0.033847	115.938387	0.008625	408
35	32.638650	3796.638052	0.000263	0.030639	116.323377	0.008597	420
36	36.056344	4206.761236	0.000238	0.027734	116.671876	0.008571	432
37	39.831914	4659.829677	0.000215	0.025105	116.987340	0.008548	444
38	44.002836	5160.340305	0.000194	0.022726	117.272903	0.008527	456
39	48.610508	5713.260935	0.000175	0.020572	117.531398	0.008508	468
40	53.700663	6324.079581	0.000158	0.018622	117.765391	0.008491	480

MONTHLY COMPOUND INTEREST TABLES

11.00% ANNUAL INTEREST RATE   0.9167% MONTHLY EFFECTIVE INTEREST RATE

	1 FUTURE VALUE OF $1	2 FUTURE VALUE ANNUITY OF $1 PER MONTH	3 SINKING FUND FACTOR	4 PRESENT VALUE OF $1 (REVERSION)	5 PRESENT VALUE ANNUITY OF $1 PER MONTH	6 PAYMENT TO AMORTIZE $1	
MONTHS							**MONTHS**
1	1.009167	1.000000	1.000000	0.990917	0.990917	1.009167	1
2	1.018417	2.009167	0.497719	0.981916	1.972832	0.506885	2
3	1.027753	3.027584	0.330296	0.972997	2.945829	0.339463	3
4	1.037174	4.055337	0.246589	0.964158	3.909987	0.255755	4
5	1.046681	5.092511	0.196367	0.955401	4.865388	0.205533	5
6	1.056276	6.139192	0.162888	0.946722	5.812110	0.172055	6
7	1.065958	7.195468	0.138976	0.938123	6.750233	0.148143	7
8	1.075730	8.261427	0.121044	0.929602	7.679835	0.130211	8
9	1.085591	9.337156	0.107099	0.921158	8.600992	0.116266	9
10	1.095542	10.422747	0.095944	0.912790	9.513783	0.105111	10
11	1.105584	11.518289	0.086818	0.904499	10.418282	0.095985	11
12	1.115719	12.623873	0.079215	0.896283	11.314565	0.088382	12
YEARS							**MONTHS**
1	1.115719	12.623873	0.079215	0.896283	11.314565	0.088382	12
2	1.244829	26.708566	0.037441	0.803323	21.455619	0.046608	24
3	1.388879	42.423123	0.023572	0.720005	30.544874	0.032739	36
4	1.549598	59.956151	0.016679	0.645329	38.691421	0.025846	48
5	1.728916	79.518080	0.012576	0.578397	45.993034	0.021742	60
6	1.928984	101.343692	0.009867	0.518408	52.537346	0.019034	72
7	2.152204	125.694940	0.007956	0.464640	58.402903	0.017122	84
8	2.401254	152.864085	0.006542	0.416449	63.660103	0.015708	96
9	2.679124	183.177212	0.005459	0.373256	68.372043	0.014626	108
10	2.989150	216.998139	0.004608	0.334543	72.595275	0.013775	120
11	3.335051	254.732784	0.003926	0.299846	76.380487	0.013092	132
12	3.720979	296.834038	0.003369	0.268747	79.773109	0.012536	144
13	4.151566	343.807200	0.002909	0.240873	82.813859	0.012075	156
14	4.631980	396.216042	0.002524	0.215890	85.539231	0.011691	168
15	5.167988	454.689575	0.002199	0.193499	87.981937	0.011366	180
16	5.766021	519.929596	0.001923	0.173430	90.171293	0.011090	192
17	6.433259	592.719117	0.001687	0.155442	92.133576	0.010854	204
18	7.177708	673.931757	0.001484	0.139320	93.892337	0.010650	216
19	8.008304	764.542228	0.001308	0.124870	95.468685	0.010475	228
20	8.935015	865.638038	0.001155	0.111919	96.881539	0.010322	240
21	9.968965	978.432537	0.001022	0.100311	98.147856	0.010189	252
22	11.122562	1104.279485	0.000906	0.089907	99.282835	0.010072	264
23	12.409652	1244.689295	0.000803	0.080582	100.300098	0.009970	276
24	13.845682	1401.347165	0.000714	0.072225	101.211853	0.009880	288
25	15.447889	1576.133301	0.000634	0.064734	102.029044	0.009801	300
26	17.235500	1771.145485	0.000565	0.058020	102.761478	0.009731	312
27	19.229972	1988.724252	0.000503	0.052002	103.417947	0.009670	324
28	21.455242	2231.480981	0.000448	0.046609	104.006328	0.009615	336
29	23.938018	2502.329236	0.000400	0.041775	104.533685	0.009566	348
30	26.708098	2804.519736	0.000357	0.037442	105.006346	0.009523	360
31	29.798728	3141.679369	0.000318	0.033558	105.429984	0.009485	372
32	33.247002	3517.854723	0.000284	0.030078	105.809684	0.009451	384
33	37.094306	3937.560650	0.000254	0.026958	106.150002	0.009421	396
34	41.386816	4405.834459	0.000227	0.024162	106.455024	0.009394	408
35	46.176050	4928.296368	0.000203	0.021656	106.728409	0.009370	420
36	51.519489	5511.216962	0.000181	0.019410	106.973440	0.009348	432
37	57.481264	6161.592447	0.000162	0.017397	107.193057	0.009329	444
38	64.132929	6887.228628	0.000145	0.015593	107.389897	0.009312	456
39	71.554317	7696.834582	0.000130	0.013975	107.566320	0.009297	468
40	79.834499	8600.127195	0.000116	0.012526	107.724446	0.009283	480

MONTHLY COMPOUND INTEREST TABLES

12.00% ANNUAL INTEREST RATE   1.0000% MONTHLY EFFECTIVE INTEREST RATE

	1 FUTURE VALUE OF $1	2 FUTURE VALUE ANNUITY OF $1 PER MONTH	3 SINKING FUND FACTOR	4 PRESENT VALUE OF $1 (REVERSION)	5 PRESENT VALUE ANNUITY OF $1 PER MONTH	6 PAYMENT TO AMORTIZE $1	
MONTHS							**MONTHS**
1	1.010000	1.000000	1.000000	0.990099	0.990099	1.010000	1
2	1.020100	2.010000	0.497512	0.980296	1.970395	0.507512	2
3	1.030301	3.030100	0.330022	0.970590	2.940985	0.340022	3
4	1.040604	4.060401	0.246281	0.960980	3.901966	0.256281	4
5	1.051010	5.101005	0.196040	0.951466	4.853431	0.206040	5
6	1.061520	6.152015	0.162548	0.942045	5.795476	0.172548	6
7	1.072135	7.213535	0.138628	0.932718	6.728195	0.148628	7
8	1.082857	8.285671	0.120690	0.923483	7.651678	0.130690	8
9	1.093685	9.368527	0.106740	0.914340	8.566018	0.116740	9
10	1.104622	10.462213	0.095582	0.905287	9.471305	0.105582	10
11	1.115668	11.566835	0.086454	0.896324	10.367628	0.096454	11
12	1.126825	12.682503	0.078849	0.887449	11.255077	0.088849	12
YEARS							**MONTHS**
1	1.126825	12.682503	0.078849	0.887449	11.255077	0.088849	12
2	1.269735	26.973465	0.037073	0.787566	21.243387	0.047073	24
3	1.430769	43.076878	0.023214	0.698925	30.107505	0.033214	36
4	1.612226	61.222608	0.016334	0.620260	37.973959	0.026334	48
5	1.816697	81.669670	0.012244	0.550450	44.955038	0.022244	60
6	2.047099	104.709931	0.009550	0.488496	51.150391	0.019550	72
7	2.306723	130.672274	0.007653	0.433515	56.648453	0.017653	84
8	2.599273	159.927293	0.006253	0.384723	61.527703	0.016253	96
9	2.928926	192.892579	0.005184	0.341422	65.857790	0.015184	108
10	3.300387	230.038689	0.004347	0.302995	69.700522	0.014347	120
11	3.718959	271.895856	0.003678	0.268892	73.110752	0.013678	132
12	4.190616	319.061559	0.003134	0.238628	76.137157	0.013134	144
13	4.722091	372.209054	0.002687	0.211771	78.822939	0.012687	156
14	5.320970	432.096982	0.002314	0.187936	81.206434	0.012314	168
15	5.995802	499.580198	0.002002	0.166783	83.321664	0.012002	180
16	6.756220	575.621974	0.001737	0.148012	85.198824	0.011737	192
17	7.613078	661.307751	0.001512	0.131353	86.864707	0.011512	204
18	8.578606	757.860630	0.001320	0.116569	88.343095	0.011320	216
19	9.666588	866.658830	0.001154	0.103449	89.655089	0.011154	228
20	10.892554	989.255365	0.001011	0.091806	90.819416	0.011011	240
21	12.274002	1127.400210	0.000887	0.081473	91.852698	0.010887	252
22	13.830653	1283.065279	0.000779	0.072303	92.769683	0.010779	264
23	15.584726	1458.472574	0.000686	0.064165	93.583461	0.010686	276
24	17.561259	1656.125905	0.000604	0.056944	94.305647	0.010604	288
25	19.788466	1878.846626	0.000532	0.050534	94.946551	0.010532	300
26	22.298139	2129.813909	0.000470	0.044847	95.515321	0.010470	312
27	25.126101	2412.610125	0.000414	0.039799	96.020075	0.010414	324
28	28.312720	2731.271980	0.000366	0.035320	96.468019	0.010366	336
29	31.903481	3090.348134	0.000324	0.031345	96.865546	0.010324	348
30	35.949641	3494.964133	0.000286	0.027817	97.218331	0.010286	360
31	40.508956	3950.895567	0.000253	0.024686	97.531410	0.010253	372
32	45.646505	4464.650520	0.000224	0.021907	97.809252	0.010224	384
33	51.435625	5043.562459	0.000198	0.019442	98.055822	0.010198	396
34	57.958949	5695.894923	0.000176	0.017254	98.274641	0.010176	408
35	65.309595	6430.959471	0.000155	0.015312	98.468831	0.010155	420
36	73.592486	7259.248603	0.000138	0.013588	98.641166	0.010138	432
37	82.925855	8192.585529	0.000122	0.012059	98.794103	0.010122	444
38	93.442929	9244.292939	0.000108	0.010702	98.929828	0.010108	456
39	105.293832	10429.383172	0.000096	0.009497	99.050277	0.010096	468
40	118.647725	11764.772510	0.000085	0.008428	99.157169	0.010085	480

MONTHLY COMPOUND INTEREST TABLES

13.00% ANNUAL INTEREST RATE   1.0833% MONTHLY EFFECTIVE INTEREST RATE

	1 FUTURE VALUE OF $1	2 FUTURE VALUE ANNUITY OF $1 PER MONTH	3 SINKING FUND FACTOR	4 PRESENT VALUE OF $1 (REVERSION)	5 PRESENT VALUE ANNUITY OF $1 PER MONTH	6 PAYMENT TO AMORTIZE $1	
MONTHS							**MONTHS**
1	1.010833	1.000000	1.000000	0.989283	0.989283	1.010833	1
2	1.021784	2.010833	0.497306	0.978680	1.967963	0.508140	2
3	1.032853	3.032617	0.329748	0.968192	2.936155	0.340581	3
4	1.044043	4.065471	0.245974	0.957815	3.893970	0.256807	4
5	1.055353	5.109513	0.195713	0.947550	4.841520	0.206547	5
6	1.066786	6.164866	0.162210	0.937395	5.778915	0.173043	6
7	1.078343	7.231652	0.138281	0.927349	6.706264	0.149114	7
8	1.090025	8.309995	0.120337	0.917410	7.623674	0.131170	8
9	1.101834	9.400020	0.106383	0.907578	8.531253	0.117216	9
10	1.113770	10.501854	0.095221	0.897851	9.429104	0.106055	10
11	1.125836	11.615624	0.086091	0.888229	10.317333	0.096924	11
12	1.138032	12.741460	0.078484	0.878710	11.196042	0.089317	12
YEARS							**MONTHS**
1	1.138032	12.741460	0.078484	0.878710	11.196042	0.089317	12
2	1.295118	27.241655	0.036708	0.772130	21.034112	0.047542	24
3	1.473886	43.743348	0.022861	0.678478	29.678917	0.033694	36
4	1.677330	62.522811	0.015994	0.596185	37.275190	0.026827	48
5	1.908857	83.894449	0.011920	0.523874	43.950107	0.022753	60
6	2.172341	108.216068	0.009241	0.460333	49.815421	0.020074	72
7	2.472194	135.894861	0.007359	0.404499	54.969328	0.018192	84
8	2.813437	167.394225	0.005974	0.355437	59.498115	0.016807	96
9	3.201783	203.241525	0.004920	0.312326	63.477604	0.015754	108
10	3.643733	244.036917	0.004098	0.274444	66.974419	0.014931	120
11	4.146687	290.463399	0.003443	0.241156	70.047103	0.014276	132
12	4.719064	343.298242	0.002913	0.211906	72.747100	0.013746	144
13	5.370448	403.426010	0.002479	0.186204	75.119613	0.013312	156
14	6.111745	471.853363	0.002119	0.163619	77.204363	0.012953	168
15	6.955364	549.725914	0.001819	0.143774	79.036253	0.012652	180
16	7.915430	638.347406	0.001567	0.126336	80.645952	0.012400	192
17	9.008017	739.201542	0.001353	0.111012	82.060410	0.012186	204
18	10.251416	853.976825	0.001171	0.097548	83.303307	0.012004	216
19	11.666444	984.594826	0.001016	0.085716	84.395453	0.011849	228
20	13.276792	1133.242353	0.000882	0.075319	85.355132	0.011716	240
21	15.109421	1302.408067	0.000768	0.066184	86.198412	0.011601	252
22	17.195012	1494.924144	0.000669	0.058156	86.939409	0.011502	264
23	19.568482	1714.013694	0.000583	0.051103	87.590531	0.011417	276
24	22.269568	1963.344717	0.000509	0.044904	88.162677	0.011343	288
25	25.343491	2247.091520	0.000445	0.039458	88.665428	0.011278	300
26	28.841716	2570.004599	0.000389	0.034672	89.107200	0.011222	312
27	32.822810	2937.490172	0.000340	0.030467	89.495389	0.011174	324
28	37.353424	3355.700690	0.000298	0.026771	89.836495	0.011131	336
29	42.509410	3831.637843	0.000261	0.023524	90.136227	0.011094	348
30	48.377089	4373.269783	0.000229	0.020671	90.399605	0.011062	360
31	55.054699	4989.664524	0.000200	0.018164	90.631038	0.011034	372
32	62.654036	5691.141761	0.000176	0.015961	90.834400	0.011009	384
33	71.302328	6489.445641	0.000154	0.014025	91.013097	0.010987	396
34	81.144365	7397.941387	0.000135	0.012324	91.170119	0.010969	408
35	92.344923	8431.839055	0.000119	0.010829	91.308095	0.010952	420
36	105.091522	9608.448184	0.000104	0.009516	91.429337	0.010937	432
37	119.597566	10947.467591	0.000091	0.008361	91.535873	0.010925	444
38	136.105914	12471.315170	0.000080	0.007347	91.629487	0.010914	456
39	154.892951	14205.503212	0.000070	0.006456	91.711747	0.010904	468
40	176.273210	16179.065533	0.000062	0.005673	91.784030	0.010895	480

MONTHLY COMPOUND INTEREST TABLES

14.00% ANNUAL INTEREST RATE　　　　　　　　　　　　1.1667% MONTHLY EFFECTIVE INTEREST RATE

	1 FUTURE VALUE OF $1	2 FUTURE VALUE ANNUITY OF $1 PER MONTH	3 SINKING FUND FACTOR	4 PRESENT VALUE OF $1 (REVERSION)	5 PRESENT VALUE ANNUITY OF $1 PER MONTH	6 PAYMENT TO AMORTIZE $1	
MONTHS							
1	1.011667	1.000000	1.000000	0.988468	0.988468	1.011667	**MONTHS**
2	1.023469	2.011667	0.497100	0.977069	1.965537	0.508767	1
3	1.035410	3.035136	0.329475	0.965801	2.931338	0.341141	2
4	1.047490	4.070546	0.245667	0.954663	3.886001	0.257334	3
5	1.059710	5.118036	0.195387	0.943654	4.829655	0.207054	4
							5
6	1.072074	6.177746	0.161871	0.932772	5.762427	0.173538	
7	1.084581	7.249820	0.137934	0.922015	6.684442	0.149601	6
8	1.097235	8.334401	0.119985	0.911382	7.595824	0.131651	7
9	1.110036	9.431636	0.106026	0.900872	8.496696	0.117693	8
10	1.122986	10.541672	0.094862	0.890483	9.387178	0.106528	9
							10
11	1.136088	11.664658	0.085729	0.880214	10.267392	0.097396	11
12	1.149342	12.800745	0.078120	0.870063	11.137455	0.089787	12
YEARS							
1	1.149342	12.800745	0.078120	0.870063	11.137455	0.089787	**MONTHS**
2	1.320987	27.513180	0.036346	0.757010	20.827743	0.048013	12
3	1.518266	44.422800	0.022511	0.658646	29.258904	0.034178	24
4	1.745007	63.857736	0.015660	0.573064	36.594546	0.027326	36
5	2.005610	86.195125	0.011602	0.498601	42.977016	0.023268	48
							60
6	2.305132	111.868425	0.008939	0.433815	48.530168	0.020606	
7	2.649385	141.375828	0.007073	0.377446	53.361760	0.018740	72
8	3.045049	175.289927	0.005705	0.328402	57.565549	0.017372	84
9	3.499803	214.268826	0.004667	0.285730	61.223111	0.016334	96
10	4.022471	259.068912	0.003860	0.248603	64.405420	0.015527	108
							120
11	4.623195	310.559534	0.003220	0.216301	67.174230	0.014887	
12	5.313632	369.739871	0.002705	0.188195	69.583269	0.014371	132
13	6.107180	437.758319	0.002284	0.163742	71.679284	0.013951	144
14	7.019239	515.934780	0.001938	0.142466	73.502950	0.013605	156
15	8.067507	605.786272	0.001651	0.123954	75.089654	0.013317	168
							180
16	9.272324	709.056369	0.001410	0.107848	76.470187	0.013077	
17	10.657072	827.749031	0.001208	0.093834	77.671337	0.012875	192
18	12.248621	964.167496	0.001037	0.081642	78.716413	0.012704	204
19	14.077855	1120.958972	0.000892	0.071034	79.625696	0.012559	216
20	16.180270	1301.166005	0.000769	0.061804	80.416829	0.012435	228
							240
21	18.596664	1508.285522	0.000663	0.053773	81.105164	0.012330	
22	21.373928	1746.336688	0.000573	0.046786	81.704060	0.012239	252
23	24.565954	2019.938898	0.000495	0.040707	82.225136	0.012162	264
24	28.234683	2334.401417	0.000428	0.035417	82.678506	0.012095	276
25	32.451308	2695.826407	0.000371	0.030815	83.072966	0.012038	288
							300
26	37.297652	3111.227338	0.000321	0.026811	83.416171	0.011988	
27	42.867759	3588.665088	0.000279	0.023328	83.714781	0.011945	312
28	49.269718	4137.404359	0.000242	0.020296	83.974591	0.011908	324
29	56.627757	4768.093467	0.000210	0.017659	84.200641	0.011876	336
30	65.084661	5492.970967	0.000182	0.015365	84.397320	0.011849	348
							360
31	74.804537	6326.103143	0.000158	0.013368	84.568442	0.011825	
32	85.975998	7283.656968	0.000137	0.011631	84.717330	0.011804	372
33	98.815828	8384.213825	0.000119	0.010120	84.846871	0.011786	384
34	113.573184	9649.130077	0.000104	0.008805	84.959580	0.011770	396
35	130.534434	11102.951488	0.000090	0.007661	85.057645	0.011757	408
							420
36	150.028711	12773.889538	0.000078	0.006665	85.142966	0.011745	
37	172.434303	14694.368868	0.000068	0.005799	85.217202	0.011735	432
38	198.185992	16901.656478	0.000059	0.005046	85.281792	0.011726	444
39	227.783490	19438.584899	0.000051	0.004390	85.337989	0.011718	456
40	261.801139	22354.383358	0.000045	0.003820	85.386883	0.011711	468
							480

MONTHLY COMPOUND INTEREST TABLES

15.00% ANNUAL INTEREST RATE   1.2500% MONTHLY EFFECTIVE INTEREST RATE

	1 FUTURE VALUE OF $1	2 FUTURE VALUE ANNUITY OF $1 PER MONTH	3 SINKING FUND FACTOR	4 PRESENT VALUE OF $1 (REVERSION)	5 PRESENT VALUE ANNUITY OF $1 PER MONTH	6 PAYMENT TO AMORTIZE $1	
MONTHS							**MONTHS**
1	1.012500	1.000000	1.000000	0.987654	0.987654	1.012500	1
2	1.025156	2.012500	0.496894	0.975461	1.963115	0.509394	2
3	1.037971	3.037656	0.329201	0.963418	2.926534	0.341701	3
4	1.050945	4.075627	0.245361	0.951524	3.878058	0.257861	4
5	1.064082	5.126572	0.195062	0.939777	4.817835	0.207562	5
6	1.077383	6.190654	0.161534	0.928175	5.746010	0.174034	6
7	1.090850	7.268038	0.137589	0.916716	6.662726	0.150089	7
8	1.104486	8.358888	0.119633	0.905398	7.568124	0.132133	8
9	1.118292	9.463374	0.105671	0.894221	8.462345	0.118171	9
10	1.132271	10.581666	0.094503	0.883181	9.345526	0.107003	10
11	1.146424	11.713937	0.085368	0.872277	10.217803	0.097868	11
12	1.160755	12.860361	0.077758	0.861509	11.079312	0.090258	12
YEARS							**MONTHS**
1	1.160755	12.860361	0.077758	0.861509	11.079312	0.090258	12
2	1.347351	27.788084	0.035987	0.742197	20.624235	0.048487	24
3	1.563944	45.115505	0.022165	0.639409	28.847267	0.034665	36
4	1.815355	65.228388	0.015331	0.550856	35.931481	0.027831	48
5	2.107181	88.574508	0.011290	0.474568	42.034592	0.023790	60
6	2.445920	115.673621	0.008645	0.408844	47.292474	0.021145	72
7	2.839113	147.129040	0.006797	0.352223	51.822185	0.019297	84
8	3.295513	183.641059	0.005445	0.303443	55.724570	0.017945	96
9	3.825282	226.022551	0.004424	0.261419	59.086509	0.016924	108
10	4.440213	275.217058	0.003633	0.225214	61.982847	0.016133	120
11	5.153998	332.319805	0.003009	0.194024	64.478068	0.015509	132
12	5.982526	398.602077	0.002509	0.167153	66.627722	0.015009	144
13	6.944244	475.539523	0.002103	0.144004	68.479668	0.014603	156
14	8.060563	564.845011	0.001770	0.124061	70.075134	0.014270	168
15	9.356334	668.506759	0.001496	0.106879	71.449643	0.013996	180
16	10.860408	788.832603	0.001268	0.092078	72.633794	0.013768	192
17	12.606267	928.501369	0.001077	0.079326	73.653950	0.013577	204
18	14.632781	1090.622520	0.000917	0.068340	74.532823	0.013417	216
19	16.985067	1278.805378	0.000782	0.058875	75.289980	0.013282	228
20	19.715494	1497.239481	0.000668	0.050722	75.942278	0.013168	240
21	22.884848	1750.787854	0.000571	0.043697	76.504237	0.013071	252
22	26.563691	2045.095272	0.000489	0.037645	76.988370	0.012989	264
23	30.833924	2386.713938	0.000419	0.032432	77.405455	0.012919	276
24	35.790617	2783.249347	0.000359	0.027940	77.764777	0.012859	288
25	41.544120	3243.529615	0.000308	0.024071	78.074336	0.012808	300
26	48.222525	3777.802015	0.000265	0.020737	78.341024	0.012765	312
27	55.974514	4397.961118	0.000227	0.017865	78.570778	0.012727	324
28	64.972670	5117.813598	0.000195	0.015391	78.768713	0.012695	336
29	75.417320	5953.385616	0.000168	0.013260	78.939236	0.012668	348
30	87.540995	6923.279611	0.000144	0.011423	79.086142	0.012644	360
31	101.613606	8049.088447	0.000124	0.009841	79.212704	0.012624	372
32	117.948452	9355.876140	0.000107	0.008478	79.321738	0.012607	384
33	136.909198	10872.735858	0.000092	0.007304	79.415671	0.012592	396
34	158.917970	12633.437629	0.000079	0.006293	79.496596	0.012579	408
35	184.464752	14677.180163	0.000068	0.005421	79.566313	0.012568	420
36	214.118294	17049.463544	0.000059	0.004670	79.626375	0.012559	432
37	248.538777	19803.102194	0.000050	0.004024	79.678119	0.012550	444
38	288.492509	22999.400699	0.000043	0.003466	79.722696	0.012543	456
39	334.868983	26709.518627	0.000037	0.002986	79.761101	0.012537	468
40	388.700685	31016.054774	0.000032	0.002573	79.794186	0.012532	480

MONTHLY COMPOUND INTEREST TABLES

16.00% ANNUAL INTEREST RATE   1.3333% MONTHLY EFFECTIVE INTEREST RATE

	1 FUTURE VALUE OF $1	2 FUTURE VALUE ANNUITY OF $1 PER MONTH	3 SINKING FUND FACTOR	4 PRESENT VALUE OF $1 (REVERSION)	5 PRESENT VALUE ANNUITY OF $1 PER MONTH	6 PAYMENT TO AMORTIZE $1	
MONTHS							**MONTHS**
1	1.013333	1.000000	1.000000	0.986842	0.986842	1.013333	1
2	1.026844	2.013333	0.496689	0.973857	1.960699	0.510022	2
3	1.040536	3.040178	0.328928	0.961043	2.921743	0.342261	3
4	1.054410	4.080713	0.245055	0.948398	3.870141	0.258389	4
5	1.068468	5.135123	0.194737	0.935919	4.806060	0.208071	5
6	1.082715	6.203591	0.161197	0.923604	5.729665	0.174530	6
7	1.097151	7.286306	0.137244	0.911452	6.641116	0.150577	7
8	1.111779	8.383457	0.119283	0.899459	7.540575	0.132616	8
9	1.126603	9.495236	0.105316	0.887624	8.428199	0.118649	9
10	1.141625	10.621839	0.094146	0.875945	9.304144	0.107479	10
11	1.156846	11.763464	0.085009	0.864419	10.168563	0.098342	11
12	1.172271	12.920310	0.077398	0.853045	11.021609	0.090731	12
YEARS							**MONTHS**
1	1.172271	12.920310	0.077398	0.853045	11.021609	0.090731	12
2	1.374219	28.066412	0.035630	0.727686	20.423539	0.048963	24
3	1.610957	45.821745	0.021824	0.620749	28.443811	0.035157	36
4	1.888477	66.635803	0.015007	0.529527	35.285465	0.028340	48
5	2.213807	91.035516	0.010985	0.451711	41.121706	0.024318	60
6	2.595181	119.638587	0.008359	0.385330	46.100283	0.021692	72
7	3.042255	153.169132	0.006529	0.328704	50.347235	0.019862	84
8	3.566347	192.476010	0.005195	0.280399	53.970077	0.018529	96
9	4.180724	238.554316	0.004192	0.239193	57.060524	0.017525	108
10	4.900941	292.570569	0.003418	0.204042	59.696816	0.016751	120
11	5.745230	355.892244	0.002810	0.174057	61.945692	0.016143	132
12	6.734965	430.122395	0.002325	0.148479	63.864085	0.015658	144
13	7.895203	517.140233	0.001934	0.126659	65.500561	0.015267	156
14	9.255316	619.148703	0.001615	0.108046	66.896549	0.014948	168
15	10.849737	738.730255	0.001354	0.092168	68.087390	0.014687	180
16	12.718830	878.912215	0.001138	0.078624	69.103231	0.014471	192
17	14.909912	1043.243434	0.000959	0.067069	69.969789	0.014292	204
18	17.478455	1235.884123	0.000809	0.057213	70.709003	0.014142	216
19	20.489482	1461.711177	0.000684	0.048806	71.339585	0.014017	228
20	24.019222	1726.441638	0.000579	0.041633	71.877501	0.013913	240
21	28.157032	2036.777427	0.000491	0.035515	72.336367	0.013824	252
22	33.007667	2400.575011	0.000417	0.030296	72.727801	0.013750	264
23	38.693924	2827.044294	0.000354	0.025844	73.061711	0.013687	276
24	45.359757	3326.981781	0.000301	0.022046	73.346552	0.013634	288
25	53.173919	3913.043898	0.000256	0.018806	73.589534	0.013589	300
26	62.334232	4600.067404	0.000217	0.016043	73.796809	0.013551	312
27	73.072600	5405.444997	0.000185	0.013685	73.973623	0.013518	324
28	85.660875	6349.565632	0.000157	0.011674	74.124454	0.013491	336
29	100.417742	7456.330682	0.000134	0.009958	74.253120	0.013467	348
30	117.716787	8753.759030	0.000114	0.008495	74.362878	0.013448	360
31	137.995952	10274.696396	0.000097	0.007247	74.456506	0.013431	372
32	161.768625	12057.646856	0.000083	0.006182	74.536375	0.013416	384
33	189.636635	14147.747615	0.000071	0.005273	74.604507	0.013404	396
34	222.305489	16597.911700	0.000060	0.004498	74.662626	0.013394	408
35	260.602233	19470.167508	0.000051	0.003837	74.712205	0.013385	420
36	305.496388	22837.229116	0.000044	0.003273	74.754498	0.013377	432
37	358.124495	26784.337116	0.000037	0.002792	74.790576	0.013371	444
38	419.818887	31411.416562	0.000032	0.002382	74.821352	0.013365	456
39	492.141422	36835.606677	0.000027	0.002032	74.847605	0.013360	468
40	576.923018	43194.226353	0.000023	0.001733	74.870000	0.013356	480

MONTHLY COMPOUND INTEREST TABLES

17.00% ANNUAL INTEREST RATE   1.4167% MONTHLY EFFECTIVE INTEREST RATE

	1 FUTURE VALUE OF $1	2 FUTURE VALUE ANNUITY OF $1 PER MONTH	3 SINKING FUND FACTOR	4 PRESENT VALUE OF $1 (REVERSION)	5 PRESENT VALUE ANNUITY OF $1 PER MONTH	6 PAYMENT TO AMORTIZE $1	
MONTHS							**MONTHS**
1	1.014167	1.000000	1.000000	0.986031	0.986031	1.014167	1
2	1.028534	2.014167	0.496483	0.972258	1.958289	0.510650	2
3	1.043105	3.042701	0.328655	0.958676	2.916965	0.342822	3
4	1.057882	4.085806	0.244750	0.945285	3.862250	0.258916	4
5	1.072869	5.143688	0.194413	0.932080	4.794330	0.208580	5
6	1.088068	6.216557	0.160861	0.919060	5.713391	0.175027	6
7	1.103482	7.304625	0.136900	0.906222	6.619613	0.151066	7
8	1.119115	8.408107	0.118933	0.893563	7.513176	0.133100	8
9	1.134969	9.527222	0.104962	0.881081	8.394257	0.119129	9
10	1.151048	10.662191	0.093789	0.868774	9.263031	0.107956	10
11	1.167354	11.813238	0.084651	0.856638	10.119669	0.098817	11
12	1.183892	12.980593	0.077038	0.844672	10.964341	0.091205	12
YEARS							**MONTHS**
1	1.183892	12.980593	0.077038	0.844672	10.964341	0.091205	12
2	1.401600	28.348209	0.035276	0.713471	20.225611	0.049442	24
3	1.659342	46.541802	0.021486	0.602648	28.048345	0.035653	36
4	1.964482	68.081048	0.014688	0.509040	34.655988	0.028855	48
5	2.325733	93.581182	0.010686	0.429972	40.237278	0.024853	60
6	2.753417	123.770579	0.008079	0.363185	44.951636	0.022246	72
7	3.259747	159.511558	0.006269	0.306772	48.933722	0.020436	84
8	3.859188	201.825006	0.004955	0.259122	52.297278	0.019121	96
9	4.568860	251.919548	0.003970	0.218873	55.138379	0.018136	108
10	5.409036	311.226062	0.003213	0.184876	57.538177	0.017380	120
11	6.403713	381.438553	0.002622	0.156159	59.565218	0.016788	132
12	7.581303	464.562540	0.002153	0.131903	61.277403	0.016319	144
13	8.975441	562.972341	0.001776	0.111415	62.723638	0.015943	156
14	10.625951	679.478890	0.001472	0.094109	63.945231	0.015638	168
15	12.579975	817.410030	0.001223	0.079491	64.977077	0.015390	180
16	14.893329	980.705566	0.001020	0.067144	65.848648	0.015186	192
17	17.632089	1174.029800	0.000852	0.056715	66.584839	0.015018	204
18	20.874484	1402.904761	0.000713	0.047905	67.206679	0.014879	216
19	24.713129	1673.867935	0.000597	0.040464	67.731930	0.014764	228
20	29.257669	1994.658995	0.000501	0.034179	68.175595	0.014668	240
21	34.637912	2374.440878	0.000421	0.028870	68.550346	0.014588	252
22	41.007538	2824.061507	0.000354	0.024386	68.866887	0.014521	264
23	48.548485	3356.363651	0.000298	0.020598	69.134261	0.014465	276
24	57.476150	3986.551756	0.000251	0.017399	69.360104	0.014418	288
25	68.045538	4732.626240	0.000211	0.014696	69.550868	0.014378	300
26	80.558550	5615.897651	0.000178	0.012413	69.712000	0.014345	312
27	95.372601	6661.595368	0.000150	0.010485	69.848104	0.014317	324
28	112.910833	7899.588246	0.000127	0.008857	69.963067	0.014293	336
29	133.674202	9365.237774	0.000107	0.007481	70.060174	0.014273	348
30	158.255782	11100.408126	0.000090	0.006319	70.142196	0.014257	360
31	187.357711	13154.661953	0.000076	0.005337	70.211479	0.014243	372
32	221.811244	15586.676066	0.000064	0.004508	70.270000	0.014231	384
33	262.600497	18465.917458	0.000054	0.003808	70.319431	0.014221	396
34	310.890557	21874.627526	0.000046	0.003217	70.361184	0.014212	408
35	368.060758	25910.171179	0.000039	0.002717	70.396451	0.014205	420
36	435.744087	30687.817929	0.000033	0.002295	70.426241	0.014199	432
37	515.873821	36344.034396	0.000028	0.001938	70.451403	0.014194	444
38	610.738749	43040.382285	0.000023	0.001637	70.472657	0.014190	456
39	723.048553	50968.133160	0.000020	0.001383	70.490609	0.014186	468
40	856.011201	60353.731845	0.000017	0.001168	70.505773	0.014183	480

MONTHLY COMPOUND INTEREST TABLES

18.00% ANNUAL INTEREST RATE

1.5000% MONTHLY EFFECTIVE INTEREST RATE

	1 FUTURE VALUE OF $1	2 FUTURE VALUE ANNUITY OF $1 PER MONTH	3 SINKING FUND FACTOR	4 PRESENT VALUE OF $1 (REVERSION)	5 PRESENT VALUE ANNUITY OF $1 PER MONTH	6 PAYMENT TO AMORTIZE $1	
MONTHS							**MONTHS**
1	1.015000	1.000000	1.000000	0.985222	0.985222	1.015000	1
2	1.030225	2.015000	0.496278	0.970662	1.955883	0.511278	2
3	1.045678	3.045225	0.328383	0.956317	2.912200	0.343383	3
4	1.061364	4.090903	0.244445	0.942184	3.854385	0.259445	4
5	1.077284	5.152267	0.194089	0.928260	4.782645	0.209089	5
6	1.093443	6.229551	0.160525	0.914542	5.697187	0.175525	6
7	1.109845	7.322994	0.136556	0.901027	6.598214	0.151556	7
8	1.126493	8.432839	0.118584	0.887711	7.485925	0.133584	8
9	1.143390	9.559332	0.104610	0.874592	8.360517	0.119610	9
10	1.160541	10.702722	0.093434	0.861667	9.222185	0.108434	10
11	1.177949	11.863262	0.084294	0.848933	10.071118	0.099294	11
12	1.195618	13.041211	0.076680	0.836387	10.907505	0.091680	12
YEARS							**MONTHS**
1	1.195618	13.041211	0.076680	0.836387	10.907505	0.091680	12
2	1.429503	28.633521	0.034924	0.699544	20.030405	0.049924	24
3	1.709140	47.275969	0.021152	0.585090	27.660684	0.036152	36
4	2.043478	69.565219	0.014375	0.489362	34.042554	0.029375	48
5	2.443220	96.214652	0.010393	0.409296	39.380269	0.025393	60
6	2.921158	128.077197	0.007808	0.342330	43.844667	0.022808	72
7	3.492590	166.172636	0.006018	0.286321	47.578633	0.021018	84
8	4.175804	211.720235	0.004723	0.239475	50.701675	0.019723	96
9	4.992667	266.177771	0.003757	0.200294	53.313749	0.018757	108
10	5.969323	331.288191	0.003019	0.167523	55.498454	0.018019	120
11	7.137031	409.135393	0.002444	0.140114	57.325714	0.017444	132
12	8.533164	502.210922	0.001991	0.117190	58.854011	0.016991	144
13	10.202406	613.493716	0.001630	0.098016	60.132260	0.016630	156
14	12.198182	746.545446	0.001340	0.081979	61.201371	0.016340	168
15	14.584368	905.624513	0.001104	0.068567	62.095562	0.016104	180
16	17.437335	1095.822335	0.000913	0.057348	62.843452	0.015913	192
17	20.848395	1323.226308	0.000756	0.047965	63.468978	0.015756	204
18	24.926719	1595.114630	0.000627	0.040118	63.992160	0.015627	216
19	29.802839	1920.189249	0.000521	0.033554	64.429743	0.015521	228
20	35.632816	2308.854370	0.000433	0.028064	64.795732	0.015433	240
21	42.603242	2773.549452	0.000361	0.023472	65.101841	0.015361	252
22	50.937210	3329.147335	0.000300	0.019632	65.357866	0.015300	264
23	60.901454	3993.430261	0.000250	0.016420	65.572002	0.015250	276
24	72.814885	4787.658998	0.000209	0.013733	65.751103	0.015209	288
25	87.058800	5737.253308	0.000174	0.011486	65.900901	0.015174	300
26	104.089083	6872.605521	0.000146	0.009607	66.026190	0.015146	312
27	124.450799	8230.053258	0.000122	0.008035	66.130980	0.015122	324
28	148.795637	9853.042439	0.000101	0.006721	66.218625	0.015101	336
29	177.902767	11793.517795	0.000085	0.005621	66.291930	0.015085	348
30	212.703781	14113.585393	0.000071	0.004701	66.353242	0.015071	360
31	254.312506	16887.500372	0.000059	0.003932	66.404522	0.015059	372
32	304.060653	20204.043526	0.000049	0.003289	66.447412	0.015049	384
33	363.540442	24169.362788	0.000041	0.002751	66.483285	0.015041	396
34	434.655558	28910.370554	0.000035	0.002301	66.513289	0.015035	408
35	519.682084	34578.805589	0.000029	0.001924	66.538383	0.015029	420
36	621.341343	41356.089521	0.000024	0.001609	66.559372	0.015024	432
37	742.887000	49459.133344	0.000020	0.001346	66.576927	0.015020	444
38	888.209197	59147.279782	0.000017	0.001126	66.591609	0.015017	456
39	1061.959056	70730.603711	0.000014	0.000942	66.603890	0.015014	468
40	1269.697544	84579.836287	0.000012	0.000788	66.614161	0.015012	480

MONTHLY COMPOUND INTEREST TABLES

19.00% ANNUAL INTEREST RATE

1.5833% MONTHLY EFFECTIVE INTEREST RATE

	1 FUTURE VALUE OF $1	2 FUTURE VALUE ANNUITY OF $1 PER MONTH	3 SINKING FUND FACTOR	4 PRESENT VALUE OF $1 (REVERSION)	5 PRESENT VALUE ANNUITY OF $1 PER MONTH	6 PAYMENT TO AMORTIZE $1	
MONTHS							**MONTHS**
1	1.015833	1.000000	1.000000	0.984413	0.984413	1.015833	1
2	1.031917	2.015833	0.496073	0.969070	1.953483	0.511906	2
3	1.048256	3.047751	0.328111	0.953965	2.907449	0.343944	3
4	1.064853	4.096007	0.244140	0.939096	3.846545	0.259974	4
5	1.081714	5.160860	0.193766	0.924459	4.771004	0.209599	5
6	1.098841	6.242574	0.160190	0.910050	5.681054	0.176024	6
7	1.116239	7.341415	0.136214	0.895865	6.576920	0.152047	7
8	1.133913	8.457654	0.118236	0.881902	7.458822	0.134069	8
9	1.151866	9.591566	0.104258	0.868156	8.326978	0.120092	9
10	1.170104	10.743433	0.093080	0.854625	9.181602	0.108913	10
11	1.188631	11.913537	0.083938	0.841304	10.022906	0.099771	11
12	1.207451	13.102168	0.076323	0.828191	10.851097	0.092157	12
YEARS							**MONTHS**
1	1.207451	13.102168	0.076323	0.828191	10.851097	0.092157	12
2	1.457938	28.922394	0.034575	0.685900	19.837878	0.050409	24
3	1.760389	48.024542	0.020823	0.568056	27.280649	0.036656	36
4	2.125583	71.089450	0.014067	0.470459	33.444684	0.029900	48
5	2.566537	98.939196	0.010107	0.389630	38.549682	0.025941	60
6	3.098968	132.566399	0.007543	0.322688	42.777596	0.023377	72
7	3.741852	173.169599	0.005775	0.267247	46.279115	0.021608	84
8	4.518103	222.195973	0.004501	0.221332	49.179042	0.020334	96
9	5.455388	281.392918	0.003554	0.183305	51.580735	0.019387	108
10	6.587114	352.870328	0.002834	0.151812	53.569796	0.018667	120
11	7.953617	439.175798	0.002277	0.125729	55.217118	0.018110	132
12	9.603603	543.385424	0.001840	0.104128	56.581415	0.017674	144
13	11.595879	669.213441	0.001494	0.086238	57.711314	0.017328	156
14	14.001456	821.144606	0.001218	0.071421	58.647086	0.017051	168
15	16.906072	1004.594042	0.000995	0.059150	59.422084	0.016829	180
16	20.413254	1226.100247	0.000816	0.048988	60.063930	0.016649	192
17	24.648004	1493.558135	0.000670	0.040571	60.595501	0.016503	204
18	29.761257	1816.500430	0.000551	0.033601	61.035743	0.016384	216
19	35.935259	2206.437425	0.000453	0.027828	61.400348	0.016287	228
20	43.390065	2677.267240	0.000374	0.023047	61.702310	0.016207	240
21	52.391377	3245.771169	0.000308	0.019087	61.952393	0.016141	252
22	63.260020	3932.211806	0.000254	0.015808	62.159509	0.016088	264
23	76.383375	4761.055238	0.000210	0.013092	62.331041	0.016043	276
24	92.229182	5761.843068	0.000174	0.010843	62.473102	0.016007	288
25	111.362218	6970.245332	0.000143	0.008980	62.590755	0.015977	300
26	134.464421	8429.331851	0.000119	0.007437	62.688195	0.015952	312
27	162.359199	10191.107326	0.000098	0.006159	62.768894	0.015931	324
28	196.040777	12318.364881	0.000081	0.005101	62.835728	0.015915	336
29	236.709632	14886.924139	0.000067	0.004225	62.891079	0.015901	348
30	285.815282	17988.333579	0.000056	0.003499	62.936920	0.015889	360
31	345.107947	21733.133503	0.000046	0.002898	62.974886	0.015879	372
32	416.700935	26254.795909	0.000038	0.002400	63.006328	0.015871	384
33	503.145960	31714.481694	0.000032	0.001987	63.032369	0.015865	396
34	607.524092	38306.784745	0.000026	0.001646	63.053935	0.015859	408
35	733.555571	46266.667644	0.000022	0.001363	63.071796	0.015855	420
36	885.732406	55877.836195	0.000018	0.001129	63.086589	0.015851	432
37	1069.478478	67482.851256	0.000015	0.000935	63.098840	0.015848	444
38	1291.342856	81495.338274	0.000012	0.000774	63.108986	0.015846	456
39	1559.233220	98414.729710	0.000010	0.000641	63.117389	0.015843	468
40	1882.697708	118844.065787	0.000008	0.000531	63.124348	0.015842	480

Index

Get the Performance Advantage on the job. . .*in the classroom*

	Order Number	Real Estate Principles and Exam Preparation	Qty.	Price	Total Amount
1.	1510-0113	Modern Real Estate Practice, 13th Edition	_____	$36.95	_____
2.	1516-0113	Key Point Review Audio Tapes for Modern Real Estate Practice	_____	$28.95	_____
3.	1510-0213	Study Guide for Modern Real Estate Practice	_____	$13.95	_____
4.	1961-0104	Language of Real Estate, 4th Edition	_____	$28.95	_____
5.	1610-0704	Real Estate Math, 4th Edition	_____	$15.95	_____
6.	1512-1005	Mastering Real Estate Mathematics, 5th Edition	_____	$25.95	_____
7.	1970-0404	Questions & Answers To Help You Pass the Real Estate Exam, 4th Edition	_____	$21.95	_____
8.	1516-0201	Real Estate Exam Preparation Software—5 1/4" IBM-Compatible Disk	_____	$35.00	_____
9.	1516-0301	Real Estate Exam Preparation Software—3 1/2" IBM-Compatible Disk	_____	$35.00	_____
10.	1970-0603	Real Estate Exam Guide: ASI, 3rd Edition	_____	$21.95	_____
11.	1970-0902	Guide to Passing the PSI Real Estate Exam, 2nd Edition	_____	$21.95	_____
12.	1970-0801	New York Real Estate Exam Guide	_____	$21.95	_____
13.	1970-0305	How to Prepare for the Texas Real Estate Exam, 5th Edition	_____	$19.50	_____

Advanced Study/Specialty Areas

14.	1520-0201	ADA Handbook: Employment and Construction Issues Affecting Your Business	_____	$29.95	_____
15.	1560-0802	Agency Relationships in Real Estate, 2nd Edition	_____	$25.95	_____
16.	1978-0302	Buyer Agency: Your Competitive Edge in Real Estate, 2nd Edition	_____	$24.95	_____
17.	1557-1007	Essentials of Real Estate Finance, 7th Edition	_____	$38.95	_____
18.	1559-0104	Essentials of Real Estate Investment, 4th Edition	_____	$38.95	_____
19.	1556-1006	Fundamentals of Real Estate Appraisal, 6th Edition	_____	$38.95	_____
20.	1556-1402	How to Use the Uniform Residential Appraisal Report, 2nd Edition	_____	$24.95	_____
21.	1556-1501	Income Property Appraisal	_____	$34.95	_____
22.	1556-1101	Language of Real Estate Appraisal	_____	$21.95	_____
23.	1557-1502	Modern Residential Financing Methods, 2nd Edition	_____	$19.95	_____
24.	1551-1004	Property Management, 4th Edition	_____	$35.95	_____
25.	1556-1202	Questions & Answers to Help You Pass the Real Estate Appraisal Exams, 2nd Edition	_____	$26.95	_____
26.	1560-0103	Real Estate Law, 3rd Edition	_____	$38.95	_____
27.	1556-1803	Uniform Standards of Professional Appraisal Practice, 3rd Edition	_____	$19.95	_____

Sales & Marketing/Professional Development

28.	1913-0401	Close for Success	_____	$18.95	_____
29.	1913-1502	Houses, 2nd Edition	_____	$19.95	_____
30.	1907-0601	How to Develop a Six-Figure Income in Real Estate	_____	$22.95	_____
31.	4105-0901	How to Profit in Commercial Real Estate Investing	_____	$34.95	_____
32.	1913-0101	List for Success	_____	$18.95	_____
33.	5608-8901	Multiply Your Success with Real Estate Assistants	_____	$79.95	_____
34.	1909-0601	New Home Selling Strategies: A Handbook for Success	_____	$24.95	_____
35.	1907-0501	Power Real Estate Advertising	_____	$24.95	_____
36.	1926-0302	Power Real Estate Letters, 2nd Edition	_____	$29.95	_____
37.	1926-1001	Power Real Estate Letters w/ 5 1/4" IBM-Compatible Disk	_____	$79.95	_____
38.	1926-0901	Power Real Estate Letters w/ 3 1/2" IBM-Compatible Disk	_____	$79.95	_____
39.	1907-0102	Power Real Estate Listing, 2nd Edition	_____	$18.95	_____
40.	1907-0401	Power Real Estate Negotiation	_____	$19.95	_____
41.	1907-0202	Power Real Estate Selling, 2nd Edition	_____	$18.95	_____
42.	1907-0701	Real Estate Agent's Guide to Listing and Sales Success	_____	$22.95	_____
43.	1965-0103	Real Estate Brokerage: A Success Guide, 3rd Edition	_____	$35.95	_____
44.	5608-7101	Real Estate Investor's Tax Guide	_____	$24.95	_____
45.	1913-2310	Real Estate Sales Handbook, 10th Edition	_____	$19.95	_____
46.	1913-1301	The Real Estate Sales Survival Kit	_____	$24.95	_____
47.	1965-1030	The Realty Bluebook, 30th Edition	_____	$19.95	_____
48.	1903-3101	Sold! The Professional's Guide to Real Estate Auctions	_____	$32.95	_____

Shipping/Handling Charges

$0-24.99	$4
$25-49.99	$5
$50-99.99	$6
$100-249.99	$8

Order shipped to the following states must include applicable sales tax:

CA, FL, IL & NY

Book total _____
Tax _____
Shipping and Handling _____
Less $1.00 off if you fax order _____
Total amount _____

Prices are subject to change without notice.

R93004

Real Estate Education Company

Where Experts Begin

a division of Dearborn Financial Publishing, Inc.

155 North Wacker Drive, Chicago, IL 60606-1719

IMPORTANT—PLEASE FOLD OVER—PLEASE TAPE BEFORE MAILING

Your Satisfaction is Guaranteed!
All books come with a 30-day
money-back guarantee. If you are not
completely satisfied, simply return your
books in saleable condition and your
money will be refunded in full.

**FOR YOUR
CONVENIENCE!**

NOTE: This page, when folded over and taped, becomes a mailing
envelope. When paying by check, please seal/tape on three sides.

**Real Estate
Education Company**
a division of Dearborn Financial Publishing, Inc.